Critical Conversations

FOR

DUMMIES

A Wiley Brand

Critical Conversations

FOR

DUMMIES

A Wiley Brand

by Christina Tangora Schlachter, PhD

FOR

DUMMIES

A Wiley Brand

Critical Conversations For Dummies®

Published by
John Wiley & Sons, Inc.
111 River St.
Hoboken, NJ 07030-5774
www.wiley.com

About the Author

Dr. Christina Tangora Schlachter, PhD, is the CEO of She Leads, where she coaches leaders who are tired of too much fire-fighting and are ready to create meaningful change based on open and authentic conversations. Christina's matter-of-fact 12-week transformation process has helped thousands of leaders around the globe build rapport, speak honestly, and deliver results.

In addition to writing *Critical Conversations For Dummies,* Christina is also the author of *Leading Business Change For Dummies* (co-written with Terry H. Hildebrandt and published by Wiley), a contributor to numerous business and communication journals and blogs, and a sought-after keynote speaker globally. Christina has been recognized as an American Express Small Business Award winner and is a Lean Six Sigma Master Black Belt.

Christina holds a PhD in human and organizational systems, MAs in education and in organizational studies, and a BBA in international finance and marketing. She is a frequent speaker and lecturer at top-ranked universities, including Stanford, where she received her first master's degree.

When not coaching, writing, or speaking with clients about leading change, Christina has swum across the 9-mile Maui Channel solo and is a two-time Ironman triathlete. She alternates among swimming, biking, running, and skiing around the mountains of Colorado with her husband, two sons, and their Nova Scotia Duck Tolling Retriever.

Christina loves to hear from her readers. She can be found on her bike or in the pool at the crack of dawn, or at christinas@sheleads theway.com or www.sheleadstheway.com.

Dedication

For all the business leaders, managers, and employees ready to start creating meaningful change and powerful relationships based on honesty, openness, and respect.

Author's Acknowledgments

My sincere thanks and appreciation to everyone who had a part in putting this book together.

I want to specifically thank the great minds at John Wiley & Sons, Inc., especially Project Editor Linda Brandon, Acquisitions Editor Tracy Boggier, and Copy Editor Sarah Faulkner. To the graphics and layout team at Wiley: You made this book come to life.

A special thanks for your dedication and for saying "yes" to my Technical Editor, Dean Savoca. And thanks to Shannon Rodriquez for making the connection.

My continued gratitude to Matt Wagner at FreshBooks; without your excitement for the project, this book would not have been possible.

To my wonderful clients who have contributed examples, experiences, and successes — your insights and triumphs are a pleasure to share.

To Beth Ornstein at Mediation Now; your expert facilitation advice and willingness to help are greatly valued. And a belated thanks to Kendra Prospero.

Thank you to my family who stuck by my side when I was working like crazy to balance writing, family, life, and clients.

And to my husband and brain trust, Michael, thank you for all your ideas, recommendations, and suggestions every step along the way. Your content, commentary, and subject-verb agreement editing make you the best husband ever.

Publisher's Acknowledgments

We're proud of this book; please send us your comments at `http://dummies.custhelp.com`. For other comments, please contact our Customer Care Department within the U.S. at 877-762-2974, outside the U.S. at 317-572-3993, or fax 317-572-4002.

Some of the people who helped bring this book to market include the following:

Acquisitions, Editorial, and Vertical Websites

Project Editor: Linda Brandon

Acquisitions Editor: Tracy Boggier

Copy Editor: Sarah Faulkner

Assistant Editor: David Lutton

Editorial Program Coordinator: Joe Niesen

Technical Editor: Dean Savoca

Senior Editorial Manager: Jennifer Ehrlich

Editorial Manager: Carmen Krikorian

Editorial Assistant: Rachelle S. Amick

Art Coordinator: Alicia B. South

Cover Photos: © Logorilla/iStockphoto.com

Cartoons: Rich Tennant
(www.the5thwave.com)

Composition Services

Project Coordinator: Patrick Redmond

Layout and Graphics: Carrie A. Cesavice, Jennifer Creasey

Proofreaders: BIM Indexing & Proofreading Services, John Greenough

Indexer: Glassman Indexing Services

Publishing and Editorial for Consumer Dummies

    Kathleen Nebenhaus, Vice President and Executive Publisher

    David Palmer: Associate Publisher

    Kristin Ferguson-Wagstaffe, Product Development Director

Publishing for Technology Dummies

    Andy Cummings, Vice President and Publisher

Composition Services

    Debbie Stailey, Director of Composition Services

Contents at a Glance

Introduction 1

Part I: The Anatomy of a Critical Conversation 7

Chapter 1: Let's Get Critical! Making Conversations Count 9
Chapter 2: The Ins and Outs of a Critical Conversation 23
Chapter 3: Critical Conversations: Key Elements to Get You Started ... 43
Chapter 4: Delivering the Message with Impact 57
Chapter 5: Knowing When It's Time to Have a Critical
    Conversation 69

Part II: Making Sense of How You Communicate ... 83

Chapter 6: Building Effective Verbal Communication Techniques 85
Chapter 7: Grasping Nonverbal Cues 99
Chapter 8: Working with Different Communication Styles 113

Part III: Getting Down to Specifics:
Creating a Critical Conversation 127

Chapter 9: Here's the Warm-Up: Getting Yourself Ready 129
Chapter 10: Keeping Challenging Situations Productive 143
Chapter 11: Closing the Conversation with Ease 159

Part IV: Putting It All into Practice 169

Chapter 12: Conversations in Good Times 171
Chapter 13: Conversations in Bad Times 185
Chapter 14: Dealing with Staff Disputes 199
Chapter 15: Identifying and Working through Workplace
    Complaints 215
Chapter 16: Resolving Difficult Behaviors with Critical
    Conversations 231
Chapter 17: Customer Conversations 249
Chapter 18: Hot Topics in Team Conversations 263

Part V: The Part of Tens 273

Chapter 19: Ten Benefits of Leading a Critical Conversation 275
Chapter 20: Ten Ways to Keep Your Cool No One Else Is 283
Chapter 21: Ten Ways to Manage a Conversation That's
    Going South 291

Index 299

Table of Contents

Introduction... 1

About This Book 2
Conventions Used in This Book............................... 2
What You're Not to Read 3
Foolish Assumptions 3
How This Book Is Organized 3
  Part I: The Anatomy of a Critical Conversation 4
  Part II: Making Sense of How You Communicate......... 4
  Part III: Getting Down to Specifics: Creating a
    Critical Conversation................................... 4
  Part IV: Putting It All into Practice................... 5
  Part V: The Part of Tens............................... 5
Icons Used in This Book... 5
Where to Go from Here 6

Part 1: The Anatomy of a Critical Conversation 7

**Chapter 1: Let's Get Critical! Making
Conversations Count** 9

Discovering the What, When, Who, and Where of
  Critical Conversations 10
    What is a critical conversation?.................... 10
    When should you have a critical conversation?........ 11
    Who should have the conversation?................ 12
    Where should you have a critical conversation? 13
Making the Effort: Benefits of Critical Conversations
  Done Right... 13
The Golden Rule of Critical Conversations: Be Genuine..... 14
Grasping the Art and Science of Critical Conversations..... 15
    The art: Making the interpersonal connection 15
    The science: Focusing on the facts 16
    Blending art and science to make a positive impact ... 17
Getting an EDGE on Critical Conversations................ 18
    Exploring and examining what's happening 19
    Deciding on options to move forward 19
    Gaining commitment and getting moving............. 20
    Evaluating next steps 20
Critical Conversations Are Everywhere............... 21

Chapter 2: The Ins and Outs of a Critical Conversation. . .23

It's Not Just Words: Critical Conversations Matter 23
    Building relationships 24
    Resolving issues 25
    Managing performance 26
Finding Out What Makes Conversations Critical 27
It's Not Easy! Why Critical Conversations Are So Hard 28
    Facts and emotions collide in the workplace 28
    A tendency to shy away from tough news 29
    Technology makes talking too passé 31
Avoiding Common Communication Pitfalls 32
    Problem/solution: One-sided conversation 35
    Problem/solution: Distracted audience 37
    Problem/solution: A lack of trust 38
    Problem/solution: Not heading in the same
      direction 39

Chapter 3: Critical Conversations: Key Elements to Get You Started 43

Playing the Right Role 43
    The initiator 44
    The recipient 45
    The support team 45
Setting Up for Success 46
    Preparing to give feedback 47
    Specifying the objective 48
    Giving fair warning 49
Kicking Off the Conversation with Ease 51
    Opening the discussion 51
    Using small talk (or not) 53
    Managing high stakes
      and higher emotions 54

Chapter 4: Delivering the Message with Impact 57

Examining Perspectives and Acknowledging
    Other Perceptions 58
    Start with facts 58
    Ask for additional information and intents 59
    Clarify consequences 61
Deciding on Options to Move Forward 62
    Identifying desired behaviors 62
    Discussing possible alternatives 62
    Gaining commitment by building agreements
      early on 63
    Making a SMART agreement 64

Gain Commitment to get a Move On: Who Does
What by When?.. 65
Closing the conversation 66
To act or not to act: That is the question.................... 67
Evaluating the Impact.. 67

Chapter 5: Knowing When It's Time to Have a Critical Conversation **69**

Your Indicator Light Is Flashing!... 69
Workplace dynamics.. 71
Performance issues 72
Overdue Notice: Time for a Critical Conversation 74
Deciding whether a problem still exists 75
Inherited issues... 75
The elephant in the room 76
Multiple Issues: Handling the Snowball Effect 77
Prioritizing what issue to focus on first..................... 78
Creating a win for everyone 79
Remembering the principle of patience 81

Part II: Making Sense of How You Communicate... **83**

Chapter 6: Building Effective Verbal Communication Techniques...................... **85**

Great Communicators Are Made, Not Born.......................... 85
Verbal Communication: When Words Matter Most 87
Facts, opinions, and gossip 88
I, you, we, and they: Pronouns matter 90
Cooperative Language: Verbal Communication
at Its Finest.. 91
Keeping confrontational language out....................... 92
Turning confrontational words into
accommodating words... 95
Using five key phrases that get results...................... 96

Chapter 7: Grasping Nonverbal Cues................. **99**

Noting Nonverbal Techniques that Speak Volumes............ 99
Expressions that count 100
Use of voice 104
Silence is golden, space is priceless.......................... 106
Nonverbal no-no's.. 107
Becoming an Expert in Active Listening 108
Practicing active silence 109
Reflecting before responding...................................... 110
Asking to clarify questions 110

Chapter 8: Working with Different Communication Styles **113**

Taking On Direct and Passive Communication Styles 113
Direct communicators 114
Passive communicators 116
Saying Yes to Assertiveness 119
Checking out assertive qualities 119
Using assertive styles to move to action 121
Knowing Your Communication Style.................................. 121
Sharpening Your Communication Style 123
Gaining insight from your peers 123
Managing your style under stress 124
Clarifying assumptions 125

Part III: Getting Down to Specifics: Creating a Critical Conversation *127*

Chapter 9: Here's the Warm-Up: Getting Yourself Ready **129**

Avoiding Pitfalls through Preparation 130
Being Physically Prepared 131
Schedule so you're not rushed 131
Eat, rest, exercise.. 131
Design the questions 132
Have a clear plan 132
Being Emotionally Prepared 133
Getting to know your motivations............................ 134
Meeting the needs of others...................................... 135
Knowing and controlling your hot buttons.............. 136
Maintaining a positive attitude 137
Starting on the Right Track: Rapport and Trust 138
Defining rapport and trust... 139
Building rapport and trust... 139

Chapter 10: Keeping Challenging Situations Productive **143**

Righting a Wrong.. 143
Okay, so you lost your cool....................................... 144
Time to ask for support 146
Get help from across the table.................................. 147
What did you say?! Handling the unexpected.......... 148
Keeping Tough Discussions Encouraging............................ 149
Motivating people gets results.................................. 150
Supporting others' needs 151
Using power wisely.. 152

Dealing with Resistance 154
    Stay flexible 154
    Know when to push and when to stop 155
    Take two steps forward and one step back 156
Gaining Focus When Conversations Go Off Track............. 157

Chapter 11: Closing the Conversation with Ease.....159

Making the Case for Closure... 159
Creating Powerful Action Plans... 160
    Agreeing on next steps.. 160
    Determining elements of an action plan 161
Following Through for Success.. 164
    Writing the perfect follow-up note 164
    Scheduling follow-up meetings 165
    Creating more formal documentation....................... 166
    Responding to ignored action plans 167

Part IV: Putting It All into Practice.................. 169

Chapter 12: Conversations in Good Times 171

Using Critical Conversation Tools to Hire and
    Develop Superstars.. 171
    Hiring the best.. 172
    Helping employees soar.. 174
    Using words that launch exceptional performance... 175
Coaching with Critical Conversations................................. 176
    Using coaching methods.. 176
    Finding coachable moments 179
Making Everyday Conversations Count.............................. 180
    Changing day-to-day talks into motivating
      moments 180
    Using feedback to create results 180
Opening Your Culture to Conversation 182

Chapter 13: Conversations in Bad Times 185

Preparing for a Performance Conversation........................ 185
Having Conversations When Performance Is Suffering..... 186
    Clarifying what's not working 187
    Looking for options 190
    Moving toward action 191
    Assessing the conversation's impact........................ 192
Turning Poor Performers into Productive Performers..... 194
Firing Employees with Compassion 195
    Be professional and empathetic 196
    No apologies necessary 197
Keeping It Close to the Chest: Confidentiality Is Critical.... 197

Chapter 14: Dealing with Staff Disputes............199

Getting Results When Employees Aren't Getting Along.... 199
  Knowing how to step aside 200
  Realizing when to intervene.................................... 202
Getting Expert Tactics for Handling Staff Disputes 203
  Using five steps to resolve conflict 204
  Turning a conflict into a positive experience 207
  Talking today to solve tomorrow 208
Resolving the Five Biggest Staff Disputes 209
  Ending offensive comments from a co-worker 210
  Dealing with an obnoxious co-worker...................... 210
  Putting away grudges.. 211
  Handling waterworks in the office............................ 213
  Discussing differing values and personal styles...... 214

Chapter 15: Identifying and Working through Workplace Complaints 215

Addressing Workplace Complaints 216
  Defining a workplace complaint 216
  Figuring out when critical conversations
    aren't enough 217
  Complaints that benefit from a critical
    conversation 219
Using Critical Conversations When an Issue Is Raised 220
Digging into Workplace Complaints 221
  Maintaining confidentiality during
    communications... 223
  Not placing blame.. 224
  Separating the personal issues from valid
    grievances... 224
Bringing in a Mediator.. 225
  What is a mediation expert?...................................... 225
  When to bring in a professional................................ 225
  How a mediator can make your life easier 226
Moving Forward after Tough Workplace Conversations.... 227

Chapter 16: Resolving Difficult Behaviors with Critical Conversations 231

Defining Difficult Behaviors... 232
Keying in on Difficult Behaviors... 233
  Looking at intentions... 233
  Focusing on behaviors, not labels............................ 235
Using a Critical Conversation to Turn Around
  Difficult Behaviors.. 237
  Paying attention to your own opinions
    and perspectives... 237
  Putting the critical conversation into play.............. 238

Building a Toolbox: Action Plans for Difficult Behaviors.... 239
　　Coaching and support 239
　　Education and mentoring 241
　　Rewarding the right behaviors 241
Finding the Words for Special Circumstances 242
　　Defusing a screamer 243
　　Quieting the back-stabbing gossiper 244
　　Cooling down the angry hostile types 245
Stepping in When Bad Behavior Becomes a Pattern 247

Chapter 17: Customer Conversations 249

Helping Customer Relationships 249
Providing Exceptional Customer Service 251
　　Using key elements to work through complaints 252
　　Noting the differences and similarities between
　　　　internal and external issues 254
　　Knowing what upset customers want 255
Handling a Customer Who Crosses the Line 256
　　Managing "I want to talk to the manager" 256
　　Facing a hostile customer 257
Delivering Bad News to Clients 259
　　Creating an open and honest environment 259
　　Identifying solutions together 260
Keeping Your Customers 260
　　Checking it twice 261
　　Renegotiating the future 261

Chapter 18: Hot Topics in Team Conversations 263

Creating a Productive Team 263
　　Facilitating team conversations 264
　　Making team decisions 268
Improving Team Behavior 270

Part V: The Part of Tens 273

**Chapter 19: Ten Benefits of Leading a
Critical Conversation 275**

Increasing Leadership Potential 275
Maintaining Confidence throughout Tough Situations 276
Influencing without Overpowering 276
Developing Healthy Work Relationships 277
Focusing on Teamwork 277
Making Work Easier 278
Developing Rapport Quickly 279
Becoming a Better Coach 279
Encouraging Different Ideas 280
Managing Conflict Like a Pro 280

Chapter 20: Ten Ways to Keep Your Cool When No One Else Is 283

Taking a Breath and a Break..283
Getting a Move On 284
Expressing Your Emotions 284
Asking for Help..285
Stating the Obvious...286
Finding the Positive...287
Keeping the Problem in Perspective 288
Knowing When to Walk Away...288
Keeping Forward Movement 289
Staying Flexible 290

Chapter 21: Ten Ways to Manage a Conversation That's Going South 291

Dealing with Texting, Typing, and Checking Messages 291
Meeting the Timekeeper 292
Wording: Me-versus-You Language 293
Checking Body Language..293
Observing When the Talker becomes Silent 294
Getting Defensive...294
Handling the Situation When the Offense Strikes Back 295
Ending the Blame Game 296
Keeping Agreements in Tact...296
Tempering Emotions 297

Index.. 299

Introduction

●●●

*W*elcome to *Critical Conversations For Dummies!*

Critical conversations are almost everywhere, from bosses who need to share tough performance messages with employees, to co-workers who have vastly different ideas on how a project should be run, to business owners who deal with customer complaints.

Although many critical conversations happen, only a few are successful in achieving productive results. Sometimes conversations fail because people are afraid of delivering bad news or offending another person. In other cases, people are so passionate about their own positions that the conversation turns into a lecture rather than a dialogue. That's where *Critical Conversations For Dummies* steps in.

Critical Conversations For Dummies helps leaders become expert communicators, ready to deliver strong messages in a single bound, while creating mutually agreed-on results and stronger relationships, all with honesty and authenticity. Okay, take out the single bound, but a critical conversation does create the impetus to do something different, and that's a powerful tool.

So what is a critical conversation? A *critical conversation* is any conversation in which two or more people have differing opinions, perspectives, or ideas on how to work, talk, act, behave, or for that matter, basically do anything. Throw in the different parties in the conversation being highly engaged and emotionally tied to their respective views of the desired results and you have a critical conversation that should be happening right now. A successful critical conversation occurs when the parties take action that's mutually agreed on and improves the current situation from all points of view. Therefore, it isn't just about having the conversation; it's about making sure the conversation results in change.

To create change that's beneficial for everyone involved, the key elements of a critical conversation need to be put into play. *Critical Conversations For Dummies* shows you how to take action and create positive productivity and desired results.

About This Book

Although most humans start talking at an early age, having a conversation when the stakes are high and emotions are higher still isn't easy for many people. In this book I give you a set of instructions and examples to help focus the conversation and create a path to success in the face of almost any conflict.

Critical Conversations For Dummies focuses on three key aspects of critical conversations:

- ✔ Understanding when and why to have one in the first place
- ✔ Building a toolkit of conversation skills to prepare you
- ✔ Delivering the message with ease and authenticity

This book gives you a roadmap to get from problem to solution when faced with almost any issue or situation. Although the discussion may not always be perfectly planned out, the tools provided in this book will help you avoid the common mistakes and pitfalls that can happen during a conversation, and the knowledge about how to address them if they do.

With more than 7 billion people in the world, about 6.9 billion probably could use a helping hand with conversation skills and can use this book to do so (which will put it on the all-time *New York Times* Best Seller list!). Although the examples in the book focus on workplace issues, *Critical Conversations For Dummies* is intended for anyone who wants an easy-to-apply framework to communicate his or her message and point of view, while building acceptance and positive relationships. And because the need for conversations and communication is one of the few constants in today's workplace, you may find yourself using this book day-in and day-out to resolve conflicts, get results, and create motivated teams.

Whether you're an executive of a Fortune 500 company who needs to encourage an executive team to work together, a manager dealing with a poor performer, an employee having a dispute with a co-worker, or anything in between, the tools in this book will help you deliver powerful messages that resolve conflict and build more productive relationships.

Conventions Used in This Book

I use the following conventions throughout the book:

✔ When I introduce a new term, I *italicize* it and then provide a definition.

✔ Keywords and actions are in **bold** and in numbered steps.

What You're Not to Read

If you're in a hurry, you can safely skip all the sidebars in this book — they're the gray-shaded boxes filled with extra information. I'm partial to them, but skipping them won't take away from your understanding of critical conversations.

You won't find any summaries in the chapters, so if you are just looking for the 10,000-foot overview, skip the details and just focus on Chapter 1.

If you only need a refresher or some ideas on what to say, jump right to the examples throughout the book. These scripts are great starting points to integrate in your own critical conversation.

Foolish Assumptions

As I wrote this book, I made a few assumptions about you, my readers. Even if only a couple of these seem to describe you or your organization, I'm confident that this book will support you in whatever change you're leading.

✔ You're a leader who wants to encourage people to collaborate more.

✔ You're faced with conflicting ideas or points of view from the people you work with.

✔ You know you need to have a conversation with someone and aren't sure where to start.

✔ You're looking for a roadmap, processes, and tools to help you lead an important conversation well.

✔ You want strategies that will help you engage employees in the decision-making process.

How This Book Is Organized

Critical Conversations For Dummies is divided into five parts. The first three parts deliver a functional, action-oriented toolkit and roadmap to put your conversation on the path to success. The fourth part dives deeper into specific circumstances that require critical conversations with plenty of examples to use right away. The last part provides the ever popular Part of Tens, featuring chapters with top-10 lists of key communication tips you can use right away. If you want information on a particular topic, the Index is a great reference guide.

Part I: The Anatomy of a Critical Conversation

Welcome to Critical Conversations 101! Part I is about getting the basics of conversations right so you can have a critical conversation wherever you may find or need one. I share why critical conversations are so important and worth the time and effort that you must invest to do them well. In Chapters 3 and 4, I walk through the key elements of a critical conversation and provide a conversation model that I refer to throughout the book. From preparing for the conversation and kicking off the discussion to closing out the communication with ease, here you get the basics of what to say and when to say it.

Part II: Making Sense of How You Communicate

Even if you aren't sure whether you need to have a critical conversation just yet, you find some great ideas on how to be a better communicator. In this part, your conversations toolbox becomes incredibly full. Because communication is the building block to a successful critical conversation, you find out how to perfect your communication techniques. In Chapter 6, I start the conversation with how to use cooperative language to keep the discussion positive and focused. Because communication isn't just about talking, Chapter 7 is devoted to honing your body language and listening skills. If you want to find out more about your own communication style and how to work with others, Chapter 8 is the place for you to start.

Part III: Getting Down to Specifics: Creating a Critical Conversation

This is where you're ready to get talking. Discover how to kick off the conversation and even how to reduce your own level of stress before the conversation starts (sorry, a masseuse is not included). In Chapter 10, you discover how to use a conversation to make decisions in the face of conflict and negative reactions, and how to keep everything on track. Because conversations don't really end when the talking is done, Chapter 11 not only helps you close the conversation with ease, but also gives you ideas on creating action plans that can guide you through what to do next so all parties take responsibility. This part provides a wealth of information about what to say and do when the conversation is rolling.

Part IV: Putting It All into Practice

Critical conversations really are everywhere and this part proves it. You discover how to communicate with impact in good times and bad. From hiring superstars and helping them hit the ground running, to firing poor performers and dealing with staff disputes, this part has it all. You get practical tips for mastering critical conversations with customers, discover how to use critical conversations during ethical and workplace complaints, and find out how to resolve even the toughest issues with the most difficult personality types. I also include a chapter on conducting team critical conversations in some hot topic situations. Check it out to be on the cutting edge of communication!

Part V: The Part of Tens

If you're in a big hurry and need ideas to get a conversation started right away, this part provides you with some essential principles and creative ideas on how to jump into the conversation. First, I start with ten personal benefits of mastering critical conversations, as well as the benefits of having them in the first place. Then, because everyone may not have read this book just yet, I give you ten ways to keep your cool when others aren't keeping theirs. Finally, for when you need it most, I give you ten ways to manage and stop a conversation that's going south.

Icons Used in This Book

Just like signposts along a road, this book uses several icons to point out helpful information that you need in order to build strong work relationships, create productive results, and make sure you don't need to have the same conversation again and again and again. Keep an eye out for these symbols throughout the book.

Throughout the book, you find lots of examples marked with this icon. You can talk all you want about conversations, but nothing makes a conversation come to life quite like words. Use the examples as scripts that you can fine-tune for your next conversation.

This icon calls your attention to important points that you shouldn't forget. These points are critical for your communication effort to bring the results you want.

This symbol provides helpful advice, tips, and words of wisdom that will support you in your conversations.

This icon points out potential mistakes and pitfalls that can derail any conversation. Pay special attention to the warnings to stay on track.

Where to Go from Here

Where should you go to get started? Anywhere in the book! You don't need to read this book from Chapter 1 onward. You're welcome to skip around and view the sections you need. However, critical conversations are somewhat of a process, and building those techniques takes some practice. Reading the book from front to back does start you with the basics and allow you to fine-tune your skills along the way.

If you prefer to start with the details, here are a few places you may want to consider. If you think you may need to have a critical conversation, but aren't exactly sure, Chapter 5 will help you recognize the signs that a critical conversation is needed. If you just want to brush up on your verbal and nonverbal communication skills before the conversation, Chapters 6 and 7 are the right places to start. Chapter 14 helps you deliver tough messages with ease; while Chapters 15 and 16 show you how to deal with workplace disputes and difficult behaviors.

Either way you choose, enjoy the read — and may all your conversations be successful!

Part I

The Anatomy of a Critical Conversation

The 5th Wave   By Rich Tennant

"A large part of our success is based on our ability to resolve conflicts before we get to work."

In this part...

What is a critical conversation and why in the world should you be having one? In this part, discover the art and science of conversations that resolve critical issues. You find out why these conversations are so important to working relationships, workplace dynamics, employee performance, and productivity. From preparing for the conversation and kicking off the discussion to closing the communication with ease, you get the basics of what to say and when to say it.

Chapter 1

Let's Get Critical! Making Conversations Count

In This Chapter

▶ Discovering what a critical conversation is

▶ Finding out why you should be having them

▶ Memorizing the golden rule of all critical conversations

▶ Excelling at both the art and science of critical conversations

▶ Recognizing the key steps in a successful critical conversation

Do you have a bossy colleague who never lets you get a word in edgewise?

Do you work with an employee who doesn't pull his own weight on the team?

Are you fed up with making the same decision again and again, but never seeming to get any traction or action?

Do you feel that sometimes you're just talking, meeting, or listening to complaints with absolutely no end in sight?

If you answer yes to any of these questions, you've come to the right place. Critical conversations are here to help turn talk into action, to boost performance and tackle difficult behaviors, and to create healthy relationships between peers.

A critical conversation is a foundation for bringing about change in a behavior, problem, or relationship. From that perspective, a critical conversation is a lot like the foundation for a house — and just as important. Without the solid foundation, even the most wonderful blueprint could result in a house quickly sinking into the ground. The solid foundation to a critical conversation is the groundwork for developing healthy work relationships, fostering teambuilding, and improving productivity.

In this chapter, I discuss what critical conversations are, when you should have one, who should be involved, and where you often see the need for them. I also cover the benefits of critical conversations and why to have one in the first place (there are many reasons). Next, I talk about being authentic and genuine when you have a conversation (something I discuss throughout the book because of its importance). Here, I pay special attention to why being genuine is so important and give ways you can make sure you're having the critical conversation for all the right reasons. Then, I move on to why critical conversations are both an art and a science, and how to excel at both. Lastly, I get into the nuts and bolts of the critical conversation so your conversations generate positive results that last.

Discovering the What, When, Who, and Where of Critical Conversations

Look around and you see that people are talking everywhere and talking about everything. But a conversation where all the parties involved examine the facts, express each person's point of view, and allow others to do the same — *and* then come to agreement about what to do next — is much harder to find. That's where critical conversations come in. The conversation itself is what starts everyone on the same track.

Before you start everyone off on the right track with a critical conversation, I lay the groundwork by covering the four Ws of what makes a critical conversation successful.

What is a critical conversation?

What is a critical conversation? A *critical conversation* is when two or more parties discuss an issue, problem, or situation in which there are different points of view. Most critical conversations involve high emotions, and the goal of the conversation is for something to change after the conversation ends. For example:

✔ A manager needs to work with an employee to improve his performance at work

✔ Employees aren't getting along and the behavior is hurting the performance of the team (The behaviors need to change so the focus can be on the project rather than personality differences.)

✔ A customer is upset with a product and wants a resolution

In all these examples, emotions are likely to be high because part of the discussion includes differing perspectives and opinions of what's happening. A manager may have examples of an employee's poor performance, and the employee may disagree if he fears his job is in danger. Or two employees may have different views on acceptable workplace behavior. Or a customer may be furious if he isn't getting precisely what he wants — and the customer may not be exactly right. A critical conversation's job is to get to the root of the problem and bring these differing perspectives to a common solution.

Another commonality in these situations is that if nothing is done, there could be negative consequences. If the performance of an employee doesn't improve, he could be fired. If employees can't work together on a project, the productivity of the entire team may be at risk. And if a customer is upset, he may stop being a customer. You want to avoid these situations. In mastering the methods of a critical conversation, you can become the hero by avoiding the negative consequences that unresolved issues bring.

When should you have a critical conversation?

People say there's no time like the present, and that's very true in a critical conversation. If you feel that change is needed in someone's behavior, skills, or performance, speaking up is better done early rather than later, after letting problems and emotions fester.

If an issue is halting performance or the ability of individuals to work with one another, it's time to focus on how to build a more productive and healthy foundation through a critical conversation. In Chapter 5, I go into more depth on the clear signs that point to an approaching critical conversation.

Of course, the idea of no-time-like-the-present has exceptions as well. You have some judgment in when to have the discussion. Some conversations need to happen while the behavior is occurring. For example, if an employee is disrupting a meeting, someone versed in critical conversations could call for a short break, and have the discussion then and there to stop the behavior and refocus the team. But many critical conversations need to happen behind closed doors in order to maintain confidentiality; those conversations won't happen at the same time as the behavior or performance is occurring. Other examples of when you may need to momentarily postpone the conversation may be:

✔ You feel the need to prepare more for the conversation. It is better to slightly delay the conversation for a day or two than to start the conversation unclear of the message or intent.

✔ Emotions are already flying high. Chapter 20 gives ideas on how to calm your own emotions down before having a conversation.

✔ If you decide a facilitator could help make the conversation more productive, you may need to delay the conversation. Chapter 15 can help you evaluate when an outside mediator or facilitator can help.

Who should have the conversation?

Many people think that critical conversations are just something that happen between a manager and employee when a performance issue comes up. Although this scenario makes for a common conversation, critical conversations can occur among a variety of people, such as two colleagues working to resolve a personality issue or an employee and a customer when changes are necessary for the relationship to continue.

Critical conversations can happen between just about anyone, but not just anyone should have them. Critical conversations shouldn't be about gossip or a he said–she said discussion. The conversation should happen between the people who are having the dispute, disagreement, or concern. Critical conversations are direct conversations — not discussions between someone's boss and someone else's boss.

If there is a large amount of resistance or there are extremely high emotions, a facilitator may need to help with the conversation (learn more about facilitators in Chapter 15). However, ideally the conversation is between the people who are having the issue.

Because all parties to a critical conversation, by definition, must be present, a manager can't have a productive critical conversation with another manager about the performance of some other employee.

I have one addition to this rule. Sometimes, the parties involved can't resolve an issue no matter how hard they try (or don't try). In Chapter 15, I cover when to bring in an outside facilitator or mediator.

Where should you have a critical conversation?

If at all possible, critical conversations should be held behind closed doors and face-to-face. Confidentiality is key, and since the conversation should only involve the people having the dispute or disagreement, find a location that dissuades other people from seeing, hearing, or eavesdropping on the discussion. Having a conversation in a quiet place helps to limit distractions and allows all the parties to focus on listening to each other rather than listening to the phone ringing nonstop.

Since nonverbal cues are so important to understanding the full message of what people are saying and hearing, having the conversation face-to-face is ideal. In today's virtual world, this is not always possible. If there is no practical way to have a face-to-face conversation, cover all your bases by finding a quiet space with no distractions (and ask for the other participant to do the same) and mastering important verbal and nonverbal communication cues, like choice of words and tone of voice. See Chapters 6 and 7 for more on mastering verbal and nonverbal communication skills.

Making the Effort: Benefits of Critical Conversations Done Right

I won't lie — critical conversations aren't the easiest conversations to have. One reason is the emotions involved; if those emotions (and the disagreements that crop up because of them) weren't present, you'd simply be having a conversation — not a *critical* conversation. Although no book can make the emotional side of a critical conversation go away, following a common process provides the comfort of following a set of guidelines that can calm your own nerves, make you less emotional, and make you better able to handle the emotions of others during the conversation. The good news is that the effort is well worth it, because you can gain plenty of benefits from mastering critical conversations.

First, you actually solve the problems at hand. If you've been trying to get your point across or resolve differences with a co-worker or employee, a critical conversation can help you finally create agreements on what to do next in an understandable plan.

The critical conversation method also helps you discover how to resolve conflict in almost any situation. If you can master how to resolve conflict when the stakes are high and emotions are flying, you surely can resolve conflict when things aren't as heated.

Critical conversations also help improve working relationships. Working relationships are at the center of almost any organization, and being willing to work collaboratively and to express differences of opinion in a clear and professional manner is what successful leaders are made of.

The Golden Rule of Critical Conversations: Be Genuine

The golden rule of critical conversations is to have a genuine desire to make the situation better. What does that mean? Being honest is the start. Opening up and expressing your own thoughts and feelings build rapport and create a safe environment for discussion. Here are two more ways to bring a genuine desire to help to a critical conversation:

- **Listen to all parties:** Listening to the other party in order to understand perspectives before trying to influence the direction of the conversation is an aspect of coming to the conversation with a genuine desire to make the situation better. During the critical conversation, you need to find out what's important to the other participants and then try to find a solution that meets these needs as well as your own.

- **Find a solution to fit everyone:** Seeking out a positive solution for all the participants involved is a visible sign of being authentic and honest during the conversation. Ask yourself whether you're willing to change your point of view if only one solution is feasible. Being genuinely interested in creating a better solution means being willing to look for the best answer, even if it isn't your answer. People are smart and can tell when you're trying to force a solution rather than open up the discussion to every possible solution.

What causes a critical conversation to run off course? Well, in addition to not being genuine and truly wanting to find a solution that benefits everyone, these two traps make it hard to resolve issues and move forward:

- **Hidden agendas:** The hidden agenda may be trying to get back at someone, fire someone, or find a way to get more credit than you're due. Regardless of the agenda, having one is a guaranteed way to make a conversation fail. On the flip side, checking your agenda at the door opens up a world of possibilities. Withholding self-serving information to make sure you get your way puts the brakes on a critical conversation and makes any forward movement fall flat in no time.

✔ **Name-dropping:** Power-tripping and name-dropping stop a critical conversation faster than you can say "I know the CEO." It's fine to use relationships you've developed to help build a better solution, but having relationships in the organization isn't the same thing as name-dropping. Name-dropping is an attempt to get your way in an argument or discussion by implying that others will support you because of a close relationship. Although this tactic may win the day, it can cause resentment among the other employees, and, if your relationship is ever discredited, it can cause others to lose their trust in you.

Throughout the book I give you many examples of what to do, how to present ideas, and even what to say during a critical conversation. However, genuinely wanting to make the situation better and being willing to put everything else aside has to come from the people having the discussion.

Grasping the Art and Science of Critical Conversations

The marriage of art and science in a critical conversation is a beautiful thing. Bringing together the art — how you approach and deliver the conversation — and the science — the facts that build the conversation — create a path to resolution success.

The art: Making the interpersonal connection

When faced with a difficult conversation, it's not just what you say but how you say it. Even with a perfect plan and a proven method, how you say something can make all the difference in the world. The art is *how* you communicate.

The art of conversation includes both verbal and nonverbal skills. Your body language, tone of voice, and eye contact can help put the other parties at ease or make them feel like they're part of the Spanish Inquisition. Words you choose can also make or break a conversation. Saying, "Wow, that was a great idea," can be interpreted sarcastically or positively depending on the tone, emphasis, and context.

I discuss nonverbal skills more thoroughly in Chapter 7; using cooperative words and phrases that facilitate working together are discussed throughout the book and in depth in Chapter 6.

But the art doesn't stop there. Being willing and able to adjust the conversation as needed helps to make the conversation flow and create the desired results. Part of this art is building rapport and trust, and the other part is just knowing how and when to be flexible. Check out Chapters 9 and 10 for more on how to build rapport during the conversation and keep challenging situations positive during the conversation.

Nothing can replace the interpersonal aspect of two people talking (and I mean *really* talking — not just texting or e-mailing each other).

The science: Focusing on the facts

The science of critical conversation focuses on the facts of the conversation to move the discussion from emotions to resolution. Even though most critical conversations involve a highly emotional issue, focusing on the facts and data first, and then how these facts make the parties in the conversation feel, defuses the emotion so a conversation — not an argument — can take place.

Yelling "I don't like you" is simply an emotional statement that leads nowhere, expect perhaps to the other person yelling back. A better alternative is to focus on the facts of the conversation: the issue, the behavior, and the impact of the behavior:

- ✔ **The situation or issue:** What event or behavior happened (or is happening) that you want to help or need to have changed? If you find someone's behavior annoying or degrading, first say what the behavior is rather than how you feel. For example, you could say, "In the management meeting today, I noticed some behaviors that you may not be aware of."

- ✔ **The behavior:** Let the individual know about the behavior. In the previous example, you may follow up by saying, "You didn't let me complete my thought three times because you cut me off midsentence."

- ✔ **The impact of the issue or behavior:** With both honesty and empathy, precisely state how you feel about the behavior or the impact it's causing. For example, you may say, "This makes me feel like my opinion isn't valued."

Sticking with the facts during the conversation keeps all parties from being defensive and helps keep relationships intact. Keeping the conversation focused on the facts also sets up the critical conversation process as a mutually beneficial one, rather than a situation in which you "let me complain and tell you everything you do wrong."

Blending art and science to make a positive impact

When you blend the art and science of conversation successfully, you get an authentic way to give meaningful feedback, confront difficult situations, and proactively recommend ways to move forward. Talk about a positive impact!

Outside of practice, one way to blend the art and science is to create agreements that build on one another throughout the conversation. The following sections tell you about the three main agreements to look for.

A willingness to work together

Do you sense a willingness to have the conversation in the first place? This part of many conversations is often ignored or assumed, but if people don't want to talk to one another, the conversation starts on the defensive and probably goes downhill from there.

Here's a good way to blend the art and science by asking whether the other person is willing to participate:

> "Hi, Josie. I noticed in the motivational meeting this morning some behaviors you may not be aware of. When I was trying to ask our sponsors to help with fundraising, you brought up all the possible things that could go wrong with our approach. This made it difficult for me to ask for help in a positive way. Are you willing to work with me to find a mutual solution for talking to our key donors next time?"

An acknowledgment of what the problem is

Most conversations jump into what needs to change, often from just one person's perspective. Critical conversations try to identify the specific behavior that's causing the problem.

The following is a masterfully blended example of how to start finding out what the real problem may be:

> "Thanks for being willing to work on this. You bring a tremendous amount of experience to our organization and perhaps I misunderstood your comments. Was there a reason you wanted to discuss all the possible things that could go wrong with our approach during the meeting?"

An approach to finding a solution

Now is the time to find solutions. You can be supportive and direct (the art) but use facts (the science) to recommend more preferable solutions.

In the previous example, after Josie explains why she was negative, or agrees that she was negative, the artful science of finding solutions would sound like this (make sure you're genuine when you say this first sentence!):

> "I appreciate your experience. You say you wanted to share your experience, but people were only listening to your negative point of view. I'm wondering whether we can work together to come up with alternative ways of balancing your experience with a positive message."

The science keeps the conversation focused on the facts and results, while the interpersonal art keeps the focus on creating mutual agreements and positive relationships. I cover all the behind-the-scenes work on how to make these agreements happen in Part III of the book.

Getting an EDGE on Critical Conversations

People are talking everywhere, but when you're faced with an emotional, critical, or high-stakes situation, just winging the conversation isn't going to fly. If you master the critical conversation process, regardless of the situation you find yourself in, you'll feel confident in making sure you're following a proven path.

Impactful and positive critical conversations follow four big steps: examining what's happening, deciding what to do next, gaining commitment about what to do next and getting moving, and then evaluating how well the actions are taking place (and how the conversation went). These steps — examine, decide, get commitment and get moving, evaluate (EDGE for short) — combined with balancing the art and science of conversation, put all the parties involved in the conversation on a common path to realizing exceptional results for everyone. Chapter 4 offers an in-depth look at putting the EDGE model to use.

Exploring and examining what's happening

Before a word is even said, as the initiator of the conversation, your job is to come to the table with the facts about what's happening. As you explore what's happening, examine the situation or concern, and determine which existing facts or circumstances support that concern. During critical conversations, the following criteria help you to keep examining the facts, even in the most heated discussions:

✔ **Acknowledge other opinions and perspectives.** A critical conversation is a two-way street. After you determine whether the other party is willing to take part in the discussion, ask him for his opinion of the situation. By doing so, you're validating the other party's opinion and perspective, even if you don't agree with it.

✔ **Make sure the behavior or issue is actionable.** To keep the conversation on track, examine and state behaviors that the receiver can do something about. Simply saying, "You're annoying," or even, "Your behavior is annoying," may be easy to say, but the person hearing it can do absolutely nothing with it. A better alternative would be to say, "Yelling across the room makes it hard for me to concentrate on work," or, "When you answer your phone during meetings, I feel you are not paying attention to our discussion."

✔ **Link behaviors to consequences.** As you explore and examine what's going on, state the facts and then link the facts to how the behavior is making a negative impact. For example, "When you don't complete your work on time, I have to spend time doing your work at the last minute," or, "When you don't respond to client e-mails, our clients are less likely to come back." Include your feelings about the behavior, as long as they're relevant. For example, "You cut me off midsentence, and that made me feel undervalued."

You can find tips and ways to prepare and deliver critical conversations in Chapters 3 and 4.

Deciding on options to move forward

After you examine the facts and acknowledge points of view, it's time to decide what to do next. Review the art and science of building agreements: Do you see a willingness to work together? How will the problem be solved?

When deciding on options to move forward, discuss how addressing the issue or concern will help achieve mutual goals and objectives. Will the company, team, or employee be better off? Even though the parties may have different views about how to solve a problem, try to agree on what you're solving.

Brainstorm ideas on how to address the problem. Although every situation is different, the best way to gain commitment to next steps is to develop the next steps together. Asking, "What solutions do you have in mind?" is a great question to generate ideas. Developing next steps together helps all parties in the conversation gain commitment about what to do next so they don't have to revisit the same conversation again, and again, and again.

Gaining commitment and getting moving

The "G" in the acronym EDGE has two key parts: gaining commitment on what to do next and then going and doing it (get moving — another important "G"!). Close out the conversation, get commitment about what's going to happen next, and start seeing meaningful results after the talking stops. Chapter 11 goes into detail about closing the conversation, and here I give you two key questions to ask before you say "let's go":

- ✔ **"Can everyone live with and support the decision or outcome of the conversation?"** The goal of a critical conversation is for all parties to walk out feeling mutual respect and mutual agreement. If one person wins and the other loses, the conversation will most likely lead to one party harboring resentment — not to progress.

- ✔ **"What is a realistic timeframe to address this issue (or make the change) and achieve the desired outcomes?"** In Chapter 11, I walk through the SMART goal-setting process and how to create action plans to support the conversation. By asking this question, you're signaling that action and accountability are needed after the conversation.

Evaluating next steps

Even if you master the critical conversation steps, if nothing happens differently after everyone goes back to work, well, it was just a conversation that resulted in the same old–same old.

At this point, the conversation is done and all the parties in the conversation have committed to an action plan. After the talking is done, it is time to evaluate how the conversation went and track progress.

To track progress, as the initiator of the conversation, you can make observations of how the behavior has changed. The recipient may track progress of her accomplishments and desired changes committed to in the action plan. The change can be behavioral, it can be in a resolution of conflict, or it can be in team dynamics. If you're having a conversation with an underperforming employee, the change will happen when the employee does his job better. If the conversation is between two employees having a dispute, the goal is to resolve the dispute.

Since the purpose of most critical conversations is to change behaviors or actions and to build a more positive relationship, it is also helpful to have a follow-up conversation to talk specifically about how the feedback was delivered and how the initial conversation went. In addition to tracking progress in follow-up conversations (for example, tracking specific short- and long-term goals on the action plan), check how the initial conversation was received. For example, you may start by asking, "I know the conversation we had last week was not easy for me. Would you be comfortable talking about how I did in delivering the feedback?" By asking this question, the initiator of the conversation can gain valuable feedback on how he or she delivered the message.

The good news is that if the parties work together throughout the process, the commitment and likeliness of action are significantly higher because the solution is built together.

Critical Conversations Are Everywhere

So where do critical conversations happen? Well, critical conversations really are everywhere. Almost anywhere you see a conflict or differences of opinion, a critical conversation can be a key tool to finding a resolution. If you master the keys to conversation, you'll soon be finding entirely new ways to communicate.

Critical conversations can happen between two people (employees and managers, peers, or employees and a customer), between groups, or between an individual and a group, or almost any combination of these participants.

One-on-one conversations often allow for more time for real discussion where all parties have the time to tell their side of the story and come to agreement.

However, some critical conversations need to happen in a group setting. When multiple people are involved in the conversation, it's more important than ever to make sure everyone listens to all sides of the issue and everyone involved agrees on the problem and is committed to a solution. Chapters 16 and 17 can help you lead critical conversations as a team and work through the difficult behaviors and situations you may experience.

You can use critical conversations to create a nonthreatening environment when highly charged, high-stakes situations exist. But in the end, the skills you have in leading critical conversations can be used anywhere and at almost any time when your needs, desires, or ideal solutions differ from someone else's. If you're looking for a way to get to the root of the problem, solve the real issues in your workplace, and have better working relationships because of it, settle in and turn the page. Critical conversations may just be the words you're looking for.

Chapter 2

The Ins and Outs of a Critical Conversation

In This Chapter

▶ Build relationships, resolve issues, and improve performance

▶ Find out why today's workplace needs critical conversations

▶ Discover — and avoid — common pitfalls

. . . .

*F*or some leaders, having tough conversations may be second nature. But for most people, delivering bad news, giving a poor performance review, or having to communicate a disappointing message can feel like a prison sentence. Critical conversations to the rescue! Critical conversations help turn challenging discussions into healthier relationships and improved performance.

In this chapter, I walk through the positive points that come out of critical conversations done well, including reenergizing and even growing business relationships, improving employee performance, and resolving long-standing problems in the workplace. I also introduce common obstacles that make even the most articulate leaders stumble when they're delivering less than perfect news to employees, customers, and colleagues. Finally, I give you expert tips on the pitfalls that can happen during critical conversations and ways that you can avoid them.

It's Not Just Words: Critical Conversations Matter

Most business leaders are comfortable with financial numbers, sales strategies, and business plans. But when it's time to deliver unpleasant news to employees or customers, they shy away from the real issues and deliver a watered-down version of what they're trying to say. Then, when the watered-down message fails to generate the results they expect, frustration, disappointment, and perhaps even anger begin to boil up all around the workplace. This cycle continues to make the situation worse.

Mastering the art and science of critical conversations helps to break this cycle and often leads to improving employee morale in the long run.

If you feel you're bringing your A-game to the table but still aren't getting the results you want from your team, or if you tend to seize up when you need to talk about performance or behavior, it's time to start using critical conversations to get your point across.

In the following sections, I show you all the good things that can happen when you deliver the precise message you want to deliver. After you understand its importance, see Chapter 3 for the key elements of a critical conversation.

Building relationships

It may seem counterintuitive, but delivering tough news can make a relationship stronger. Here's why: working relationships are the result of credibility and trust among all parties. Trust and credibility take time to develop, but if you tell the whole truth, employees are usually more receptive to any type of feedback you give and are more willing to provide you with their own feedback in the future.

Although pleasant information is always more enjoyable to deliver, the honest, tough message builds relationships by creating an open, honest dialogue rather than the parties in the conversation resorting to playing mind games, hiding their own opinions, or resorting to outright hostility. Good relationships are built when everybody involved has a chance to present their opinion and needs without fear of retaliation.

If building or repairing a relationship is a goal of your communication, here are a few tips to keep in mind:

- ✓ **Be willing to listen to the other person's point of view.** Come into the conversation with an open mind. If you genuinely agree with this sentiment, I suggest simply saying that you want to keep everyone's best interest in mind while working on a resolution.

- ✓ **Find a common goal.** Disagreeing on how to achieve a goal is much easier if you can at least agree on an overarching goal that all parties have in common.

Here's a drastic example of finding a common goal. If you have to let an employee know that you have to cut his paycheck to help the company meet its financial targets, you and the employee have goals that seem to be polar opposites. On one side, the employee wants to make money to pay his bills; on the other side, you need to make your numbers so you can keep your job. In truth, you share a common goal: The company stays in business and everyone stays employed.

✔ **Be supportive.** If at all possible, show support of the other person's goals or perspectives. You don't need to agree with them, but letting the other parties know that you respect their opinions and ideas, even if you don't agree with them, can go a long way toward building relationships during tough conversations.

Resolving issues

Nine times out of ten, the reason for a critical conversation is to resolve an issue in the workplace, so of course you want to resolve the issue at hand! But if you don't deliver a message clearly, the issue can (and usually does) continue to get worse.

An issue can only be resolved if all parties come to the table with the opportunity to voice their opinion and feel their opinions are heard. But don't just take my word for it, from the research at top-ranked universities to the acts of great leaders everywhere, successful and respected leaders communicate openly rather than hiding their ideas or attacking others.

Most business professionals have faced or have seen unresolved conflict that has led to friction in the workplace or even deterioration of relationships and performance. I recently observed a discussion between ten directors on an upcoming change with the company's technology systems. The conversation went along just fine, until the Senior Vice President walked into the meeting, listened for three minutes, and then informed the rest of the group that the option was her way or no way. The room went silent. The opinions from the ten other directors on possible roadblocks, concerns, and opportunities were shut down faster than you can say *critical conversation*. It was not until one of the mid-level directors stood up and pointed out that while the Senior VP was right about the timing of the system implementation, perhaps encouraging discussion rather than forcing her answer could avoid some of the issues the company had with the past technology system.

Was the director nervous about telling the boss how her behavior was causing conflict rather than resolving the issues? Yes! If you feel unusually anxious during conversations, your anxiety is likely crippling your ability to resolve any issue and it may even be making the issue worse. Being anxious during a conversation is one of the biggest deterrents of effective critical conversations, but when you overcome the anxiety and start talking, the tensions often quickly go away and progress starts to be made. For ways to get ready for the conversation, head to Chapter 9.

Managing performance

Improving the performance of an employee or team is one of the best outcomes of a critical conversation done correctly. It's pretty powerful to know that with the right delivery, you can really change how things are done in the workplace. Imagine walking out of a meeting room knowing that you helped improve your employee's aptitude or attitude. In order to do that, the message must be clear and understood, in other words, don't leave it up to someone else to decipher what you're trying to say.

Before going into ways a critical conversation can help performance, first make sure the performance issue is not a conduct issue. If an employee is unable to perform their job satisfactorily, a critical conversation can help give guidance and coaching. Chapter 13 is full of examples on how to use critical conversations to turn around performance. However, if an employee is unwilling to perform her job, the issue is more likely to do with conduct (or lack thereof). If the writing is on the wall and conduct is the reason, you may want to knock on HR's door and bring the second half of Chapter 13 along.

Critical conversations help employees improve their performance because they create an open climate with ample feedback, ask for the employee's perspective, and create actions for improvement. Take a look at these factors a little more closely:

- ✔ **Open climate for feedback:** Critical conversations are based on honest feedback, rather than allowing emotions and opinions to stay bottled up. By starting a dialogue on what is not working, employees and managers are free to ask for additional feedback, share concerns, and get guidance on what to do (rather than just guessing).

- ✔ **Ask for the employee's perspective:** Some employees have no problem speaking their mind, but others may feel intimidated or unsure when asking for tools and training to get their job done. A critical conversation gives employees a chance to ask for what they need. Job roles and tasks change quickly in today's environment, and it is not unreasonable for an employee to be overwhelmed by the speed of change.

✔ **Create action plans for improvement:** Actions plans not only outline specific steps of what to do next, they also create specific times to check back on progress and answer any questions or concerns that come up after the conversation ends. This open cycle for performance improvement is one of the best ways to make sure performance continues to meet expectations in the future.

Finding Out What Makes Conversations Critical

In Chapter 1, I give you the dictionary definition of a critical conversation. In this section, I expand on what makes a conversation so critical and give you a few examples. A critical conversation is

✔ **A conversation for which the desired result is to change performance or behaviors.** Critical conversations can often focus on behaviors in the workplace or provide feedback on poor performance. But this is just the tip of the iceberg when it comes to using critical conversations to change performance. You can use the critical conversation steps on anything from building consensus around a problem (and how to resolve it) to identifying (and agreeing on) the consequences of undesirable behaviors or actions. You can also use a critical conversation to set or reestablish goals or even to elicit feedback from employees or customers.

✔ **A Critical conversation in which information is not just delivered between a manager and employee.** In fact, if your team is having critical conversations that help resolve issues, improve performance, and build relationships, you have the potential to have a highly functioning team delivering exceptional results. A critical conversation can happen between a manager and employee, a manager and a team, two or more colleagues, a supplier and a customer, or any combination of these roles.

✔ **A conversation that leads to a key business or employment decision.** These conversations may include hiring, firing, transferring, or promoting employees. They can also include letting customers know about price increases, potential quality issues with a product or service, or changes to the services customers are used to having.

A critical conversation is a conversation that provides information that will significantly change the environment, dynamics, relationships, or performance in the workplace. These critical conversations can happen quite often — just with varying scales of complexity.

It's Not Easy! Why Critical Conversations Are So Hard

Chances are good that you've been talking since you were about 1 or 2 years old. With all this experience, why is it so hard to deliver critical conversations? The answer isn't as easy as "people don't like to give bad news," but that's at least part of it. Balancing different emotions and perspectives with the facts is also part of it. Now add into that mix the new technology that makes it that much easier to blast off good or bad news, and "reply all" e-mail shouts, and you have the potential for issues, performances, or relationships turning south rather quickly if the fundamentals of critical conversation aren't in place.

In this section, I share with you some reasons why critical conversations don't happen as often as they should in the workplace. Understanding these reasons will help you identify when critical conversations need to happen in a timely manner (more on that topic in Chapter 4).

Facts and emotions collide in the workplace

All people have their own personalities, styles, perceptions, and beliefs. Leaving these traits at the front door of the office and acting like a robot from 9–5 are next to impossible. Because all these characteristics walk in the door with employees, and because employees work together, you should expect differences of opinion in the workplace. These differences can be anything from how to run a project to what's considered appropriate language in the workplace. Now marry these emotions, perceptions, and styles with the facts — or the perception of facts — and disagreements can quickly occur. A company may have a workplace rule about acceptable and professional behavior, but managers are often expected to decide right and wrong among the many shades of gray.

Table 2-1 shows some examples of facts and emotions colliding.

Table 2-1   Fact versus Emotion in Critical Conversations

Scenario	Fact	Emotion
A company is going through a restructuring, and employees may lose their jobs.	A company needs to operate efficiently, which may mean cutting costs.	A leader needs to tell someone he no longer has a job and this will most likely result in the employee feeling sadness and distress.
An employee applied for a promotion as a branch manager and didn't get it.	The leader has to set up the new branch manager for success.	The leader has to deliver the news to the employee who didn't get the job and help the employee find ways to continue to support the new branch manager without being jealous.
An employee believes another employee talks too loudly on the phone when dealing with customers.	Customers have never complained, but the tension is a barrier to getting work done.	Both employees have different opinions about acceptable behavior at work and will need to find a way to agree.

These examples show how emotions and facts often cause different perceptions of the same issue, which is why critical conversations are so important. The balancing act of keeping or finding a way for everyone to work together (emotion) and getting the job done (fact) is always a challenge, but also a great opportunity to deliver a critical conversation to make things better in the long run. Because these conversations are never easy and the balancing act takes both patience and persistence, sometimes leaders shy away from even having the conversation in the first place.

A tendency to shy away from tough news

Critical conversations are hard because people know that others have emotions. Most people don't want to intentionally hurt someone's feelings, so they may just avoid the conversation altogether. When a manager is shying away from giving bad news, he may push off a meeting time after time, shuffle an employee from one department to another department, seize up when it's time to talk about the issue, or simply say nothing.

Keep these two big things in mind when you want to back down from giving bad news:

- **Take the word "bad" out of the discussion.** Rather than thinking of the message as good news or bad news, just think of it as news. In Table 2-1, I give you an example about a company going through restructuring and employees losing their jobs. Telling someone he's losing his job isn't pleasant, but it can be done in a compassionate and genuine way. Firing someone is rarely easy, but it is the fact, and dancing around the issue or waiting until the last minute can make the situation even more uncomfortable.

- **Not delivering news to an employee, customer, or colleague may seem like the easy way out in the short term, but it rarely leads to anything positive in the future.** If you have an aspiring accountant on your team but he can't add, wouldn't it be better to let him know that sooner rather than later? If you have to let a customer know that the product may have a quality issue, wouldn't it be better coming from you instead of from a rumor posted on a blog?

Here's an example of how to constructively confront an issue that has been avoided in the past:

A customer has been getting increasingly irate at the customer service team. Alex, the customer service manager, has been hoping the entire thing will just resolve itself with communication training and conflict resolution webinars. Nothing is getting better. After reading about critical conversations, Alex delivers this message:

"Hi, Mr. Customer. I want to address something that seems to be hurting our ability to provide exceptional service. It seems like most of the calls end up without resolution because they end with raised voices [the situation presented as fact, neither good nor bad]. That is different from the way we usually operate, and I'd like to see what we can do to resolve the issue [not waiting any longer to resolve the issue]."

This conversation works for a few reasons. First, since Alex used "I" messages, the reaction will more likely be rational rather than defensive. The information was specific but did not fall into the parent-kid trap of telling the customer exactly what they should do. Second, Alex focused on one issue at a time and did not lay blame. In this example, saying conversations end with raised voices is a statement, not an opinion. If the customer can work on not raising his voice, there would be a much higher chance the situation could be resolved.

Slowing down is the new fast

Leadership and time management guru Stephen Covey stated that slowing down in relationships is the only way to move fast. Critical conversations help you to do just that. Sending off an e-mail, typing a text, or dictating orders may seem like a fast way to get your point across, but when you try to hurry up in relationships, it almost always results in costing more time in the end. Often, impatience is returned with an equally hasty response, and sometimes hostility. It may take about 30 seconds to send a colleague a note to let them know you are frustrated, but it could potentially take years to repair the relationship if the other person takes offense.

If you still find yourself shying away from delivering critical conversations, turn the tables. If you weren't living up to your manager's expectations, you'd probably want to know so that you could change. You probably also wouldn't want to have to guess at the real message if the message was watered down.

Technology makes talking too passé

Technology can remove a number of barriers that get in the way of conversations. Technology can give you the ability to more easily find time on calendars to meet, chat virtually with someone many time zones away, or visually share information in real time. Technology can also help communication happen more quickly and efficiently. Outside of the standard e-mail, messaging, and knowledge management tools, enterprise tools like Chatter and other real-time collaboration platforms help employees share information more quickly than ever before. However, technology still can't do one thing quite yet — it can't think for you. Sure Siri can find the closest sushi restaurant, but she can't build relationships or resolve conflicts.

With texting, chatting, e-mailing, and all the other tools at business leaders' fingertips, sometimes getting up and having a face-to-face conversation just doesn't happen, or at least doesn't happen as frequently as it did before. Typing something and pushing send may seem easier than having a face-to-face (or at least voice-to-voice) exchange of ideas. By no means should organizations go back to interoffice mail and logistically challenging meetings, but *critical communication can't be done in an e-mail*. There's no way around it. Cutting and pasting the company policy with a few concise comments at the end isn't going to solve anything. Sending a note in ALL CAPITAL LETTERS TO GET YOUR POINT ACROSS does little to build relationships in the face of conflict.

Think about how you may react to these two different ways of approaching a critical conversation with someone who has been late to work.

> **Option 1: The technology option.** In an e-mail, write: Dear Lauren, Per your time card you have been coming in after 1 p.m. three times in the past three weeks. Your official start time is 10 a.m. Please see our policy (included in the attachment) and let me know if you have any questions. Sincerely, Your Non–Critical Conversation Informed Boss.

> **Option 2: The critical communication option.** Communication Savvy Boss asks Lauren if she can talk in private for a few minutes during a convenient time and then starts the discussion with: *Hi, Lauren. I've noticed you've been coming in around 1 p.m., three times over the past three weeks. Our team really depends on everyone being at our morning meetings to talk through project issues. I'd like to talk about how this can be solved. Are you willing to talk about this?*

Sending a stock response is faster than investigating the problem to find a specific solution, but the end result of these two approaches will most likely be very different. In Option 1, Lauren is automatically on the defensive. In Option 2, the boss genuinely wants to find a solution to the problem.

Technology has given employees the opportunity to check in from anywhere and do more with time that may have once been spent doing nothing. Use that technology to support conversations rather than to have them. (For more on using technology in closing out conversations, check out Chapter 1.) In the previous example, if the boss wants to document the conversation, he could use an e-mail after the face-to-face discussion.

Avoiding Common Communication Pitfalls

If you've ever been part of a conversation (critical or not) that has gone dreadfully wrong, know that you're *not* alone! You may feel like it, but struggling with getting a message across clearly and struggling with getting the desired results after the conversation ends is far more common than most people think. If it was easy, you wouldn't need this book, right?

Being effective in critical conversations isn't about having a grab bag of scripts. Successful critical conversations are the result of preparing for the discussion, asking the right questions, listening to the other parties, and engaging in constructive dialogue. Not surprisingly, hazards crop up to keep that perfect formula from coming together.

The good news is that I can tell you the common reasons why critical conversations fail, as well as the proven ways to recover from these errors and avoid the pitfalls in the future. Knowing these pitfalls and avoiding them will help create that perfect formula for effective conversation.

If you just finished a conversation and feel amazing, you know you did something right. But if you're exhausted and don't quickly see the results from the discussion, take the time to find out what went wrong and fix it, ASAP. Here are a few questions to ask if the conversation didn't go as planned:

- ✔ **Did someone talk too much?** Critical conversations are successful when all parties ask questions and are given time to answer them. No one likes to be talked "at," especially when a critical message needs to be understood and accepted. Did all the parties in the conversation ask questions and have acknowledgement that they were heard? Was there enough time to allow people to express their ideas and emotions? Did people have time to think? If not, one of the parties may have *talked too much* — a big no-no in the critical conversation world.

- ✔ **Were people distracted?** Being present is one of the most valuable tools in the conversation toolkit. Was everyone present in the meeting, or did you see texting, typing, and cellphone yapping? Did the body language reflect engaged participants or people who wanted to be elsewhere? If people looked like they weren't listening, they probably weren't, and the message may have fallen on deaf ears.

- ✔ **Was there trust?** Building an atmosphere of trust and openness is the first step to building or rebuilding relationships. Did you come into the meeting with a genuine desire to make something change or happen? Did you probe to understand the employee's concerns? Is the relationship between the parties healthy or fragile? A healthy relationship, even in the face of conflict, creates results; a hostile environment needs to be addressed before any change can happen.

- ✔ **Was everyone headed in the same direction?** Gaining clarity on specific goals helps keep the conversation and the action after the conversation focused. Did all parties in the conversation have a chance to voice their personal outlook on the problem? Did all participants in the conversation share at least one common goal? Did you elicit feedback and expectations for what happens next? If you didn't set common goals and expectations, they probably won't be achieved. Having specific and agreed on goals is especially important if other parties don't want to hear the message.

Many of these pitfalls focus on what the initiator of the conversation can do to make the conversation go more smoothly. Sometimes, you'll find a challenge that's outside the control of the initiator, like one party not being receptive to the message or outright hostility. Although you can't force anyone to change or listen, making sure the common mistakes are mitigated can move the conversation in a positive manner. For more techniques on keeping challenging situations and people moving in a positive direction, check out Chapter 10.

Although the following sections may not address absolutely everything that could go wrong during a conversation, these questions are a great place to start and will help you improve critical communication skills. Read on to fix and avoid these hazards in the future. And take a look at Table 2-2, which gives you a quick guide to the problems and their solutions.

Table 2-2	Problems and Solutions in Critical Conversations	
Problem	*Solution*	*Example*
One-sided conversation	Acknowledge the behavior and then redirect the conversation.	Thanks for that information, Kathy. I know many things can get in the way of getting work done, so let's come up with a plan on how to remove the three main barriers you talked about [acknowledge what was said]. More could come up, but I recommend we start with these three. What do you see as some potential solutions [redirect the conversation to the next step]?
Distracted audience	Ask questions about what is happening.	Ted, you look confused. What part of the goal would be helpful for me to go over in more depth?
	Be respectful. Help people think.	Sue, you look like you are spending lots of time on your phone. I know everyone is busy. Is there anything I can do to help you be part of the conversation?
		Dan, I would love to hear your opinion. What are your ideas on how to solve the problem?

Problem	Solution	Example
A lack of trust	Trust builder #1: Give meaningful feedback.	Are you open to feedback about the meeting this morning?
	Trust builder #2: Be authentic.	I plan on researching more about the issue and will give you an update next Monday.
	Trust builder #3: Speak now.	I honestly don't know the answer, but I am happy to try to find the solution.
	Trust builder #4: Keep commitments.	
Not heading in the same direction	Be clear on goals. Identify motivations.	It seems like we may not be in agreement on the expectations of the job. Would you be willing to talk about what you feel is most important to the job and your performance?

Problem/solution: One-sided conversation

Critical conversations can get sidetracked when one person dominates the conversation. Individuals may talk too much when they're nervous, want to make sure they're heard, or simply have a habit of talking a lot. Regardless of the root cause of the talking, one person dominating the conversation can prevent the conversation from creating the results needed to help change the behavior or situation.

If an individual is talking and not letting others get a word in edgewise (or not letting you get to the point of the meeting), here are two techniques that work:

✔ **Acknowledge:** In the meeting, acknowledge the comments. If you ignore the individual, he may get angry or louder — neither is good for a productive, critical conversation.

✔ **Redirect:** During a natural break in the conversation or when the talkative party comes up for air, repeat what you heard, and then redirect to get results. After acknowledging the information from the other individual, reflect on his comments and then redirect the conversation to help it move to the next step.

Here's how redirecting the conversation may sound:

Suppose Expert Communicator Eddy is having a critical conversation with Chatty Kathy about her performance. Kathy has been late on a number of projects and is talking quite a bit about why these projects are late.

> **Chatty Kathy:** "And I was late on that project back in 2009 because I didn't have access to the files . . . [4 minutes later] . . . and that caused this project to be late." [Kathy comes up for a breath.]

> **Expert Communicator Eddy:** "Thanks for that information, Kathy. I know many things can get in the way of getting work done, so let's come up with a plan on how to remove the three main barriers you talked about [acknowledge what was said]. More could come up, but I recommend we start with these three. What do you see as some potential solutions [redirect the conversation to the next step]?"

Expert Communicator Eddy politely summarized the reasons Kathy explained and immediately asked permission to move on to solving the issue at hand. Eddy may even take Kathy's knowledge of all the reasons things have gone wrong and redirect them with a simple question: "With your experience in project management, Kathy, how would you recommend we start identifying ways to deliver the best results possible in the future?" An even more pointed alternative may be: "We've been discussing the problems for most of the meeting; how are we going to implement solutions in the future?"

With both of these statements, Kathy will realize that you're paying attention to her and that she needs to redirect and focus on the solution, rather than just rambling on about the problems of the past.

But what if the person who talked too much was you? If you're initiating the conversation and find that you're doing most of the talking, here's a simple method to redirect the conversation, either during or after the conversation. Try following these steps:

1. **Let the group know you recognize what happened.** Simply saying, "I realize that I spoke for most of the meeting about quality issues with the new product line, and we weren't able to get the group feedback on the issue at hand" is a great way to build trust through being honest.

2. **Let the group or individual know what you plan to do about it.** "This Friday I'm going to open my door and let

anyone with ideas for helping to solve the quality issues participate in a problem-solving session."

3. **Be specific about why the conversation will be different the next time around.** Instead of just saying the conversation will be different, cite the actual behavior that will change. For example, you may want decide to delegate facilitation to another team member or ask for feedback in another way.

If you catch yourself talking way too much during a conversation, you can redirect the discussion right then and there. You may say something like, "Wow, I've been talking for way too long. What do you think?" A little humor and humility can go a long way.

Problem/solution: Distracted audience

When people are distracted during a conversation, it will be fairly apparent that the message isn't getting across. Most people have witnessed some form of distracted individuals: Typing Ted types away on his phone, Sidetracked Sue checks e-mail during a meeting, and Disruptive Dan not-so-politely excuses himself to take an "urgent" call during a meeting. Typing Ted, Sidetracked Sue, and Disruptive Dan aren't the only individuals who may not be listening to your message, but they're often the biggest offenders of a message falling on deaf ears.

People are distracted during a conversation for many reasons, and only one of them is that the individual is just plain old rude (more on that in Chapter 16). The individual may have personal issues at home, be worried about another project, or not understand why *this* conversation is so important.

Involvement is the best way to redirect distracted parties in the conversation and get everyone focused on a common goal. The following techniques even work when someone is distracted or pretending to be distracted because he just doesn't want to acknowledge or "hear" the discussion.

- ✔ **Ask questions.** If the other individual or party in the conversation is quiet or exhibiting Typing Ted, Sidetracked Sue, or Disruptive Dan behavior, ask questions that will encourage participation. For example, "Ted, you look confused. What part of the goal would be helpful for me to go over in more depth?"

- ✔ **Be respectful (even when the other party isn't).** Be careful not to ask sarcastic questions, like "Wow, Sue, it looks like you're an expert in creating calendar entries. Can you schedule our next meeting to discuss this issue?" Catching people who are distracted is easy, but being sarcastic could alienate them more. A better option may be to take Sue aside during a break and say, "Sue, you look like you are spending lots of time on your phone. I know everyone is busy. Is there anything I can do to help you be part of the conversation?" This direct statement lets Sue know you have noticed her behavior and want to help her be less distracted without you sounding rude or sarcastic.

✔ **Help people come back to the conversation.** Even though people can multitask quite well, multitasking and thinking rarely go hand in hand, so make the other party think. When you're trying to involve a distracted individual, the worst thing you can do is ask a yes-or-no question. Asking, "Dan, did you understand that last point?" will surely get a "yep," even though Dan may have been out of the room for the entire conversation. This tactic will destroy your credibility, because the rest of the group involved in the conversation will think you've asked a silly question, and they may even respond with silly responses in the future. Instead, ask an open-ended question like, "Dan, I would love to hear your opinion. What are your ideas on how to solve the problem?" This type of question brings a distracted Dan back into the conversation in a firm and participative way.

 The best way to focus a critical conversation when someone is distracted is to involve them with respect and make them think. If these techniques don't do the job, an alternative may be as simple as stating the obvious: "Ted, it looks like you're distracted. This conversation is important. Do you want to have it at another time, or is there something we need to work through first so that both of us can focus?"

Problem/solution: A lack of trust

A healthy relationship can make any critical conversation successful, while an unhealthy relationship can make every conversation futile. Relationships aren't built overnight, and a trusting relationship can't be forced on an employee, peer, or manager.

In addition to being open, honest, and genuine every day, here are some specific actions that can lead to better relationships and that, in turn, will launch critical conversations more positively — even when you need to deliver a negative message.

✔ **Trust builder #1: Give meaningful feedback.** Don't wait until you need to have a critical conversation! Proactively provide specific and tangible feedback, rather than staying quiet and withholding your point of view. You don't have to hold formal meetings to give feedback or make recommendations. You can do it right after a meeting, when you're walking in the hallway, or on a weekly one-on-one call. The longer you wait to give feedback, the more critical it becomes.

✔ **Trust builder #2: Be authentic.** Express your opinions and feelings, even if the other individual disagrees with them. Saying what you think the other person wants to hear never leads to a productive, long-term relationships.

✔ **Trust builder #3: Speak now.** Waiting for the other person to take the next step or assuming they know what to do without talking about it can lead to a tricky situation. Down the road, the other person may ask, "Well, if you knew I should do something else, why didn't you tell me?" Rather than be dictatorial, make recommendations and allow for frequent discussion between parties. The same goes for smoothing over the issue, hoping it will go away. Often, employees or managers avoid or smooth over the issue, but doing so just momentarily pushes the issue to the side. At some time, you will need to address the issue, and there's no time like the present.

✔ **Trust builder #4: Keep commitments.** A good rule of thumb is to produce what you promise. If you say you are going to do something, do it, and if you cannot keep your promise (which sometimes will happen), let people know what happened and what you are going to do about it.

Problem/solution: Not heading in the same direction

At the beginning of the conversation, making sure everyone is headed in the same direction (as much as possible) will save time and effort downstream. The initiator of the conversation comes to the discussion with a goal in mind, but so does the other party. To get your audience to head in the same direction, make the goal of the conversation clear, and identify the audience's motivations.

Be clear on goals

The first step is to be clear about the goal of communication *at the beginning* of the discussion. Yes, this step may be difficult, but that's why critical conversations aren't called a-walk-in-the-park conversations. They're difficult!

Wondering how to kick off the conversation, especially when you have disappointing news? First, be honest and genuine.

In Chapter 13, I walk through examples of how to kick off less-than-positive conversations, but here's an example of how to get everyone on the same page quickly, even when you're delivering negative news:

> Discussing layoffs: You may know that our company is going through tough financial times. This means we have to cut costs and let employees go. The point of today's meeting is to let you know the process, which departments are impacted, and what will happen next.

Heading in the same direction and agreeing with the same direction may not be the same thing. Rarely do employees agree to be fired for performance issues. Rarely does a manager agree that she has done something unethical. However, even when all parties don't agree with the particular outcome, they can agree to engage in the conversation.

Look at how an expert critical communicator may get the other party headed in the same direction when it involves firing an employee for poor performance.

> Hi, Jarod. As you know, you've been on a performance improvement plan for 90 days. We've met weekly to discuss the plan and, as we agreed, the goals of the performance plan weren't met. I've worked with Human Resources, and at this time we will be terminating your employment. I'd like to walk you through the next steps and determine how we can make sure you feel respected throughout the last part of your employment.

The termination of employment wasn't an agreed-on direction, but the respect on Jarod's last day was something everyone could agree on.

Identify motivations

Stating the goal of the conversation up front is an absolute must. In some conversations (especially those that involve staff disputes, differences of opinions between peers, or confronting a difficult situation for the first time), you should take one more step: identifying the other person's motivations. Heading in the same direction during a critical conversation is tough when both parties don't know or understand each other's motivations.

Adapting style may be all you need

Communication is a two-way street, but it can seem to come to a dead end at times. A common mistake leaders make is to communicate only in a way they're comfortable communicating. When having a critical conversation, take into account the personalities and styles of the other party in the conversation. Don't change personalities or pretend to be someone else, but be careful not to overuse or assume everyone likes a particular style. Here are some examples of how people in a conversation may have to adjust their way of communicating:

Situation: Participant A likes to talk fast and take action quickly, but participant B is more reflective and reserved.

Solution: Participant A may need to slow down the pace when talking and allow time for reflection. Participant B may need to agree to specific timelines to show commitment to getting to results sooner rather than later.

Situation: Participant A is reflective and uses few gestures, but participant B uses hand gestures and likes to express emotions.

Solution: Sitting around a table rather than behind a desk creates an open environment with some space to put both participants in the conversation at ease.

You don't have a magic wand you can use to find out the motivations of others. You need a solid relationship and an open and honest conversation. Does the other individual have an ambition to quickly move up the ladder? Does he want to be seen as a superstar? Does he want to manage his work-life balance better? Motivations can come in any shape or size. Here's a sampling of some motivation-seeking questions:

- ✔ What do you enjoy most about work?
- ✔ What aspects of work give you the most personal satisfaction?
- ✔ If you could design the perfect role, what would you keep and what would you delegate in your current role?
- ✔ What motivates you the most?

 Motivation could come in the form of anything from enjoying being known as the go-to person, to a large paycheck, to having flexibility to take time off from work.

You don't have to agree with the other person's motivations — just understand them. If you understand the other individual's motivations, finding a way to satisfy everyone's needs and meet the goals of the conversation will be much easier.

During critical conversations, don't make the mistake of believing that the other person has or should have the same motives you have.

Chapter 3

Critical Conversations: Key Elements to Get You Started

In This Chapter

▶ Identifying the roles that make the conversation successful

▶ Preparing for a critical conversation with ease

▶ Kicking off a conversation with effortlessness

Critical conversations abound in the workplace, and they include everything from hiring and firing employees to having performance management discussions, and from telling a client bad news to working through workplace conflict. The good news is that regardless of the type of conversation you need to have, all critical conversations follow a similar pattern to achieve a successful outcome.

In this chapter you discover the elements of the critical conversation pattern and the roles that make a critical conversation successful. I discuss how to prepare for the conversation and provide tips on how to kick off a conversation so that you can get to the point quickly and focus the conversation on the facts rather than opinions.

Playing the Right Role

Critical conversations bring significant value to all the parties involved when they're handled correctly. A critical conversation done right keeps the relationship intact, even if conflicting opinions and ideas continue. A critical conversation can also validate the process of communication instead of causing participants to avoid it in the future with the excuse that "last time was too painful."

Although the goals of each critical conversation may differ, the practical aspects of the conversation remain consistent.

The fundamentals of a conversation include:

- The people taking part in the conversation
- The prep work for the conversation
- The actual conversation
- The follow-up after the conversation ends

Next, you break each of these fundamental steps down into manageable chunks so that you can start reaping the benefits of a conversation done right.

Critical conversations are a place to exchange information and build relationships. Critical conversations build a climate of trust; they're not just about presenting information. Almost all conversations have three main roles: the initiator, the receiver, and potentially a facilitator, advocate, or mediator.

The initiator

The initiator of the critical conversation is the person or people who want to make a difficult change happen. It's as simple as that. The initiator not only delivers the message, but he also helps create the space for open, honest, and direct communication and can influence someone to choose to change. The initiator is responsible for bringing facts to the discussion in order to create positive, meaningful change that lasts. (Check out *Leading Business Change For Dummies*, written by yours truly and Terry H. Hildebrandt, and published by Wiley, for more on making change last.)

The initiator of the conversation has three roles:

- **Ensuring that the objective for the meeting is clear:** The initiator must be able to clearly answer why the conversation is happening.

- **Maintaining an open environment that will help meet the objective of the conversation:** When stakes are high and emotions heated, an honest, respectful, and open environment keeps the discussion moving.

- **Giving feedback:** Providing specific and actionable feedback that is well-timed will help to keep the conversation focused. Verifying that the feedback was received will increase the likeliness that the conversation will lead to change. For more tips on giving feedback head to Chapter 4.

I delve into these jobs in the "Setting Up for Success" section of this chapter.

The initiator's role isn't done when the conversation ends. The old saying "finish what you started" is true in delivering critical conversations, because initiators are responsible for making sure the feedback is understood during the conversation and coaching and supporting changes that will happen because of the conversation.

The recipient

The recipient may be a person or an entire team, which can make delivering the message and respecting everything the receiver brings to the table even more complicated. Even if your conversation involves discussing a low-par performance, the other individuals aren't novices. They have unique experiences, values, and interests that you must acknowledge during the conversation. Here are some examples of receivers of the tough, but critical conversation:

- ✔ Employees not performing well or not following professional conduct guidelines
- ✔ Teams or an entire organization that isn't meeting goals or expectations
- ✔ Individuals who have differing opinions on how work gets done
- ✔ A boss who's not providing feedback
- ✔ Customers who are unhappy with a product or service

The list could go on and on. Almost anyone can be the recipient of a critical message at some point in their career. At times you may be providing a message and at others you may be receiving one. The common point for anyone receiving a critical message is that the receiver is doing or expecting something that isn't what the initiator of the conversation is expecting or is hoping to have happen. Keep in mind that just being an initiator does not make your opinion the right one, just as being a recipient does not make your opinion wrong. It simply means there is a need to create the space for open, honest, and direct communication.

The support team

Some conversations involve more than just the initiators and recipients of the information. Third parties, including human resources professionals, the next level of management, expert facilitators, or mediators, can support the conversation (Chapter 15 will help you determine when a third party is the right choice). Strong communicators may even be called on to help direct another conversation (which of course means you may be asked to help with many critical conversations after reading this book). Regardless of title, here are additional details about these roles:

- Third parties can help the initiator with decision making regarding how to hold the conversation and prepare the feedback. A leader initiating a conversation may ask a coach or mentor to review the feedback for clarity or how to support action plans coming out of a conversation. Human resources departments are usually brought in when there is a significant and habitual performance issue or when there are ethical or legal concerns.

- Third parties must maintain absolute confidentiality throughout the process. Regardless of the role, confidentiality is critical for all parties in a critical conversation, and lack of confidentiality erodes trust.

- Facilitators can help with the conversation. If emotions are extremely high or if a number of parties are involved, bringing in a neutral facilitator can help ensure that everyone is heard and the process continues to move forward. For example, if a manager wants to initiate a conversation with her team but also wants to provide ideas on the topic, a facilitator would take responsibility for making sure the conversation process is followed so the manager can participate. They can help initiators know when to allow for more discussion and when to move toward agreement and closure. The role of the facilitator is to make sure everyone is involved. Her job is to apply cohesion to the issues being discussed, especially when she sees disagreement within the group.

- Mediators are considered a step between a facilitator and legal counsel. For more on involving mediators in the process, check out Chapter 14. The parties may choose to have a mediator help with the process, especially when there have been previous unsuccessful attempts at creating an open environment for discussion.

Setting Up for Success

Successful critical conversations require some planning before you speak even the first word. To keep the conversation running smoothly and to maintain a good productive level, make sure you do the prep work. The prep work for the conversation involves a lot more, however, than just setting up a meeting. The prep work involves deciding on a clear objective for the conversation, preparing the feedback in a constructive manner, and getting a grip on any emotions people may be feeling before the meeting takes place. Preparing for the conversation also includes understanding different communication styles, motivations, and values. Chapter 9 will help you as you emotionally and physically prepare to give a critical message.

Preparing to give feedback

Feedback provides focused and descriptive information that will either encourage the recipient to repeat a desired behavior or stop an undesired behavior.

Constructive feedback will help improve not only the situation, but also attitudes and relationships within an organization.

Although so many people say that feedback is a gift, most people still have a good amount of apprehension about how and when to provide feedback.

Feedback can be challenging for people to give because they may not want to hurt the other person's feelings or have had a bad experience with giving or receiving feedback in the past. Using collaborative language, focusing on facts and consequences, and using "I" statements to avoid defensive reactions will create a positive feedback environment. Head over to Chapter 6 for more examples on these verbal communication techniques.

Consider these two different approaches to giving feedback and decide which one you'd rather be on the receiving end of during this critical conversation.

Discussion #1

The Recruiter: "I want to give you some feedback on your recent (job) interview. You just weren't a fit for the role."

Interviewee: "Can you give me an example or go into more detail?"

Recruiter: "I really don't know what they meant, but they just don't think you are a fit."

Interviewee: "Hm. Not much I can do with that now, can I?"

Discussion #2

Manager: "I wanted to give you some feedback on your recent (job) interview. Do you have some time?"

Interviewee: "Of course."

Manager: "We picked a different candidate, but I wanted to give you some constructive feedback. You have deep experience creating financial reports, but because you haven't managed anyone in your career, managing 100 financial analysts could be too much of a stretch. It may make sense to get a little more management experience, and then start exploring the CFO position."

Interviewee: "Thanks. I thought my lack of management experience would be an issue. I really appreciate the feedback and ideas. Perhaps I can apply for another position after I lead a few project teams. Wow, I really want to work for your company because you give such great feedback."

I would definitely choose to be part of the second discussion! Not only was the feedback in the first example done by a third party, there was no specific description of what the interviewee could improve. The manager in the second discussion did her homework and had specific examples to provide to the candidate. These specific examples take time to uncover but steer the discussion to a rewarding outcome.

Remember to be specific when preparing the feedback. Comments such as, "You don't handle customers well," aren't specific enough to drive action after the conversation is done. Consider giving a specific example like, "When you picked up the phone and continued to carry on a side conversation instead of greeting the customer, it made her think you weren't professional and wanted to focus on your personal problems rather than the issue she was calling about that day."

 Write down the feedback you want to give. After all, emotions can get high during the discussion (I cover this issue in the later section "Managing high stakes and higher emotions"). If an employee is late, write down when she was late. If a customer is abusing your employees during customer service calls, write down the specific examples of when the customer stepped over the lines of professionalism. This prep work isn't meant to be a witch hunt! Quite the opposite. Having facts to back up why you're initiating the conversation helps the receiver know that you care enough to get to the bottom of the problem, and that you aren't just presenting hearsay.

Specifying the objective

The initiator of the conversation is responsible for setting the objective for the meeting.

Before you schedule the meeting, think about what you're trying to achieve with the conversation based on specific examples and desired behaviors. Setting specific objectives focuses the conversation on the task at hand and makes sure the conversation delivers the desired results.

If a third party is helping you in the critical conversation, confidentially speak with her about the objective of the conversation and making sure it ties to the specific feedback and examples you will share.

Objective statements may include:

- ✔ My objective is to improve the long-term performance of a team or individual. (I cover performance improvement in detail in Chapter 12.)

- ✔ I want to foster a professional work environment where everyone feels their opinions are valued every day. (Resolving staff disputes and addressing workplace complaints are the focus of Chapters 14 and 15.)

- ✔ I must deliver bad news to a client and rebuild the relationship. (I walk through this scenario in Chapter 17.)

The commonality in all these objectives is to have some action happen after the conversation ends.

The objective is one of the first things the initiator will communicate during the critical conversation. As the initiator, you may say, *Thanks for agreeing to meet with me. I called this meeting because I want to foster a professional environment where everyone feels their opinions are valued every day.* If you are giving news to a client or someone you don't have a healthy work relationship with, you may share the objective when setting up the meeting. *My objective for the meeting is to share information with you and find ways we can work together in the future. Would you be able to meet next week to kick off this discussion?* Ideally, the objective would be shared verbally, since an e-mail or text could be misinterpreted or lead to more concern than the meeting itself.

Giving fair warning

After you've done the prep work, you're ready to move into action mode. No one likes having a critical conversation sprung on them, but few people like seeing a meeting with the boss scheduled for a few months out, leaving them to wonder every day what you want to tell them. Giving fair warning that a critical conversation needs to happen means finding the right time and place to have a discussion.

Keeping reasons close to the vest

In some cases, like when you're dealing with ethical concerns or already emotional staff disputes, you may not be comfortable letting the recipient know about the meeting ahead of time. After all, the recipient may retaliate or simply not show up for the meeting. In these cases, be brief and hold the meeting as soon as possible. If the employee probes for more information, you can either hold the meeting right away or provide a general example of what the discussion will include. For example, if the critical conversation may be about a staff dispute, you could say, "It seems like our team is working through a few problems, and I want to help us get to the bottom of it so we can all succeed." This statement is to the point, honest, and positive — the exact way you want to kick off the actual critical conversation.

Find the right time

If at all possible, try to schedule and hold the meeting during the same week. Letting recipients question what the meeting is about and what will happen for an extended amount of time will only add to the problem. As long as you're prepared for the conversation, sooner is always better than later. Letting problems fester is one thing (and I address this problem in Chapter 5), but letting emotions fester with a meeting in the future will certainly lead to even higher emotions when you finally have the meeting.

There are many recommendations on when to hold a conversation and when not to hold one. I've heard people say don't hold them on Fridays, since recipients may go into the weekend upset. I've heard don't hold them on Mondays, because there may be negativity in the office all week if the conversation does not go well. I've heard don't hold them in the morning or last thing in the day, because people are tired. So, that leaves about nine hours during a 40-hour work week for any critical conversation to take place, which, in my expert opinion, is just impractical. Instead of focusing on the perfect millisecond for the conversation, spend the time taking into consideration who may be impacted, how they may react, and what you can do to end the conversation on a positive note.

If at all possible, let the employee or employees know (either face-to-face or on a phone call) that you want to talk about a few concerns and ideas instead of just putting a meeting on their calendar. This is a good place to let the recipient know the general objective of the meeting. No one likes surprises, especially when the surprise is a critical conversation. You had time to prepare, so give the same courtesy to the recipient if at all possible.

Schedule the meeting for at least 30 minutes longer than you expect the meeting to go. This extra time ensures that no one will be knocking on the conference room door to hold the next meeting scheduled there, and neither party will feel rushed as you're coming up with solutions and next steps.

Find the right place

Finding a place to hold a conversation in today's virtual and open workplace can be a challenge. Ideally, critical conversations happen face-to-face in a private setting, free from interruptions. If you can't find a room without windows through which interested onlookers can pry, try to have the meeting somewhere away from all the action in the office to provide privacy and limit potential distractions.

If meeting face-to-face just isn't possible, using videoconferencing or a web-based meeting space is your second choice. Yes, the phone is much easier, but as I discuss in Chapter 7, nonverbal cues are important. They can and do tell a lot about how the message is being received and how sincere the initiator is about the discussion. If you must have the conversation on the phone, find a quiet place and a landline phone, and ask the recipient to do the same.

 Regardless of the place, turn off your cellphone, turn off calendar notifications on your computer, and do your best to remove any other potential interference.

Kicking Off the Conversation with Ease

Often the hardest part of the conversation is getting to the real issue. You're sure to see some nervousness in the room before the conversation starts, so here are some ideas on how to put the other individuals at ease and get to the point quickly but not abruptly.

Opening the discussion

You can imagine how awkward it would be to walk into a room and have the initiator of the critical conversation jump right into the problem. Kicking off the conversation shouldn't take a third of the meeting time, but the opening should be distinct and everyone should be ready to move into the main part of the conversation when you're done with the opening. Here are the three parts to the opening of a critical conversation:

- ✔ **Greet everyone:** Say hello and thank the other person for coming to the meeting.

- ✔ **Describe what success looks like:** Pre-frame what the end of a successful meeting will look like at the opening. Explain the objective of the meeting, the meeting process or agenda, and what a successful meeting would result in. For example: *I called this meeting to talk about behaviors I have been seeing in our office. My goal is to create an environment where everyone is respected and feels valued (objective). During the meeting, I would like ask for feedback and ideas (process) so after the meeting we feel our team has a clear action plan to work together that we can support (pre-framing success).*

- ✔ **Ask for agreement to work together:** At this point, you're not asking for agreement on the problem, you're simply asking for agreement that everyone in the room is willing to explore (and potentially solve) the critical issue at hand. Stating "We need to come up with a solution to the problem," may seem very directive. Instead, ask "Are you willing to work together to find a solution?" This immediately starts the conversation off in a collaborative environment.

Here's an example of a not-so-great opening during a small-group conversation:

> "Everyone is here today because we're all aware that there is a problem. The problem needs to be fixed, so let's find out how to do that." (People in the room will then roll their eyes and soon tune out from the discussion.)

Why is this opening not so great? First, some people may not be aware of the problem. Even if people know of a problem within the team, you're unlikely to have consensus of the real reason for the problem. If you did, it most likely would have been solved by now. Second, when an adult is told they "need" to do something, there is a high chance the person will immediately go on the defensive. There are always alternatives in the workplace, and telling the parties involved in the conversation they need to do anything creates a directive mode of conversation rather than a facilitative one.

Here's a better example of how to kick off the same critical conversation:

> "Hi everyone. First, thanks for taking the time to come to this meeting. I know the subject of the meeting may have left a few of you questioning what we're going to discuss, so I appreciate

you having faith that this is worth your time. As a manager, my role is to make sure you all feel like you're part of the team and can contribute openly to discussions to make the team better. Over the past month, I've noticed some behaviors from team members that seem to stop this type of open communication and innovation. I'm not exactly sure what the main issue is, or how to solve it, but I'm willing to work on it. Does everyone agree that this is something we can explore and potentially begin to solve?" (And then the crowd answers with a wave of, "Yes, let's work on it!")

In this example, the initiator warmly welcomes individuals, states the reason for the meeting without placing blame, and asks for consensus to continue the discussion. The tone and outcome of the second example is more likely to generate positive involvement than the first, which is ideally how you'll start every critical conversation.

Using small talk (or not)

When people are nervous, one reaction is to engage in small talk. Although you want to set the tone for the meeting with a friendly greeting, small talk may make everyone even more nervous. If you can see that the other parties are fidgeting or have anxiety written all over their faces (check out Chapter 7 to find out how to read these nonverbal cues), small talk can make the situation worse. Who wants to talk about what they did last weekend when they think they may be getting fired or disciplined? The best thing to do in this situation is to get right to the point. You can even acknowledge what you're feeling as a way to gently move into the main message of the conversation.

"Hi, Jim. Thanks for coming to the meeting. I always get a little nervous when I have to deliver a difficult message, so why don't we jump right into the discussion? Over the past three months, I've noticed on your time card that you've been coming in 15 minutes late and taking a two-hour lunch. I want to have a discussion with you about how this behavior is impacting the team and what can happen to turn it around. Can we have a conversation about this now?"

Other situations may call for a little more warm-up before diving into the critical issue. Deciding how much small talk to use often depends on the following:

- The relationship you already have with the parties involved
- The urgency of the critical issue
- The style of the individual (more on this in Chapter 8)

For example, if you know the individual well and the issue is focused on performance improvement, it may feel more comfortable to start with a little more relaxed conversation, as the following example shows.

"Hi, Jim. Thanks for coming to the meeting. How was your weekend? . . . [small conversation here]. Well, I'm glad to hear that you had a good weekend. You may be wondering why I called this meeting, so why don't we jump right into the agenda? I wanted us to talk today about some areas of improvement that could really benefit our department. Are you willing to have this conversation now?"

If you choose to have a little small talk, remember to keep it short and quickly move into the meeting agenda within five minutes of the meeting beginning. If you think small talk will just make the situation worse, acknowledge that and jump right in.

Managing high stakes and higher emotions

A critical conversation, by definition, will bring high emotions and high stakes into the room. If poor performance is an issue, someone's job may be on the line. If a customer is upset, losing her business could mean lost revenue for the organization. If a conversation about workplace conflict has been imminent, you need to acknowledge — and perhaps heal — at least a few feelings before the team can move forward. And of course you'll have pressure as the initiator as well, because dealing with any confrontation can create physical and emotional stress.

You have three main options, as a facilitator, to alleviate the stress and manage high stakes and high emotions during a critical conversation:

✔ **Support the discussion.** Acknowledge that all parties in the room are critical to the success of the discussion. Let the other person know that you need them to be involved verbally by saying that they're part of the discussion, not just the recipients of the discussion. Then back up your words with nonverbal cues like sitting around an open, round table rather than behind a desk or try uncrossing your arms as the discussion occurs.

✔ **Provide gentle relief.** I never ask any executive to be a comedian, but if a little humor fits the situation, it can help all the parties let off some steam. For example, if you realize there is more tension in the room than you expected, you may say something like, "I feel the tension in the room may be growing, not decreasing. I don't think we have a masseuse in the room so are there other ideas on how to relieve this tension?" I'm not talking slap-stick comedy, but humility and honesty can do wonders to bring relief to a stressful situation. If humor isn't a forte (or if humor starts hiding the seriousness of the conversation), a simple smile and nod of the head can also add relief to the room.

✔ **Keep the discussion focused on the objective.** During the conversation, the initiator sometimes needs to listen and let the conversation go at its own pace. At other times, you need to refocus the process to meet the objectives of the discussion. If emotions are high and leading the discussion off track, state the obvious and then ask for agreement to get the meeting back on track. If this happens during a group conversation, you could ask, "I feel like there are a number of opinions and emotions being presented. Can we agree to focus on the objective of the meeting or should we switch gears and resolve the other issue first?"

Getting started with a critical conversation takes a lot more effort than simply sending a calendar invitation. If the initiator is unclear of the message or reason for the meeting, you can be certain that the receiver will also be confused.

Taking a little more time to prepare for the conversation will pay off with less stress during the meeting. It helps to create an open and collaborative environment that includes a common understanding of goals and objectives. In Chapter 9, I cover more on how to prepare for the conversation, including managing stress. In Chapter 4, I walk you through how to use all this preparation to keep the conversation moving in the right direction.

Chapter 4

Delivering the Message with Impact

In This Chapter

▶ Using the EDGE model to have meaningful conversations

▶ Taking a look at the facts

▶ Moving forward in the SMARTest possible way

▶ Assessing the critical conversation after the fact

*H*olding a critical conversation correctly leads to better relationships, increased productivity, and better leadership. Three guidelines that support delivering an honest, empathetic, and impactful message include:

✔ Focus on maintaining and building relationships so that all parties have confidence in each other and are willing to work together to create a solution.

✔ As the initiator, do your homework to gather information as a starting point.

✔ Use the conversation to discuss that information so that all parties can commit to reasonable next steps with mutual acceptance and support.

A process called the EDGE model helps all parties meet these three lofty, but indispensable guidelines. EDGE stands for

✔ **E**xamine data and perspectives and acknowledge other perceptions

✔ **D**ecide on options to move forward

✔ **G**ain commitment and get moving with a powerful action plan

✔ **E**valuate the impact of the discussion

In this chapter, I break down the EDGE model and show you how to apply its rules to critical conversations.

Examining Perspectives and Acknowledging Other Perceptions

When you're ready to initiate the conversation (see Chapter 3 for information on how to get the conversation started), quickly get to the point so that you can create an open environment and build agreement on how to change the situation (the ultimate goal for a critical conversation). The goal of this part of the conversation is to clearly and concisely present your feedback and findings and then allow the recipient to explain their view or position (see Chapter 3 for more on preparing feedback). Finally, you will clarify the critical issue and check for understanding from all the parties involved.

Start with facts

During the preparation work, you gather feedback to use in the conversation (see Chapter 3). After opening the conversation, describe the situation that led to the critical conversation and give facts and examples to support why the critical behavior or performance has consequences.

Identify the situation

Describe the situation. Be brief, but provide enough detail so the recipient understands the feedback is based on actual events, not just general impressions.

Here are some brief but well-defined ways to describe the situation:

"In the staff meeting yesterday, I noticed some behaviors you may not be aware of."

"In the past two project team meetings, I observed a few actions that I'd like to talk about."

If you are delivering a message to a team, you may start with: *I know we have had a quality issue with our product, and this has led to a number of returns from our customers. I would like to talk about how we can fix the process.*

State the facts and give examples

After you identify the situation, move straight into facts. Keep these facts simple, specific, and jargon-free. Give the information in blocks, so you don't overwhelm the other party.

Here's an example of how to focus on the facts:

> "In the past three meetings with our project team, I observed a few actions that I'd like to talk about. I saw you typing on your phone when I was asking a question. During our project team call last week, I heard you putting the conference phone on and off mute a number of times and typing in the background."

Describe the impact or consequences of the behaviors

After the facts are on the table, close with describing why the performance isn't ideal, how you feel, or stating the consequences that are resulting from the other party's behavior. During this part of the conversation, you're helping to clarify the importance of coming to some resolution.

In this example, I show you how to use facts to describe the impact of poor behavior on a project team:

> "The behaviors and actions are causing me to feel I can't have a meaningful discussion with you about how the project is going."

If you have many examples or if the situation has been going on for an extended amount of time without being addressed, stick to the Rule of Three: Give three examples that are the most meaningful. Anything more will just seem like a laundry list and anything less may not drive home the point that the issue isn't limited to one situation. For example, if a manager is dealing with poor performance she may say:

> "Jeff, over the past few weeks, I have noticed three different times when your communication may not have gotten the desired results. In the meeting last week, you raised your voice at Sally. Earlier this week, you sent an e-mail to our customer team saying they did not know how to do their job. And yesterday I noticed arguing in the team break room. The communication seems to be creating tension on the team."

Ask for additional information and intents

After you examine the data from your point of view, ask the other parties about their perspectives and intents, and whether they believe the information is accurate. This step is important because if you don't have consensus on the facts, you're unlikely to have consensus on the solution.

Ask the other parties whether they agree with the facts and the reason for their actions. Even if you think you know, don't jump to conclusions. Try to assume their intent is positive — even when it appears negative. This positive spin can do wonders in propelling the conversation forward to a better outcome, even when you're faced with difficult behaviors or unwilling receivers of the information (more on difficult behaviors in Chapter 16).

Here is how the conversation may go after an employee has been told their arguing with other employees nonstop is negatively impacting the team:

> **Kathy (super manager):** "Do you agree with what I observed?"
>
> **Sam:** "Yes, I guess so. But I don't think it's that important."
>
> **Kathy:** "Having the team work together is important to the success of the project. What is your perspective on what is happening?"
>
> **Sam:** "I just don't see it as an issue."
>
> **Kathy:** "What can I do to help get our team to better work together?"
>
> **Sam:** "I do have a lot on my plate, and I just want to get work done. Sometimes I think some of my team members just talk too much and that just stresses me out."
>
> **Kathy (manager extraordinaire):** "Thanks for sharing that. I know you have a lot on your plate. Are you willing to come up with some options that are productive for the entire team?"
>
> **Sam (acknowledging he perhaps could improve):** "Sure, let's think of some options."

While gaining additional information, encourage all the parties to ask questions. Make sure to have time to understand the main issue or reflect on the facts you just shared.

Allowing parties to ask questions helps to make sure what the recipient heard is what the initiator was trying to say. It is easy to have one fact misinterpreted, even from the best communicators. Simply ask, "Do you agree with the information I am sharing?" Or state, "I want to make sure I am communicating the message right. Do you see how the consequences are tied to the examples I gave?" You may even just ask, "Do you want me to clarify anything we talked about?"

I get into gaining commitment and action planning later in the chapter, but when the recipient has a chance to respond and provide input, there is a better chance that both parties will be able to find an agreeable solution.

Clarify consequences

Before moving into deciding on options to move forward, this is the right time to understand why the recipient of the information agrees (or disagrees) the change is needed and if the recipient wants to do something different. You may be able to simply ask, "Do you agree this action may need to change?" Depending on the answer, you may need to do a little more work and point out how the other party's intent is actually making the situation worse and what could make the situation better. Be supportive, yet direct, and make sure the key point is clear.

Back to the example from the previous section:

> "You agreed that you have so much on your plate that you just want to get the project moving (intent). But every time you interrupt team members, people are paying attention only to the fact that you interrupted them or were doing something else, and the discussion about the project plan stops. The team was paying attention to you typing on the call, not the expert opinions you can bring to the table. A better option may be to listen to everyone's opinions and then incorporate your own ideas. What do you think?"

In this example, the initiator presents the intent of all parties and the consequences of the actions in a positive way — and one that's hard to disagree with. By continuing to focus on the facts, you keep emotions at bay and help all parties find a solution.

As the initiator of the conversation, keep in mind that most people have good reasons for doing what they do. Rather than fighting or arguing with those reasons, find out what these are to help propel the conversation forward toward resolution. For more on uncovering motivation, head to Chapter 9. For example, a customer may be returning every product you ship because they did not realize your product changed. An employee may be micromanaging his team because he wants to make sure the project is perfect. On the other hand, a manager may not be managing enough because she trusts her employees will do a good job without her help.

Before moving forward with options for a resolution, describe the situation, identify facts about the behavior, describe the consequences, and ask for other facts or perspectives.

Deciding on Options to Move Forward

In order to move forward with the discussion, you need to talk about the desired actions or change, and then all parties can work on finding possible solutions and alternatives. Throughout the process, mutual agreements continue to be a priority and everyone should be ready to put action items on paper to mark a clear pathway to the desired outcome.

Identifying desired behaviors

After examining the critical issue, all parties should be ready to identify what should be happening to reach the desired end result. The transition from focusing on the past to focusing on the future can be as easy as saying, "Are you willing to walk through other ways to get the project moving faster?" or, "Are you ready to start looking at ways to move forward?"

The initiator can continue to be supportive but direct when identifying behaviors. If the critical conversation is about the performance of an employee, link these behaviors to what's acceptable in the company or what's expected for someone in his job or role.

 As you share the list of desired behaviors, keep in mind that the behaviors should focus on something the receiver can do something about. Telling someone he needs to stop sweating in the office isn't really actionable; asking someone to perhaps take a shower after going for a 3-mile run at lunch is actionable.

Discussing possible alternatives

Wouldn't it be great if everyone agreed on all the alternatives and options to change behavior? Yes, it would. But most likely you'll have to acknowledge that differences exist, and therefore all parties will have to develop multiple options to achieve the desired outcome.

Follow these steps to find the best alternatives to the solution:

1. **List the different alternatives and discuss the pros and cons of each.** Aim to list three or four possible alternatives (anything more can be overwhelming).

2. **Ask all the parties to state their preferences.**

3. **State your own preference.**

If preferences to the possible alternatives are still different, identify what everyone can and can't support. Although all parties may not get their ideal solution to the problem, you have a strong opportunity to let all parties decide on the most favorable options that everyone can support.

For example, if you have a critical conversation with an employee about his tardiness, the employee may not be able to commit to being at the office at 8 a.m. every morning. But perhaps he can commit to being at the office at 8:10 and taking a lunch that's 10 minutes shorter. If the alternative works for the organization and the employee, a good solution that everyone supports is better than the perfect solution that only half the parties support.

Gaining commitment by building agreements early on

Experts in critical conversations know that an agreement to move forward with a solution isn't a single moment at the end of the discussion. By using critical communication skills, you build agreements throughout the dialogue.

By developing agreements along the way, no matter how small, you have a much higher chance of reaching the desired goals.

In the beginning of the conversation, the agreements may be focused on consensus about working toward a solution or even sitting in a room together to discuss what's happening. At the end of the discussion, the agreements may focus on how to move forward and what behaviors will be expected in the future.

Here are examples of the agreements used during a critical conversation:

> **Agreement #1:** Gaining agreement to work together. "Although we may disagree on how to solve the problem, can we agree to work together?"

> **Agreement #2:** A problem exists based on the facts. "Looking at the facts, do you agree that there might be a problem?"

> **Agreement #3:** Everyone wants to solve the problem. "Before jumping into solutions, is there value in solving the problem?"

> **Agreement #4:** All parties agree on the possible alternatives and options. "Now that we've walked through a number of alternatives and options to move forward, are there any other

ideas we should discuss? Okay, do we agree that these are the possible alternatives and options we want to work with?"

Agreement #5: The parties are committed to the next steps. "Now that we've discussed the specific next steps, do I have your commitment to get moving on the action plan?"

As you can see from the questioning technique, no one agreement finds a resolution to the problem or issue, but each agreement builds on the previous agreement, making the path to success a bit clearer and a bit easier to work toward together.

Keep a mental note of each agreement you make. If the conversation gets stuck or if emotions get high, back up the process by reinforcing the last agreement the group made, and proceed from there.

You may have instances when all the parties reach an impasse and can't come to a conclusive agreement. In these cases, agree on how you'll escalate the process through other channels. For example, if the conversation is at a standstill, the recipient or the initiator may ask, "Do you think it makes sense to ask someone to help with the discussion? Maybe we can ask human resources or a facilitator to work with us."

Making a SMART agreement

When you're developing agreements on what to do next, it's time to get SMART — that is, to set a goal that's specific, measurable, agreed-on and action-oriented, realistic, and time bound.

SMART agreements help move a critical conversation from just talk to action. SMART goals (and agreements) are easy to understand, clear for all parties involved, and are able to be evaluated objectively. When an action plan is being created, take a minute to consider how SMART the agreement is:

> ✔ **Specific:** Are the goals well defined to each party and clear to anyone who may read them?

> ✔ **Measurable:** Will you know when your goal is achieved?

> ✔ **Action-oriented and Agreed-on:** This A gets double duty. The goal of a critical conversation is to see a change in behavior or performance, and all parties need to agree on what will happen next. If all the parties don't agree to next steps, you're no better off than when the conversation started.

> ✔ **Realistic (and Risk):** Is the goal realistic? If an employee is late to work, asking him to come in to work on time is realistic. If an employee isn't creating a positive team environment,

expecting him to be seen as a superstar in 30 days isn't realistic, but asking him to use professional language in all his conversations is realistic. The R also stands for Risk, since the goal or change could be a challenge if the individual has to work outside of their comfort zone.

✔ **Time bound:** When will the actions be accomplished? Have a clear deadline to make sure actions happen. A good rule of thumb when having a critical conversation is to have a 30-day timeline for the goal to be accomplished.

Here are examples of a not-so-smart and a SMART goal:

✔ **Not-so-smart agreement:** Employees will be happy with their manager.

✔ **SMART agreement:** The manager will ask human resources to complete a feedback survey (specific and action-oriented) to gather information on how the manager can specifically improve by September 30th (time bound and realistic). And this agreement is measurable, because the manager will do it or not.

Gain Commitment to get a Move On: Who Does What by When?

Developing action plans is what turns a critical conversation into action. These action plans help ensure that all the parties involved in the conversation understand what should happen next and what they can specifically do to commit to meeting the objective of the conversation.

Action plans may need to happen at both team and individual levels if you're dealing with workplace conflict. These plans often occur concurrently but are closely aligned. For example, the team action plan may be to hold brainstorming meetings to create a more innovative environment; an individual action plan may recommend a specific employee take a class on how to use assertive rather than aggressive communication techniques. For more on action plans, check out Chapter 11.

Whether you're working with a team or an individual action plan, they have several common characteristics. Action plans are:

✔ **Linked to the goal:** Clearly link action plans to the original objective of the critical conversation.

✔ **Doable:** Can everyone imagine how these actions will be done?

- **Measurable:** Can everyone answer the question "How will I/we know if I've/we've achieved this?"

- **Supported:** Does everyone appreciate the different approaches to achieve the objective? The more all parties are involved in creating the action plan, the more commitment they will have to execute.

Closing the conversation

Closing the conversation is a crucial step in the critical conversation process. In order to make sure you don't have this same conversation again in a week, month, or year, properly close the conversation with an action plan that makes everyone satisfied. If you prep for the critical conversation correctly (see Chapter 3), you put yourself in line to get the positive results everyone desires.

For most people, a critical conversation is a stressful event. The goal of closure is to make all parties feel valued and motivated to move forward and to accelerate productivity in the near term. The best way to make people feel valued is to come to the conversation with a genuine desire to help make the situation better while being respectful of all people involved. (See Chapter 1 for more on this golden rule of critical conversations.) Ultimately the change will not be successful if the initiator does not focus on the other person's intents, motivations, and needs first.

The best way to close out a conversation is to bring the conversation back to the person and, if the situation allows, discuss how the future will be better. Here are three perfect ways to close out even the toughest of conversations:

- **Performance Improvement Discussion:** "Thanks, Joey, for the time and your focus today. I appreciate you being willing to work hard on this action plan. I know with these improvements, you will be on the path to a successful project. Please let me know when you need help, and I will set up time for us to review the action plan early next week."

- **Customer Complaint Discussion:** "Thanks, Mr. Customer, for your time. I will put this plan into action today so we do not have the same problem in the future. If you need help on this in the future, please call me directly or e-mail me."

- **Firing Discussion:** "Jim, I know this conversation has been tough. I wish you all the best in the future. Would you like some time to pack your desk, or should we schedule a time to come back and gather your things when fewer people are in the office?"

To act or not to act: That is the question

In all the previous scenarios, you may feel like every conversation ends with "they lived happily ever after." Well, that is not always the case. There may be times you will find the best thing to do is for the recipient and initiator to go separate ways. What happens if all the parties can't agree on next steps? Here are a couple of the most common "what if's" and how to deal with them:

- ✔ **What if the other individual disagrees with everything you're saying?** Agreeing on next steps may be as simple as saying, "I think we can both agree that we have different opinions. The next step for me will be to talk with my manager about other options. Would you like to take some time to think about alternatives based on our discussion today?"

- ✔ **What if the conversation's end result is firing a poor performer?** At the end of a tough conversation, an employee may simply decide the effort to improve performance is something they do not want to do. Or, you may find the employee is not willing to make changes. In this case, you may need to change course and let the employee know the choice is to change or to be fired. The conversation would go something like this, "Bill, it seems like we cannot agree on how to improve performance. The choice to make now is to find agreements on how to improve performance or I can work with human resources and start the termination process."

Whether your conversation ends in action, or if you realize there is no resolution, keep in mind that the goal of a critical conversation is not only to make a change, but to create an open and honest discussion. Every critical conversation will build on the environment you created and start to make communicating fairly and openly part of the organizational culture.

At the end of most conversations, there will be a need to evaluate how the conversation went and, even more importantly, if the actions discussed during the conversation changed for the better. This means evaluating the impact of everything you just said and heard.

Evaluating the Impact

Evaluating a critical conversation comes down to one question: Did the behavior or performance change? Ideally, all the parties will see a change in behavior or performance. I recommend having a weekly meeting over the first 30 days to give feedback on the changes and identify any additional next steps to keep the improvement on the right track.

During the weekly meeting, ask the employee whether he needs help removing any obstacles in his way, and whether he finds the action plan beneficial. Now is also the time to (hopefully) give positive feedback on the changes. After a conversation between two peers resolving a dispute, this is also a good time to thank the other party for having the conversation and being committed to making the change. If you see someone making an effort to change, acknowledge it. If the other party is having difficulty, offer suggestions on other ways he could address the issue.

You'll get a good reputation as a leader if you're fair with individuals and hold them accountable to deliver on their part of the action plan. In the end, the follow-up will make your job much easier in the future by establishing clear guidelines for behaviors and performance. This check-in is perhaps one of the most beneficial things for employees receiving feedback and for teams that need intervention, because it gives them extra time and space to process information (much more than any single meeting could give them). Checking in for progress also helps people see the importance of the conversation and your commitment to helping the situation change for the better.

You may need to have more than one follow-up meeting to check in on the progress, especially if problems have been occurring for quite some time or are significant (and most issues that lead to critical conversations are!). During each of the check-ins, you can continue to summarize your commitment and expectations to making things change, and ask what the other parties need and can expect of you in the months ahead.

Chapter 5

Knowing When It's Time to Have a Critical Conversation

In This Chapter

▶ Looking for signs that a critical conversation is necessary

▶ Knowing what to focus on

▶ Finding out when and how to tackle problems

*I*f you're short on time, I can sum up this chapter in one word: now. With a few exceptions, there really is no time like the present to have a critical conversation. In fact, if you picked up this book, you probably know that you should address an issue. In an ideal world, critical conversations are just conversations that happen every day: managers continuously provide feedback to employees, employees speak freely to their leaders, and employees work out any differences with direct, yet respectful dialogue. Because this ideal world usually exists only in corporate fairy tales, this chapter helps you figure out when you need to have a critical conversation.

In this chapter, I cover some critical conversation indicators, including signs that a critical conversation may need to happen. I also address what to do when a critical conversation is long overdue. Sometimes problems multiply into more issues, so this chapter reviews which problem to address when you're dealing with several; I even tell you how to pick the right one to focus on first and help you put the issues in the right order.

Your Indicator Light Is Flashing!

Critical conversation is a powerful tool that can change behavior, improve performance, and improve the workplace environment. Yet, so many otherwise successful leaders fail to deliver a powerful and impactful message, especially when the organizational culture or leader's background is resistant to disagreements or conflicting opinions. The irony is that critical conversations actually help create relationships and resolve conflicts (see Chapter 2). I'll walk through the indicators for some of the most common critical conversations: workplace dynamics and performance issues.

Use critical conversations to address (and solve) two different types of issues:

✔ **Objective issues:** By definition, objective issues are usually based on facts that are fairly black and white (I say "usually" because you can always find some room for interpretation between parties). Objective-focused conversations tend to be a bit easier to identify because strong facts support having a critical conversation. You may need to have a critical conversation in the following scenarios:

- When an employee isn't completing part of her job (missed project deadlines, coming in late to work)

- When you need to discuss a definite customer issue (a late delivery or quality issue)

- When you're questioning an ethical behavior (sending an inappropriate e-mail or taking company supplies for personal use)

✔ **Subjective issues:** These critical conversations are harder to have, because personality differences and differences of opinion aren't as concrete as objective issues and are more difficult to pinpoint. These issues often impact how a team or organization functions together. Examples include the following:

- When a team isn't working well together (team members gossiping about one another, people are not willing to compromise, results are promised but not delivered)

- When a customer or employee may be crossing the line from direct and critical to abusive and aggressive (one team member may be dominating conversations, arguing with others habitually, or personally attacking people)

Both types of issues indicate that a critical conversation is looming. You follow a similar approach in both cases, but the subjective issue may take a little more work during the preparation and a lot more work when dealing with emotions during the conversation (I go into more detail on how to prepare for the conversation in Chapter 9).

Critical conversations can come from hard facts or from the interpretation of facts. The following sections cover some of the indicators that point to the need to have a critical conversation.

Workplace dynamics

Workplace dynamics can make a good team perform at an extraordinary level or a great team fall to pieces. Look at the sports world as an example. When an underdog team wins a game, it's often because the team came together. The United States Olympic hockey team that beat Russia in 1980 did it because their workplace (the ice rink) dynamics flowed perfectly. Teams may not be going after an Olympic gold medal, but if a workplace seems to be stumbling more than striding, you may need to have a critical conversation.

Many workplace dynamic critical conversations come about because of subjective issues (see the next section). So before you have the conversation with individuals or the group, diagnose what is causing the problem. In other words, look for actions that are causing the problem or resulting in undesirable consequences, not just impressions or symptoms of the problem. You may find employees do not support one another in achieving the team's goals, but then dig a bit deeper to find no one even knows what the goal is.

As you look at events and actions in the workplace that are driving undesirable consequences and results, you may begin to see that dysfunctional workplaces can come from almost anywhere. If you are having trouble pinpointing what is causing a team to not work effectively, here are a few places to look:

- ✔ **Actions of individuals.** The saying goes that a chain is only as strong as its weakest link, and in workplace dynamics this is often the case. Any action by an individual that disrupts a group's ability to work successfully together warrants a critical conversation. Whether an individual is consistently late to meetings or goes against the team's decisions or is aggressive in his communication, the individual may be destroying the environment.

- ✔ **Interactions between individuals.** In most organizations, individuals communicate and interact. These interactions may be anything from sending e-mails to attending team meetings to small talk over coffee. A few interactions that may lead to a critical conversation include individuals cutting each other off during discussions or ignoring comments during a meeting. Ideally, individuals would be able to work out differences of opinions or work styles, but if the dysfunctional relationship has a negative impact on the team, it may be time for a critical conversation facilitated by a neutral party or leader.

Try to avoid making this critical conversation look like a visit to the principal's office when kids are arguing on the playground. Your first step should always be to recommend that the people not working well together have a critical conversation with just the two of them first. Perhaps buy each of them a copy of this book. Or, individually coach them on two areas: first, how to have a conversation, and, second, show how their actions or behaviors are impacting the business and your request for them to change. Then offer your support and try to let the employees work it out with one another.

✔ **Patterns of behavior within the group.** Critical conversation can come out of one or two specific tasks or incidents, but often they're the result of patterns in behaviors within a group. Team members may be purposefully avoiding one another or not wanting to work together on project teams. Or you may have a situation in which stress levels are high, and the usual respectful behavior turns into an emotional battlefield.

When you're observing action, interaction, or patterns, you're likely to be somewhat biased. You are, after all, only human. Everyone has emotions and biases about how things should be done. To limit your own bias, follow these steps: reflect, engage, and commit. First, reflect on what you may be biased against (or for). It may be helpful to use work, communication, and leadership style assessments (including DiSC, Myers-Briggs, Strengths Deployment Inventory, and Thomas-Kilmann Conflict Mode Assessment) to get a different perspective on what generalizations or bias you may have. For more on what information these assessments can provide and how to take them, head to www. leadingchangecoach.com. Second, bias is usually caused by past experiences, so take the extra step to engage with groups or individuals you may have a bias or prejudice against. You may find your biases to be unfounded. Third, make a commitment to be more aware of your biases and try to stop them before they get in the way of a potentially great work relationship.

Performance issues

Performance issues are often the most common problems in the workplace. Unfortunately, many managers wait to address them until it's too late and the problem has become much bigger than when it started. For example, an individual may start acting indifferent about a project, and then they begin to let others carry the load, and then they completely withdraw from the project entirely. It would be much easier to just address acting indifferent.

Or, even worse, managers wait until the official annual performance review to let an employee know she's missing the mark. Most people would want to know right away if they were not meeting the expectations of their boss so they could do something about it, rather than be surprised in a performance review. Having up-front agreements on performance expectations will make a critical conversation easier to have.

When is a good time to intervene with a critical conversation, without being a micromanager? The simple answer is before the behavior or action becomes a trend. I am not asking you to make a chart and plot three points on a graph, but if an employee changes her behavior (the employee once was a super star and now is dragging her feet) or if an employee does the same action that results in negative consequences three times, it may be time for a critical conversation. The way I look at it is, once is a bad day, twice is a tough time, and three times starts a trend.

I just described when *to* intervene, and here's an example of when *not* to intervene:

> Rachel has been a great performer on your team and usually actively engages in discussion. During a critical debate, she doesn't add anything to the team discussion.

Rachel's lack of engagement in this case may mean she has nothing to add and agrees with everyone. No reason to question anything at this time.

However, if Rachel continues to be silent, if she exhibits a significant change in behavior, or if her performance begins to suffer, that's a pattern. When you have a pattern, it's time to have a critical conversation about performance and participation.

Letting someone know that her performance needs improvement isn't easy, but you can do it in a way that's beneficial to all the parties involved. Lucky number Chapter 13 covers performance conversation in detail, but this should get you started on the right track. Here's how to do it:

- ✔ **Be specific.** Give specific examples of what did or did not happen. Generalities don't add value; examples do. For example, "I noticed you have not given any ideas in the team meetings over the past few weeks," rather than, "You seem to be withdrawing from the group."

- ✔ **Add value.** Make sure the conversation will add value to the performance at hand. Help the employee to understand why the behavior needs to be changed or what actions from the past you would like to see repeated in the future. Keeping with the example, the manager may say, "One of your job roles is to provide feedback on the product design, and the team does not have anyone providing this type of input."

✔ **Ask for their perspective.** Encourage the employee to share her reasons, feelings, or opinions about the feedback. You may need to go back and forth between adding value, examples, and gaining perspective. This open dialogue will help both the employee and the leader to agree on the specific concern and action steps. The manager may ask, "Are you willing to talk about what might be stopping you from performing at your best or offering your ideas?"

You may be thinking, this seems like a lot of work when someone is just starting to not perform. Yes, you may be right. But, the alternative is to do nothing and then have a critical conversation when someone has not been performing for a long time. I would always take the first, more proactive option. The goal of a critical conversation is to improve performance and strengthen relationships, and you don't need to make the conversation a huge deal. If there is a trend or concern with performance, build an open, honest, and direct dialogue right away. This environment will make discussions about performance (both good and bad performance) much easier in the future.

Overdue Notice: Time for a Critical Conversation

Issues get swept under the rug rather than discussed openly and promptly for a number of reasons. The main reason is often that managers don't have the time or energy to address an issue. Having a critical conversation isn't as easy as just scheduling a meeting. It takes work, time, and follow-up. But you've come to the right place to find out how and when to have a conversation that ultimately gives you back both time and energy, after you solve the problem.

When you address people problems with respect and honesty, you will gain energy, time, and most likely get people working rather than arguing, which leads to more profit, productivity, and a better work environment. Cha-ching!

Deciding whether a problem still exists

When past issues need to be resolved, you have a choice: address them or hope they go away. Addressing them is the only right answer! If you've given the issue a few weeks (or months or years) to get resolved on its own, and it hasn't been, you need to have a critical conversation.

Start with the most recent example first. Make sure feedback reflects actions that are happening now. You may need to reference past actions, but focusing on two or three key actions that are causing negative behaviors right now may be enough to start turning behavior around.

Second, focus on actions, not generalizations. Saying, "Well, no one wants to work with you because you never pull your weight on projects and are always late with your work," is accusatory and a generalization. Instead, say, "I noticed you have not updated the presentation for our client in over 13 weeks. I have also seen that during this project you have not turned in your time reports for six weeks and I have to redo the invoices for the client."

Next, make it relevant. Nothing is worse than dragging up old issues that are no longer relevant or highly subjective. If concerns are no longer relevant, don't hold a critical conversation of grudges — just move on.

Finally, just get it done. Addressing an issue or concern that occurred months ago — if not years ago — is never a glamorous job, but it needs to be done. The sooner you can start the conversation, the sooner the actions or behaviors can change.

Having a critical conversation on issues that are long overdue follows the same steps as any other critical conversation, there may just be more examples and emotions involved. But examining what is happening and providing specific examples and consequences, tied together with honest talk and follow-up will hopefully put all the past issues to rest and allow all parties to start fresh.

Inherited issues

Past problems can come your way from a change in personnel — such as when you change roles and move to a new team, or when another manager sends an employee to your department so she doesn't have to deal with the issue. However the problem comes to you, deal with it quickly to get the team off and rolling on a positive note.

Smart managers know that ignored problems rarely go away. If you didn't observe past behaviors, having a critical conversation based on any fact, rather than hearsay, is difficult. If, for example, you suspect that an employee is one who's been passed around, keep opinions and bias at bay.

Some inherited issues may come from an employee making excuses for why work was not done before (her computer crashed, she threw her phone in the bath, the dog ate her report, and then her computer crashed again when a meteor struck her house). Still others come from projects that may have never been completed. My advice is to focus on the issue directly, openly, and honestly (you probably guessed that, right?). For example, if an employee has been passed around, treat the employee as you would a new employee, and if her performance isn't meeting expectations, speak up and speak up fast.

If the issue is related to an old project that left resentment in the organization, state the problem and then quickly move to focusing on the solution. For example, you may say, "I know last year's project was not as successful as we thought it would be. I would like to recommend we learn from what went right and repeat those steps to make this year's project perfect."

Secondhand issues often look like performance or workplace dynamic issues (see the earlier section, "Your Indicator Light Is Flashing!" for more on these kinds of issues), but during the conversation you hear something like, "Oh, well, my old manager just let me do what I wanted," or, "My previous manager has been letting me do this for years." When you hear this response, keep to the facts and the consequences of the behavior. Don't start the blame game.

The elephant in the room

Elephant issues are those things that most people in the organization are automatically thinking about, but may not talk about because of legal or cultural reasons or simple politeness. Yes, everyone knows the issue is there. And everyone is looking away.

Here are some elephants that organizations may need to address head-on before they become unresolved issues from the past:

- ✔ The CEO or top performer on a team just quit this morning. Everyone is waiting to find out why.

- ✔ The company just lost its biggest client. Everyone is wondering what happens next.

- ✔ Yesterday afternoon, the boss and someone else got into a screaming match. No one knows why, but everyone is thinking about it.

The best way to handle the elephant in the room is to tackle it straight on using the critical conversation steps, just like any other conversation: focus on the facts, tie in the consequences of the behavior, and then discuss opinions, ideas, and perspectives.

Keep with the critical conversation model by stating the facts and help others understand how the situation is impacting them. For example, if you just lost your biggest customer, you may start the conversation with, "You may have heard that we have lost our biggest client. I want to talk about the facts, how it impacts you, and help everyone get to work to deliver the best service we can for all our customers." If the superstar on the team just quit, you can start by saying, "Jill has left the company, and we wish her the best. I would like to use this time to talk with the team to look at ways we can work together to keep the project on schedule."

Most often, when one person starts talking about the elephant in the room, there is a big sigh of relief. Most likely everyone has been thinking of it, and the team will be relieved if the initiator takes the lead and states the facts and then helps the group understand how the situation may impact them and what they can do to make the situation better.

Multiple Issues: Handling the Snowball Effect

If you tackle an issue or concern in a timely manner, you focus the conversation on one main area that's critical to change. But sometimes a problem starts as a simple discussion and grows into a discussion about other problems. For example, you may have a discussion about interrupting people during meetings. Sounds simple until you find yourself also talking about not listening to others' points of view and never allowing others to talk in any conversation, which may ultimately lead to poor performance and a negative team environment. A problem is often like a snowball — it keeps getting bigger and bigger until someone stops it.

When you face multiple concerns with an individual or team, the task may seem overwhelming, but the time and effort you spend to resolve the situation will pay off, and pay off quickly.

As the initiator of the conversation, you always play a big role in setting the tone of the conversation. When you have multiple issues to address, your role is even bigger. Make sure you do the following when you're dealing with multiple issues:

- ✔ Present facts.

- ✔ Select the most pressing concerns.

- ✔ Balance giving enough information with the emotions of the other individual thinking everything is wrong. Try to deal with one or two concerns or ideas at a time. Even if you have a number of examples, focus on the two or three most important examples instead of just running through a laundry list.

- ✔ Give a clean slate if the other parties are willing to make meaningful change in their performance or behavior.

The goal of working through multiple concerns is to keep the other parties engaged and motivated, and to accelerate their productivity.

The following sections help guide you through the critical conversation when you're dealing with multiple issues.

Prioritizing what issue to focus on first

If you have a laundry list of issues that need to change, prioritizing what you need to work on first is key. Decide which issues you need to discuss and which ones can wait or even never be discussed if the other areas change. Here are a few things to keep in mind when prioritizing what to focus on during the critical conversation:

- ✔ **Consider the biggest consequence:** To prioritize all the issues, start with the facts and the impact the facts have on the organization or team. What issues have had the biggest consequence? Although you may see a difference in work styles, the most important issues are the ones that have the biggest negative impact. For example, sure someone forgetting to do his financial report at the end of the month is a big issue, but not delivering on client commitments (which could lead to the client asking your competitor to do the work) may be more important.

- ✔ **Start with two:** Perhaps the receiver of the information doesn't deliver projects on time, and the quality is poor; she talks too loudly, treats others with disrespect; and so on, and so on. But throwing out *all* this information will surely fall on deaf ears. Even if all parties agree to work through the issues at hand, too much data will just overwhelm the other party. Start with the most important concerns that are leading to the most negative consequences, and create action plans for those concerns. If you feel there is still room for improvement, add in the third concern or idea but try to stop there. Work on those two or three issues, and if there are still concerns later, have another conversation at a later date. The first conversation will open the dialogue, and if you group the concerns together, fixing two or three important behaviors may do the trick.

✔ **Combine concerns:** Combining or grouping concerns can be the right way to go when you're dealing with multiple issues. Although you need to base the critical conversation on facts, finding general themes may make the information more manageable and easier to understand and retain. You may be able to give specific examples of when a person did not collaborate with the team, for example, they did not attend team meetings and did not participate in discussions when they did show up. In this case, you may summarize this with the following three examples: "I have noticed you are not participating actively in team meetings. Last month you did not attend any of our Friday calls, and this week I know you were on the call but you did not offer your opinion on possible solutions for the client."

✔ **Use the most recent data:** Timing is everything, and digging up issues from a few years back is only going to de-motivate the other party. If the data you use isn't from the last three to six months, it may no longer be relevant, and the recipient very well could think, "You knew this for a year and never told me!"

As with all critical conversations, for each of the areas you plan to present, come prepared with the future expectations in order to create mutual agreement in the conversation. Nothing is worse than presenting facts on where improvement needs to take place but never giving the other party support or ideas on how to improve.

Creating a win for everyone

The term win-win may seem a bit cliché in the corporate world, but considering the alternatives of lose-lose or win-lose, helping everyone succeed doesn't sound so bad.

Here's why a win-win is necessary during a critical conversation.

✔ **Win-lose:** If one person wins the conversation and another loses, you have little chance to build a relationship or maintain a positive environment after the conversation ends. A win-lose mentality creates competition, just as it does in sports, and positions people who should be partners as sides working against one another. The fact is that the individual or team does need to change something (the goal of critical conversations), but that something shouldn't be dictated to them. An example of a win-lose mentality is when the initiator comes to the conversation with the mindset that the other person is wrong.

✔ **Lose-lose:** If you start with a win-lose mentality, your only other option for the outcome of the conversation is lose-lose. If an initiator presents information to the other party and the other party gets hostile or angry, the meeting may turn into a "If I'm going down with the ship, so are you!" scenario.

✔ **Win-win:** When everyone walks away from the conversation feeling that the decisions for next steps were made together, and everyone can support the decisions, you'll have positive results. The easiest way to create a win-win (after prioritizing the two critical topics that deserve a critical conversation) is to come to the table with data and the intention to create lasting change rather than to just get a point across.

Leading a successful conversation means that all the parties agree on next steps, the relationship is strengthened (or at least not worsened), and people are motivated to do something different. While data and facts are important, people are important too. One part of this process is closing the conversation with ease (see Chapter 11). The other part is creating an environment that leaves people motivated, even when they need to do a good amount of work after the conversation ends. Most people have heard of sports teams who come back with a fire in their eyes after losing a game. In this case, you shouldn't use sports as an analogy for generating results. In a critical conversation, getting back at someone comes from losing; motivation to do better comes from winning.

Know your own motivations: Be honest about your own goals for the conversation and, as appropriate, state them up front. I presented a few ideas on how to address your own bias, and in Chapter 8 I talk a bit more about working with your own style and goals.

This conversation will be a stressful event. The other party needs time to absorb all the areas that may need to change, so build reflection time into the discussion. Having a rushed conversation only leaves the other party with questions and uncertainty.

Problems don't pop up overnight

Critical conversations usually don't pop up overnight. No one book can spell out every issue that could lead to a critical conversation (and if such a book existed, it would be like *War and Peace* and then *War* again!). The important thing to remember is that no person in an organization or relationship operates as an island. Look at all the behaviors, actions, and dynamics that could and should lead to a critical conversation from the point of view that everything operates as a whole. Some actions may need a quick and focused response, but in other cases critical conversations are the result of patterns and reactions rather than just one snapshot in time.

Remembering the principle of patience

Because the issues you discuss during a conversation didn't pop up overnight, it makes sense that the solution won't happen overnight. The critical conversation may have to take place over multiple meetings, and perhaps even with different audiences. Patience will be not only a virtue, but also a requirement.

An expert communicator knows that being patient goes hand in hand with being flexible, but still in control. Chances are good that you'll witness the second coming of Mount Vesuvius when addressing multiple concerns. The two main topics you bring to the table will explode into many more. The conversation may start off with one focus, but often the initial problems you want to address are simply symptoms of more issues. Be flexible with the discussion. The best way to keep flexible, especially when you are not sure which way to bend, is by stating the obvious (see the earlier section "The elephant in the room"). Say "I sense that this topic is a hot point in the room. We can continue talking about past issues, or we can focus on next steps. What does the group want to do?" One of the issues may have to be put on the back burner, but listening and showing that you're willing and able to work on any problem is always better than getting through a pre-planned agenda.

Part II

Making Sense of How You Communicate

The 5th Wave   By Rich Tennant

"...faster than a speeding bullet...more powerful than a locomotive...these attributes are great. It's the X-ray vision that we need to talk about."

In this part...

Effective communication is the building block to a successful critical conversation. You take a deep dive into how to use body language, listening, and tone of voice to develop expert communication skills. I also walk through how to work with different communication styles so you can resolve issues quickly and start building productivity and improving employee morale.

Chapter 6

Building Effective Verbal Communication Techniques

In This Chapter

▶ Communicating clearly and effectively in every situation

▶ Discovering how the smallest words can have a big impact

▶ Turning a confrontational conversation into a cooperative one

*I*n everyday situations, people rely on the familiar back-and-forth of verbal communication. You probably don't walk down the street in the morning and pause to think about what to say or what to do when a neighbor says hello. Instead, you have a fairly common pattern based on an existing relationship; you smile, say "hi" back, perhaps engage in small talk, and go on with your day. For most of your relationships, this process works fine. During critical conversations, however, the intent changes the process. For this situation, you need effective and explicit communication techniques to manage the dialogues and to ensure that the results are focused and clear. Building effective communication techniques will catapult the success of a critical conversation.

In this chapter, I give you the 411 on how to communicate clearly and effectively. I give techniques that help build productivity and improve employee morale with different verbal cues you can use in every conversation, especially the critical ones. I devote part of the chapter to examples of open, authentic, and explicit conversations. Finally, I show you how to turn confrontational language into cooperative discussions that get results.

Great Communicators Are Made, Not Born

Although people have been communicating for most of their lives, critical conversations are different. Critical conversations are deliberate events that are targeted on results. In most cases, the main goal of the critical conversation is to improve working relationships or organizational results. That goal is a lot different from leading a project meeting, sending an e-mail about a status update, or even presenting the company's results to shareowners.

A leader may be a wonderful speaker who communicates frequently and with transparency. But even the best communicators can get caught up in the message when delivering a critical point.

To understand why communication skills are so critical to a successful conversation, briefly walk through what happens when people engage in dialogue. First, the sender has an idea, translates this idea into words, and sends it. Then the receiver gets the message, applies meaning to the idea, and gives feedback, making the receiver the new sender. Every back-and-forth exchange of words (and even nonverbal cues) continues with this process. Figure 6-1 shows this interaction.

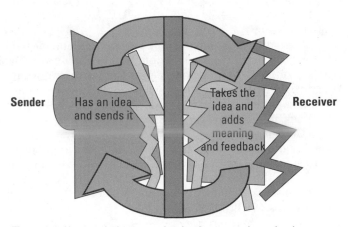

Figure 6-1: How verbal communication is sent and received.

Communication is a transaction in which both parties continuously send and receive messages. Even before the initiator speaks, the receiver is observing nonverbal signals. For more on nonverbal techniques, check out Chapter 7.

Now imagine a chain of this communication. Back and forth, each time with the other party interpreting what was or wasn't said and adding meaning to the information. A message's meanings can easily become distorted.

Here's an example to show how the simple act of communicating can turn a bad situation into a horrible one.

Kate: "Hi, John. Thanks for agreeing to meet with me today. I wanted to talk with you about a concern I have with your behavior in team meetings recently."

John (getting a bit defensive): "A concern. What concern?"

Kate: "Well, it's hard for me to believe that you did this because I wasn't in the room, but Kasha came into my office complaining that you have been raising your voice, and —"

John (cutting in): "How can you give me any feedback when you weren't in the meeting?"

Kate: "Sounds like you're mad. If you'll let me speak, I can help."

John promptly rolls his eyes and tunes out the conversation, allowing Kate to speak all she wants.

Right off the bat, Kate sends the message that she has a concern, which may seem like a fair statement. What Kate does wrong is to use words that lead John to believe the problem is entirely on his end ("your behavior"). The situation just gets worse when Kate says "it's hard for me to believe this." Perhaps she's trying to add some humor or use a less accusatory tone, but John interprets this statement as an accusation that his actions are so wrong even his boss can't imagine they happened. (I get into how tone and other nonverbal cues impact the conversation in Chapter 7.) Words make a giant difference in how the receiver accepts and agrees on the desired result of the critical conversation.

The good news is that with simple strategies, you won't fall into Kate's slip-ups. When you communicate well, participants will be committed to improving their working relationships in the course of improving the business. When you don't communicate correctly, the other parties will be put on the defensive and refuse to engage in the conversation. You can see how the former option gives you a much better outcome.

Verbal communication and nonverbal communication are the building blocks to a successful critical conversation. In Chapter 3, I go into the basics of a critical conversation; in this chapter, I dig a little deeper into how to deliver the message and get results with the right verbal exchange.

Verbal Communication: When Words Matter Most

Effective verbal communication employs a number of simple and not-so-simple tools during different situations. The goal of mastering critical conversation is to know what the tools are, without using an overformulaic "toolkit" approach. Success depends on the relationship the two parties have before the conversation takes place and whether they can understand and respect each other. Being interested in and respectful of others' points of view through your choice of words will contribute greatly to open communication and cooperation.

According to some communication experts, body language and other nonverbal communication skills account for more than 90 percent of the way an individual receives information from a sender. I dive into all the nonverbal cues that facilitate a successful critical conversation in Chapter 7.

Facts, opinions, and gossip

In Chapter 3, I introduce the importance of using facts to support a critical conversation. But just having the facts doesn't guarantee a successful critical conversation. You have to present the facts as facts; this is when words matter most. During a critical conversation, present factual information and avoid the temptation to use opinion or hearsay. These steps leave no room for question and distrust, which could lead to one of the parties closing off the flow of communication.

Although this chapter is far from an English lesson (if you need one, check out *English Grammar For Dummies* by Geraldine Woods [Wiley]), here are some clear-cut definitions to help guide you through what to do (and what not to do) during a critical conversation:

- ✔ **Fact:** An action you witnessed. Use facts during critical conversations — they can't be disputed. Lead with, "When I was in the meeting, you were pacing around the table while everyone else was sitting down."

- ✔ **Opinion:** A personal judgment. Try to avoid opinions as much as possible during critical conversations, because they leave room for misinterpretation and uncertainty. Although your opinion may be right, you have no proof. Believing that someone left the room during a meeting because he thought the meeting was going nowhere, or that he crossed his arms because he didn't agree with the group's opinion, is just that — opinion. Opinions that can wreck a critical conversation include, "The administration believes you lied," or, "People who are usually so angry often aren't good workers."

- ✔ **Gossip:** Anything that comes secondhand or through the rumor mill. Gossip has no place in a critical conversation. Statements like "People have told me that you're a boozehound in the office," or "Lots of people have told me you aren't working that hard," open the conversation to doubt and mistrust.

Words create meaning

The following table shows a few key words and phrases that may have negative meanings during a critical conversation. I also show you how to turn these phrases into positive ones that can help create an open environment for honest discussion.

Poor Word Choices	Examples	Why It's a Poor Choice	Better Alternatives
"You should . . ."	"You should work harder." "You should do things differently."	The words "should" and "could" may be taken as an order and put the recipient on the defensive. "You should work harder" will derail a conversation faster than the blink of an eye.	"Would you be willing to look at different ways of working?" "Based on this feedback, can we agree on how to create more positive results?"
"You need to . . ."	"You need to change your behavior and listen to me."	Letting someone else know that she needs to do anything may put her on the defensive. Instead of telling someone what she needs to do, focus on talking about why changing is good and focus on the positive.	"Can we look at ways to make a more positive impact with the behavior I mentioned?"
"They" and "them"	"They told me you are a bad presenter." "They have issues with your presentation style."	Using "them" or "they" instead of "us" or "we" can create a competitive environment. Instead, try focusing on what people can achieve together.	"I'd like to share some presentation examples I saw in last week's meeting."
"Horrible" and "bad"	"You have a horrible presentation style." "Your communication skills are bad."	Although someone's behavior may truly be horrible, these negative adjectives tend to create a defensive environment. Instead, try to focus on positive solutions rather than problems. If in doubt, simply drop the negative adjective.	"I want to talk about your presentation style." "Are you willing to discuss your communication skills?"

I, you, we, and they: Pronouns matter

No one wants to be brought into a conversation and told that she's doing things wrong or that she's going against the company. During a critical conversation, limit the words "them" and "they," and stick to "I" and "we."

Think of the different reactions these statements generate:

> *Situation:* A client relationship manager walks into his manager's office right after losing a key customer account.
>
> **Manager (who didn't read *Critical Conversations For Dummies*):** "Because *you* didn't get along with our client's executive team, *you* lost us a giant book of business."

Note how this statement immediately pits "you" versus "us."

> **Manager (using a revised approach):** "I realize there were different perspectives on the right approach with Company ABC, especially during the last project. How can we work together to prevent losing another client, and perhaps even get Company ABC back?"

Here's another example to demonstrate the nuances of word choice:

> *Situation:* At an engineering conference, one of the senior engineers partied every night and word got back to her manager.
>
> **Manager (not using the right words):** "They shouldn't be as sensitive when it comes to how other people behave when they aren't officially in the office, but you really need to watch your behavior when it comes to how you act at conferences."

I see a double-whammy here! The recipient is already on the defensive with "they" and "you," and then is hit again with a conditional verb, "should." (See the nearby sidebar "Words create meaning" to discover more positive alternatives to these words.)

Here's a better approach to the conversation from the previous example:

> **Manager (making good use of verbal skills):** "I know that during conferences, it's important to be social. This has to be balanced with maintaining professional behavior. Can we work together to talk about which activities are better than others?"

Accusations make people defensive. *Collaboration* makes change possible — and change is the ultimate goal of a critical conversation. During critical conversations, the smallest details, like the use of pronouns, can set a positive tone or create an argumentative or confrontational environment. Using the right inclusive words creates a higher level of commitment to the conversation because all the parties can take part in the discussion instead of being talked to by the other parties.

Cooperative Language: Verbal Communication at Its Finest

Although the goal of some communication may be to excite or shock the audience, the intent of critical conversations is to engage and perhaps educate all parties on how to work together more effectively in the future. Cooperative language is the cornerstone of critical conversations.

The polar opposite of cooperative language is confrontational and argumentative language. When a difference of opinion arises, many people want to win while the other person loses (check out Chapter 5). In some situations and cultures, arguing or using rank to influence is seen as a sign of strength. Critical conversation is not one of these times.

Don't think that critical conversations will never involve a debate about the best possible solution. Parties will have to discuss (and even debate) during a critical conversation; the tone and words of the debate, however, are most productive when they're cooperative rather than confrontational.

Corporate speak, buzz words, and jargon

Talking in corporate speak, buzz words, and jargon — even if all parties are part of the same organization — usually results in glazed eyes or, worse, rolling eyes. A critical conversation isn't the time to demonstrate how smart or with-it you are; it's time to get to the point clearly and make sure the message is heard.

Keeping confrontational language out

When you have a difference of opinion on how to solve a problem or concern, getting caught up in the moment is easy to do. One misinterpretation or difference of opinion can cause someone to lose her cool, causing the conversation to spiral out of control. Just like that, a critical confrontation — rather than a critical conversation — begins.

Confrontational language blocks each party from listening to the other's interests and needs. The focus becomes protecting or standing your ground rather than finding a common and agreeable ground. Confrontational language is often emotionally charged or even defensive, and lets the other parties in the conversation know that you're not there to help build relationships and create something better; you're there to win.

Here's an example of a critical conversation that starts as a simple misunderstanding between two peers about who was responsible for doing a final review of a proposal document before it went to a customer. Notice how one piece of confrontational language can belly flop an entire conversation.

> **Erin:** "Julian, I'm not sure if you knew this, but the final proposal that went to the client didn't include all the answers we had developed. What were you thinking?"
>
> **Julian:** "What do you mean, 'What was I thinking?' I've been at this company 15 years, and in all my life I've never seen such a mess. The lawyers changed the meaning of all our responses in the document. It wasn't my fault. It was their fault. You really need to tone down your attitude and stop accusing me of things."
>
> **Erin:** "Attitude? I don't care how long you've been at this company; if you read the proposal before it went out to the customer, this wouldn't have happened."
>
> **Julian:** "It isn't my job to proofread what the lawyers said."

You can almost feel the negative force escalating in the conversation. Taking a step back, the goal of the conversation is to find out what happened to the document, where the process broke down, and perhaps even solve the problem. All Julian hears was that she was wrong ("What were you thinking?"), and the conversation tumbles downward from the beginning.

Table 6-1 shows you the areas that turn the conversation sour. In this example, you can see two of those confrontational triggers:

✔ Erin thinks she's right, and she says so by accusing Julian with "What were you thinking?" and "If you read . . ." Erin goes as far as saying, "I don't care." It doesn't matter what comes next — this language immediately signals Julian to give up or get defensive, neither of which is good for a critical conversation. Giving up is one of several defensive reactions.

✔ Blame starts from the very beginning with Erin saying, "What were you thinking?" which can be interpreted as, "Why did you do this?" This conversation has plenty of blame to go around, and the blame isn't just between Julian and Erin. By the end of this simple conversation, Julian is fed up and starts sharing the blame. The only solution Erin presents is for Julian to recognize that if she "read the proposal before it went out to the customer, this wouldn't have happened."

Table 6-1 Spotting Confrontational Language (And Turning It Around)

Confrontational Triggers	Examples	Why It's Confrontational	Better Alternatives
One individual or party thinks she's unconditionally right	"What were you thinking?" "If you read . . ."	Because one individual thinks she's right, that person is unwilling to consider other opinions, ideas, or positions.	"Are you willing to work together and explore other ideas that may work?"
A lot of blame	"What were you thinking?"	Because the individual believes she's right, the only solution is for the other party to agree. This ultimatum leaves little room for finding a common ground in a solution all parties can agree to work with in the future.	"Let's focus on the solution. What can we do to avoid the situation from happening again?"

(continued)

Table 6-1 (continued)

Confrontational Triggers	Examples	Why It's Confrontational	Better Alternatives
Attacks	"Fine, talk with my supervisor." "I don't care." "You're wrong."	Confrontational language that's emotionally charged puts people on the defensive and shuts down collaboration, period.	"I want to resolve the issue, but if you do want to talk with my supervisor, I can help you do that." "I may not agree with your actions, but let's talk about how we can create a positive solution."
Absolutes ("always" and "never")	"We always do it this way." "You never show up to work."	Saying something always happens or never happens leaves no room for discussion or interpretation. It is better to state a fact in place of absolutes.	"That's different from how I usually solve this concern." "Based on this week's time report, I noticed that you didn't come into work all week."

Confrontational language can also give the impression that a party's only choice is to fight back, just like Julian starts doing as soon as Erin asks what she was thinking. The principles of physics can be applied to the principles of conversation: For every action there is an equal and opposite reaction. If one person tells another person that she's wrong, the second individual has a choice to either combat one negative with another negative, or to react in an equal but more positive way.

In the previous example, Erin and Julian are going back and forth with negative force in the conversation. The conversation goes in a completely different (and better) direction when Erin starts the discussion like this:

> **Erin:** "Hi, Julian. We just sent out that proposal to the client, and the final version wasn't the same version we created last week. Can we sit down and find out how we can correct it?"

> **Julian:** "Yes. Let's sit down and find out how we can fix it."

Erin may also choose to use an "I" statement, like "The proposal just went to the client, and after it was sent, I noticed it wasn't the same version we created last week. Can we sit down and find out how we can correct it?"

Unless Julian saw Erin rewrite the proposal and press send, blaming her for the error is not only premature, but also does nothing to correct the situation now or in the future. In almost all critical conversations, what's done is done — the parties can't go back in history to redo the events. Create an open and honest environment to help direct the future rather than try to find out who should be blamed.

The good news is that even if one individual begins to use confrontational language, the other individual can respond in an equal but more positive manner. The next section shows how to turn confrontational language into accommodating words that get results.

Turning confrontational words into accommodating words

The goal of critical conversation isn't to win, but to approach a problem as a collaborative effort and seek solutions that are beneficial to all parties involved. Whether you're kicking off the critical conversation or on the receiving end of a potentially confrontational situation, moving from argument to collaboration will create more positive results.

With a little practice, almost any confrontational situation can be flipped into a collaborative and accommodating discussion. The following sections give you some ways to turn confrontational words into more accommodating ones.

Tip #1: Focus on the process and the future, not the person and the past

> **Argumentative:** "I never received any e-mails. You must have made a mistake."

Accommodating: "I don't remember receiving the e-mail. If you like, I would be happy to look into the process together and find out what happened and how we can fix it."

What changed and why: In one sentence, you can see three big changes. First, "you made a mistake" turns into presenting an opportunity to work together. Second, instead of accusing a person, the focus of the meeting is on the process and how it can be fixed. Third, rather than accusing the other party of doing anything wrong, the accommodating sentence focuses on the future and how to prevent the problem from happening again.

Tip #2: Lead with fact and options

Argumentative: "You have to change your behavior."

Accommodating: "Emotions were high last week in the office. I noticed that the yelling in the office made team members withdraw and stop sharing their ideas on the customer meeting."

What changed and why: Remember that no one needs to do anything during a critical conversation, so telling someone that she has to change anything, especially her behavior, could easily be met with hostility. Instead, state the facts and their impact from an objective point of view. It can also be helpful to turn possibly harsh statements into questions. Genuine questions help gather more information and open a dialogue, which is perfect for a critical conversation.

When using questions to turn possibly hostile conversations into cooperative ones, be careful not to start the Spanish Inquisition. Come to the conversation with a genuine desire to make things better, not to sarcastically or critically accuse someone. A comment isn't necessarily cooperative just because you add a question mark to the end.

Tip #3: Things are always possible, even if they aren't probable

Argumentative: "That's just not possible."

Accommodating: "That's different from how we usually solve problems. Are you willing to look at other alternative solutions?"

What changed and why: Using the words "never" or "not possible" immediately closes the discussion and limits the number of solutions that are possible.

Using five key phrases that get results

No one has a magic wand to make all critical conversations go perfectly, but you can draw on key phases to get the discussion going in the right direction and redirect the discussion if it gets off track.

Using the five key phrases in the following sections when they're appropriate lets the other parties know you want to help make the situation better. Although all these phrases (and all the tactics in this chapter) need to come from a genuine desire to help, using them signals to the other parties that you want to create a critical dialogue to solve the issue instead of giving a one-way lecture on what needs to change.

Take a look at the following sections and put the following key phrases to use.

Why don't we work together to solve . . .

In the heat of a debate or emotional discussion, having at least one common goal helps the conversation move forward. "Why don't we work together on . . ." gives the other individual an opportunity to have some control in the discussion. She can control whether or not she's there, and she can have a voice in the conversation. This phrase is also helpful to go back to as common ground if the conversation gets off track. For example, you may say, "It seems like we may have gotten off track. In the beginning of the conversation we agreed to work together to solve the problem. Can we keep doing that?"

It's difficult to . . .

When providing critical information during a conversation that may not be well received, you'll probably feel stressed. Opening up can help set a genuine tone that you're there to help. This openness can neutralize confrontational individuals so you can move toward talking about the real issues. As the initiator of the conversation, you may begin with, "It's difficult to deliver bad news to a great employee, and this situation is no different."

 Don't use this phrase if you don't genuinely feel the situation is hard. For example, if your job is to fire people, saying "It's hard to fire you" could be seen as insincere. If it's true, you can say, "I'm in a position to deliver tough news more often than others, but that doesn't make the situation any easier. I can understand how you may be feeling."

The receiver of the information may also use this tactic. "It's hard to hear this information. I'm feeling a bit overwhelmed with the information you provided. Do you mind if we walk through that example again?"

Were you aware . . .

Asking another individual whether she was aware of behavior, rules, or policies is one of the most underutilized tools during a critical conversation — and in communication in general. At times, information may just go unnoticed. A person may really not be aware of the impact a behavior has on the team. A customer may not be aware of a policy. "Awareness" is a safe word that helps the other party to save face, and it provides a great opportunity to give critical information or education.

A critical conversation should open the doors of communication and create an honest environment for discussion. If one individual feels that she lost the discussion and the other person won, or if any party feels embarrassed, the safe environment of conversation can quickly deteriorate.

Don't phrase this statement as "Did you know . . ." Meeting space tends to be ego space, and asking "Did you know . . ." can be interpreted as the other individual not having the intelligence or ability.

That is different from . . .

Saying "That is different from the way other situations have been solved" is a great and positive alternative to saying that something will never happen or isn't possible. Using the phrase "that is different" doesn't accuse or blame; it simply states a fact. Suppose a customer is complaining on the phone and demanding more than a customer has received in the past. Rather than saying that what the customer wants is impossible, simply say, "That is different from the way we usually work through problems." The information the customer gave has been acknowledged, and the customer service representative has refocused the conversation on the solution. Maybe you have a magic wand for making critical conversation productive after all!

If someone is outright lying about a situation, make sure you focus on the ethical issue at hand. Chapter 15 covers dealing with ethical issues in more detail and addresses how a mediator may help in tricky situations.

How might [problems] be solved?

Keeping the conversation focused on the future keeps the discussion positive. This phrase is especially useful when a conversation is focusing on excuses or things that have happened in the past that can't be changed. Although looking at facts is important for making critical conversations successful, the goal of a critical conversation is to change behavior — not just to present information. This phrase also takes the burden off the initiator of the conversation. One person doesn't need to have all the solutions to every problem, so asking for other alternatives is a good way to get buy-in and agreement on what will happen after the conversation ends.

Chapter 7

Grasping Nonverbal Cues

In This Chapter

▶ Identifying nonverbal cues that help deliver critical messages

▶ Actively listening to move a conversation forward

▶ Assessing unspoken signals

*N*onverbal cues during conversations include everything from body language to the use of space, and from moments of silence to eye contact. Nonverbal cues can be defined as broadly as almost anything that's not verbally communicated, and they can be interpreted in just as many ways.

In this chapter, I introduce nonverbal techniques that speak volumes during a critical conversation. I then walk through the process of active listening and give you examples to make sure you can really hear the concerns in the room. I also give you tools that you can use to assess your own cues and the cues of the recipient of the message. This chapter gives many examples of how to become more aware of the way nonverbal cues are perceived and how they can help (or hinder!) a critical conversation.

Noting Nonverbal Techniques that Speak Volumes

Nonverbal techniques in communication encompass everything from how you sit or stand, your facial expressions, eye contact, nerves and stress, dress and appearance, and even voice quality. Nonverbal cues often reflect emotions and may be unconscious and unintentional. For example, blushing often means embarrassment, and clearing the throat or a cracking voice can mean nervousness. Even the most positive critical conversation needs the right unspoken communication methods to make sure the message is delivered appropriately and understood.

The following is an example that uses just a few of the nonverbal elements that can influence a conversation:

> Sally is moving an employee into a new position after the employee did not get a promotion. If you were the employee, which conversation, noted in Table 7-1, would make you more likely to want to accept the offer?

Table 7-1 Considering Nonverbal Elements in Conversation

	Conversation One	*Conversation Two*
What is said	"Jim, I know you've wanted the manager position. I have another opportunity I would like you to consider . . ."	"Jim, I know you've wanted the manager position. I have another opportunity I would like you to consider . . ."
Body language	Sally's arms and legs are crossed, or her hands are tightly clasped.	Sally is sitting at a round table, both feet on the ground, shoulders relaxed.
Eye contact	Sally switches from looking at Jim to looking at her phone every five to ten seconds.	Sally is leaning in slightly, looking at Jim as he talks.
Dress and appearance	Sally just got back from the gym over lunch hour and is running late.	Sally is poised and dressed in work clothes.

Even though the words are exactly the same in conversations one and two, you may think that the Sally in conversation one is just too busy to care about an employee and simply wants to fill a role in the organization. Conversation two, on the other hand, has more sincere nonverbal cues and genuine interest. In conversation two, it seems like Sally really cares about the conversation — the key ingredient of critical conversations! What you don't say is just as important as what you do.

Expressions that count

A key to unlocking the nonverbal cues treasure chest is to be mindful of how you're expressing your message. Pay attention to facial expressions, the way you display nerves and stress, and voice quality. The upcoming sections help you master these nonverbal languages.

Table 7-2 is a handy guide on effective nonverbal expressions during a critical conversation. For more examples on how to master nonverbal expressions, check out `www.leadingchangecoach.com`.

Table 7-2	Comparing Effective and Ineffective Nonverbal Expressions	
	Supportive and positive	*Unsupportive and negative*
Body language (lower body)	Feet on ground, ankles crossed slightly	Legs crossed
Body language (upper body)	Sitting up straight, relaxed shoulders, arms on the table — ideally at waist height	Slouched shoulders, hands in front of mouth, leaning against a wall, waving arms around, pointing fingers
Eye contact	Looking at the other individual or individuals as they talk; concentrating on their voice, movement, and eyes	Staring at the other individuals or never looking at their eyes during the conversation
Dress and appearance	Dressing appropriately; holding the conversation in a clutter-free zone	Rushing from one meeting to the next; papers everywhere; being flustered; food on face or clothes (this really does happen!); wearing outdoor gear when you're inside (rain jacket, wool coat, hat, gloves)
Facial expressions	Smiling appropriately	Raising eyebrows, smirking, grimacing, resting or putting your head in your hands
Voice quality	Steady and clear, may be a bit slower than your usual conversation speed but not exaggeratedly slow	High, fast, too soft, too slow; using *um, ah, you know*, and *like*
Nerves and stress	Taking a deep breath and being aware of sudden changes in body language or nervous habits	Tightly crossing hands; toes/hands tapping; legs shaking; pacing the room; spinning pens or pencils between your fingers; jingling loose change in your pocket; vocal sighs, hmmms, and throat-clearing

Imitation is the best form of flattery

A good way to increase the comfort level of the other party is to focus on your own nonverbal cues when you're listening to and delivering a message. People not only listen to you during a critical conversation, but also watch you and can even start mirroring your behavior. If you have your hands relaxed on the desk and are listening intently, the other individual may begin to do the same thing. This imitation often is unconscious, so try not to force the issue by overemphasizing the behavior you want the other individual to imitate. For example, if you want the other person to slow down the pace, slow down your pace slightly, but don't go into extreme slow motion. If you do, the other person may focus on the pace of the conversation rather than the conversation itself. As with all nonverbal techniques, moderation is the key.

Mirroring positive nonverbal communication from the other party can also relax everyone in the conversation. For example, if the other party is gently leaning toward you (often a sign of interest), you may want to lean your head toward the other party as well. If you see the other party backing away, you may tone down your own arm or body movements and perhaps even take a step back to show respect for the other individual's desire for space.

Most of the body language techniques in Table 7-2 are common in some Western cultures, but be careful not to make assumptions about the meaning of nonverbal cues in all geographic or organizational cultures. Nodding a head in one culture may mean agreement, while in another culture it may simply mean that you're being heard. *Cross-Cultural Selling For Dummies,* by Michael Soon Lee, Ralph R. Roberts, and Joe Kraynak (Wiley), can help with ideas on how to adapt your message and get a crash course in building multicultural rapport.

With so many expressions to be attentive of, becoming overwhelmed is easy to do. But nonverbal expressions don't need to be overwhelming if you find ways to become aware of them. Improving nonverbal techniques takes practice. Try this exercise during a non–critical conversation, such as a relaxed talk with a colleague. Notice how you sit; what you do with your hands, arms, and legs; how you physically change when the other person is talking; and how often you look away to check what's outside the window or who's texting you on the phone. Although few communicators are ever perfect at all these expressions, little changes can make a big difference during a conversation.

Bring a light jacket or sweater to a critical conversation! No, your mother isn't writing this book. But crossing your arms can signal a number of reactions: being uninterested in the conversation, disdain for the topic or person, or anxiousness. Crossed arms can also just mean that you're trying to stay warm in an air-conditioned meeting room. Be sure not to cross signals, and if you happen to get cold quickly, keep a light jacket or sweater on hand. Sounds simple and perhaps silly, but it will be one less thing you need to be aware of during a conversation — and that's significant.

Keep your body relaxed, but don't be a slouch

Think back to your primary school teacher and sit straight and confident, but don't be tense. Crossing your arms can give the impression that you're guarding some piece of information. Remain open to giving and receiving information during the conversation by sitting straight, either with both feet on the floor or your ankles crossed, and keeping your arms open and shoulders down.

Maintain appropriate eye contact

Being in a deadlock stare with another individual during a conversation can be intimidating or downright creepy. Look at the other person's eyes and mouth throughout the conversation, but move your eyes every three to five seconds to avoid making the conversation feel like a police investigation rather than a critical conversation. Sometimes gently nodding helps to maintain the appropriate level of eye contact as well — but remember to keep it in moderation. Nodding is good; being a bobble-head doll is annoying.

 When you create eye contact, you aren't just doing it because this book told you to. Eye contact helps you to look for signals like fidgeting (the other person is nervous), darting glares (an individual may be getting defensive), and glancing at the clock (the person is distracted). All these signals indicate that you may need to make an adjustment in the conversation.

Use genuine facial expressions

Even during tough conversations, relaxing is okay. A gentle smile and leaning your head in slightly can help put the other person at ease. When you make an agreement during the conversation, a smile can be appropriate to show a sincere appreciation for the way the conversation is progressing. Be sure not to touch your face or lay your head in your hands in a show of frustration or desperation — both are distracting and can indicate that you're nervous.

Keep dress and appearance professional

You don't need to go out and buy a nice suit, but tuck in your shirt, don't leave old coffee cups out on the table, and have enough empty space to avoid distractions. When your outward appearance and the location for the conversation are professional, the recipient of the conversation knows that you're taking the matter seriously.

As simple as it may sound, looking in the mirror before having a critical conversation may help catch a piece of food between your teeth. Limit visual distractions from a critical conversation.

Acknowledge and control nerves

Every critical conversation comes with some nerves and stress. If appropriate, acknowledge these reactions verbally, and then control them physically. For example, if you find your voice cracking and your hands shaking, simply say, "I'm a little nervous about this conversation," and then move on. Make sure your shoulders stay relaxed, keep your hands unclenched, and try not to shake your legs or tap your fingers. If you tend to talk with your hands, don't change your body language to look like Frankenstein's monster. Instead, use moderate gestures or even point to a part in the notes you may be taking. For more on handling high emotions when the stakes are high, jump to Chapter 3.

Know how your voice sounds

Vocal quality is a lot more than the words you choose during a conversation. Watch out for extremes in volume, pace, pitch, and diction. You don't need a speech coach, but nervous tension can tighten your body and vocal cords, so remember to breathe and take time for the conversation instead of being rushed through it. These techniques help in the overall presentation of the critical message. Finish one statement before starting another, and leave plenty of time between the two, especially when emotions and nerves are high.

The way you use your voice dictates how recipients listen to the message: a fast delivery can make individuals nervous or overly stimulated, while a delivery that's too slow may seem a bit dramatic and controlled.

Use of voice

Your voice can work wonders in creating a safe and productive environment for the conversation. It's important to plan and prepare for a conversation, but the use of voice sets the tone (literally) of the meeting. Tone can either build rapport and trust, or put up an iron curtain.

Using the right style and tone of voice is directly related to how the receiver perceives your point of view on the conversation. Open, enthusiastic, and patient use of voice leads to trust and collaboration. And I probably don't need to let you know what pessimism, sarcasm, and a rushed tone do to the conversation!

So what is the right tone? There is no one right answer, but if you're attentive and genuine, you can generate the right tone of voice for the situation.

The following sections give you a look at how tone can influence the conversation. You can also listen to how the tone of voice can make or break a conversation online at `www.leadingchange coach.com`.

Friendly and open

Is your voice friendly and open? You don't have to be best friends with the other parties in the conversation, but if you offer information, the recipient is more likely to offer information back to you. This openness establishes a constructive dialogue.

Even in black and white, you can hear the use of voice in these examples:

> **Good use of tone:** "I understand there is a difference of opinion on the team, and the goal of the conversation is to find a solution we can all live with and work toward."

> **Questionable use of tone:** "There is a difference of opinion and we need to solve it."

Appropriate level of enthusiasm

Simply having a genuine desire to help change the situation creates a positive environment with the appropriate level of enthusiasm needed for the discussion. If you are watching every minute tick by during the conversation or thinking that you would much rather be playing a game on your phone, your interest for the topic at hand is probably fairly low. On the other hand, if you genuinely are interested in working with the other parties, all the parties involved will see and hear that you care and they will be more inclined to mirror your positive behavior. You don't have to be a cheerleader or oddly excited to be enthusiastic.

Here are a few examples of what the right level of enthusiasm could sound like:

> **Overenthusiastic:** You can imagine the reaction to a chipper boss saying, "Hey everyone, I asked you to come to this meeting to let you know your paychecks are cut in half! Yeah! Sis-boom-bah!"

> **Underenthusiastic:** On the other hand, having a critical conversation at 5 p.m. on a Friday after a long week of deadlines may not be the best time. "Thanks for working so hard this week. I'm so exhausted from the week too (yawn). Your paychecks are cut," won't go over well either.

Appropriately enthusiastic: A better use of voice (and choice of words) may be, "I know everyone has been putting in long days during the recession to keep our company in business. It's hard to let you know this, but even with the extra work, we need to make pay cuts. I'd like to walk through the details to answer the many questions you may have right now."

Patient and calm

Perhaps the easiest use of voice to control is making your voice patient and calm. Because many critical conversations deliver a message that could lead to disagreement or focus on a difficult topic, try to slow down your words and not rush the recipients. Being rushed can make people nervous. Rushed conversations can also be seen as blunt or tactless.

The easiest way to slow down the conversation — especially if you're prone to speaking and acting fast — is to be clear and leave enough time for discussion. Don't schedule back-to-back meetings, and don't hold the meeting right before lunch hour or at 5 p.m. If you find yourself rushing through a conversation, take a breath or take a break. Taking a break to slow down doesn't mean going out for a coffee or taking a walk. Simply allow the other party to speak. For example, "Let me take a break and let you do some of the talking. Can you tell me any more about how the meeting went with our customer?" Although these may seem like minor details, they can make a big difference.

Silence is golden, space is priceless

Two other nonverbal techniques can keep a critical conversation on target for success. The first is silence and the second is space.

Giving pause for silence

Listening is very important in a critical conversation, but listening and silence are two different things. Silence does one thing that no other verbal or nonverbal technique can do: It gives everyone time to process information and to think.

Silence doesn't need to be long, and if it is, it may seem unnatural. Use silence between thoughts, before responding to a question, or when you feel yourself getting impatient or nervous. You need only three seconds to take a breath, allow words to sink in, and clearly think about what to do next.

Making good use of space

Look around you and notice how the space is being used during the conversation — both the physical space of the room and the space around your body. Try to keep the space suitable for the conversation. If the conversation is happening between two groups, don't try to cram everyone into the only tiny conference room available. A circular table immediately conveys inclusion, while a boardroom table can signal intimidation. When looking at how you use the space around you, try to lean in to the conversation, but don't tumble over. Leaning in signals interest, leaning back signals indifference, and leaning in too far can feel like intimidation.

Also consider where you sit or stand during the conversation. Standing too close to someone can cut into her personal space, but having a critical conversation from across the room becomes a critical yelling match. Bottom line with the use of space: Use moderation and practice what's comfortable.

Nonverbal no-no's

It's nice to think that although critical conversations may be stressful, they will at least be professional. Unfortunately, not everyone thinks this way or acts this way. Emotions can be expressed by words, but they're often first exhibited through nonverbal cues.

If you find yourself making the following nonverbal mistakes, or if you're the recipient of them, stop the conversation immediately and either redirect it (discover how to do this in Chapter 10) or call in a mediator (see Chapter 15):

- ✔ **Disrespect:** Rolling eyes, smirking, interrupting, and audible sighs are not only annoying but also disrespectful. Come to the conversation with a genuine desire to help make the situation better, and this type of disrespect for the other party in the conversation quickly disappears.

- ✔ **Anger and hostility:** Nonverbal examples of these emotions include pounding on a desk or table or hitting a wall. Critical conversations aren't always pleasant, but violence and anger should never be part of the discussion.

- ✔ **Intimidation:** Waving a finger in someone's face is one of the more subtle examples of nonverbal intimidation. Also, if you see someone getting up close and personal, it signals that she may be trying to bully the conversation.

- ✔ **Destruction:** Throwing things or ripping paper or other property is a not-so-subtle signal that tells you to redirect the conversation, most likely with a mediator involved.

Becoming an Expert in Active Listening

When people say they have trouble communicating, they often mean that they're having trouble understanding the other person's perspective or opinion. The best way to understand what the other person is saying is to actively pay attention to the speaker's verbal words and nonverbal cues. Doing so is called *active listening*. As an active listener, you use nonverbal cues to show your interest and understanding when the other party is talking.

You'll discover a few differences between listening and active listening. Take a look at Table 7-3 for an explanation.

Table 7-3	Listening versus Active Listening
Listening	*Active Listening*
To determine whether or not you agree with the other person's point of view: When you're listening, you may begin judging the value of the other party's statements before he has a chance to finish saying what he's saying.	**To understand the other person's point of view:** Hold back forming an opinion until the individual is done talking. If someone is nervous, his first words may not be perfectly stated. Often the real meaning comes out in the second half of a statement. Actively listen so you can hear everything being said — not just selective words.
To decide what to say next: When someone else is talking, you may be thinking about your next statement rather than listening to what the other person has to say.	**To hear what the other individual has to say, and then respond to his statement:** Active listening slows down the pace of the conversation, engages the other person in a discussion of what to do next, and eliminates the other individual thinking "Did that person not listen to a word I said?"
To decide what to say and when to say something based only on the words being said: Often this kind of listening happens during phone calls because nonverbal cues aren't available.	**To deal with the topic at hand by taking into account verbal and nonverbal cues:** Active listening gives you feedback on how the message is being received. For example, if the speaker is saying, "I totally agree with you," but his body language is closed and he's looking at the clock, he may just be saying he agrees to try to end the conversation as quickly as possible.

Stay positive

One cue can help turn around almost any professional critical conversation: Keeping a genuine, positive attitude. A genuine desire to help the situation not only drives the tone of the conversation, but also makes a big difference in body language and other nonverbal cues. And it goes both ways. Smiling and listening to other people creates sincerity.

Because active listening can also help a leader decide how to move a discussion forward, it's a good skill to have during a critical conversation.

Use the active listening process to clarify ambivalence to an issue. Actively listen to what someone *doesn't* say, as well as to what she does say.

Active listening involves three steps:

1. **Engage in active silence while the other individual is talking.**
2. **Reflect before responding.**
3. **Ask to confirm that you received the right message.**

Practicing active silence

During active listening, one party is speaking and the other is using active silence to understand what the first individual is trying to communicate. Although you need a lot of practice to be an expert in silence, the first step is to simply be present. Here are some additional hints:

- ✔ Try to maintain eye contact and an engaged posture.
- ✔ Look at the other party, lean in slightly, and focus on what the other party is saying.
- ✔ Try to use only small gestures that are appropriate for the conversation.
- ✔ Keep hands and arms at waist height and try to control any nervous activity (see the earlier section "Expressions that count" for more details).
- ✔ Make sure the environment is conducive to engaged silence. Having a critical conversation in a loud coffee house or in a meeting room with large glass windows is just begging for distraction.

These nonverbal techniques will help create an interested silence that helps you listen for content and emotions. You may detect a difference in what's being said and the emotions being felt. If the other party is nodding his head in agreement and saying, "Yes, I understand," but tears are building up in his eyes or his face is turning red with either anger or embarrassment, his emotions and his words aren't the same. Use the verbal questioning techniques from Chapter 6 to find out what the individual is really thinking before moving on with the conversation.

Active silence isn't easy, and the numbers prove it. People can talk at a rate of 120 or more words per minute, but most individuals can comprehend about 300 to 400 words per minute. When you listen to someone speak, you're using only part of your brain's capability, which makes it easy to tune out and think of other things. Really focusing on 120 words per minute takes a good amount of mental effort. Use the extra processing space in the brain to pay attention to intent and emotions. You can clarify the intent later in the active listening process, but often, the intent and emotions clarify the message more than the content of the message does.

Reflecting before responding

For some people, silence isn't comfortable. Many people think that silence shows weakness or ignorance. During active listening, you need some time for silence so that you can reflect on what was said. If the listening party is paying attention to what's being said by being present (not thinking about what to say next), silence is the necessary processing time to reflect on what to do or say next. A bit of natural silence helps to keep the conversation at a steady but unhurried pace. The time doesn't need to be uncomfortably long; you can imagine how odd the conversation would be if a speaker took 30-second pauses after every sentence.

Reflection also ensures that the speaker can finish his thoughts. Jumping in to respond may interrupt the speaker in the middle of a thought, intentionally or unintentionally.

Asking to clarify questions

After you really listen and take time to reflect on the information, clarify what you heard. The goal of clarifying questions is to confirm that the message, intent, and emotions you heard and noticed were the message the speaker intended to convey. You have a few ways to clarify information:

✔ **Paraphrase, don't parrot:** Repeating the speaker's exact words is annoying to most people. Instead, rephrase the statement by using your own words.

> Suppose Sam comes to you (his manager) and says, "I'm feeling really upset about this layoff."
>
> **Don't say:** "So, Sam, what I heard is you are feeling really upset about this layoff?" *(Polly wants a cracker! Squawk, squawk.)*
>
> **Do say:** "Sam, it's natural to feel upset about this process. I'm going to do everything I can to help."

✔ **Perception check:** Having biases and opinions is only human, but those biases and opinions often lead you to jump to conclusions, especially if a critical conversation is long overdue. As hard as it may seem, suspend judgment for the conversation and use reflection, hearing the other party out. When clarifying perceptions, don't blame or accuse. Instead, simply state what you observe.

> **Don't say:** "It's obvious you're disappointed."
>
> **Do say:** "It sounds like you're disappointed."

✔ **Open-ended question:** Use open-ended questions to clarify the message, intent, or emotions so that you don't jump to conclusions (see the previous bullet). You can also use open-ended questions to probe for more information when the message is unclear.

> **Don't say:** "It seems like you're not open to any of my ideas to improve the team's performance."
>
> **Do say:** "What ideas do you have to improve the team's performance?"

Try to keep the clarifying questions in manageable chunks of one or two sentences. Anything more makes it difficult for the other party to adequately reflect when he's bombarded with questions and statements.

Active listening ends when the listener becomes the speaker. After the listen-reflect-clarify cycle is completed, respond to the message. The cycle of active listening may have multiple repetitions. Remember that this repetition is normal and valuable to the conversation. Spending more time clarifying words, emotions, and intentions up front is better than making assumptions and stalling the conversation later.

Assess others' unspoken cues through active listening

Nonverbal communication isn't just about the speaker's behavior. Being aware of how the other party is responding, both verbally and nonverbally, provides insight into how your message is being received. Don't jump to conclusions, however, when you're looking at nonverbal cues. Active listening helps you assess how the other party is receiving the message and his emotional reaction to the message.

When assessing nonverbal communication, keep in mind the situational context and how behavior changes during the conversation.

- ✔ **Situational context:** Thinking that someone will start jumping for joy when you give him bad news is unreasonable. Some nonverbal cues can be expected during a conversation, but keep the environment and the situation in mind. Feet tapping on the ground may just show expected nervousness, but feet tapping, legs swinging, and fingers tapping probably mean that you need to address an emotional side of the issue before moving forward.

- ✔ **Changes over the course of the conversation:** One nonverbal communication assessment technique that leaves little to interpretation is how behavior changes over the course of the conversation. Is the person open and smiling when he walks in and then quickly becomes upset and irrational after hearing the message? This change probably indicates that his emotions are high. Is the person agitated from the beginning? This behavior may be fueled by the conversation, but it could also mean that he's simply having a bad day.

Chapter 8

Working with Different Communication Styles

In This Chapter

▶ Discovering which communication styles do (and don't) work

▶ Finding out your preferred approach to conversations

▶ Sharpening your communication style

*I*f everyone talked alike, had the same communication habits, and understood messages similarly, you wouldn't need a book on critical conversations or the progression of an entire industry on how to communicate effectively. Back in reality, you'll find as many different styles of communication as people communicating.

The differences in communication style make work and life interesting. Although there is no one right way to communicate all the time, there are definitely wrong ways to communicate. In this chapter, I walk through the pros and cons of being overly assertive or passive when communicating. I also present a model of assertive communication that works wonders during a critical conversation. Because understanding your personal style of communication helps others to respond better to different situations and environments, I also give you an opportunity to discover more about your own communication strengths and weaknesses. Finally, I help you avoid making assumptions about different communication styles. By adapting the approach to communication and assumptions, each critical conversation can conclude objectively.

Taking On Direct and Passive Communication Styles

Chapter 3 provides a roadmap of what to do during critical conversations. Now take the elements of a critical conversation and deliver them effectively. Effectively delivering a message comes down to style. I'm not talking about the style on runways each season; style is the way you deliver the message, not necessarily which words you deliver.

Individual style and behaviors can greatly impact the message. Most individuals have to adapt their personal style during conversations, or at least be aware of their own style. This chapter uncovers the three main types of styles out there: direct, passive, and assertive.

The message you deliver and the way you deliver it are equally important.

This chapter provides high-level groups of communication styles. To better understand your own style and how to best use and adapt it, turn to the many communication and conflict assessments that provide specific insights and compatibility recommendations when working with other styles. A few of the more common assessments include Myers-Briggs, DiSC, and the Thomas-Kilmann Conflict Mode assessment.

Direct communicators

People who are direct communicators often tell it like it is, with very few exceptions. They also like to drive action and continue forward momentum during meetings and discussions. At times they may argue just for the sake of arguing. Although direct communicators can be seen as aggressive or forceful, their behavior is often driven by a passion about what they believe is right or wrong.

Perhaps unsurprisingly, politicians and executives who seem decisive and driven are direct communicators. Direct communicators are nearly perfect at public speaking because they can energize others with their passion. During critical conversations, however, the direct style can come across as a bit overbearing. Because the goal of critical conversations is to make meaningful change to behaviors or to create a mutual agreement toward a behavior change, being driven to get immediate results isn't always the best policy.

If the other party thinks you have a one-track mind for the right way things are done, she may feel that her opinions and ideas don't matter. How do you know you're working with a direct communicator and what can you do to balance such a powerful communication personality? Table 8-1 gives you a few ideas on how to balance directing and driving results with getting mutual agreements that make behaviors change. A direct communicator may naturally do some or all of the behaviors I list in the table.

Table 8-1	Behaviors of a Direct Communicator		
Behavior	What You May Observe	How to Adapt If You See This Behavior	What to Do If You Behave This Way
Talking fast and moving fast	Few breaths, a rapid conversation pace, quickly moving from one topic to another, perhaps even pacing around the room. Conversation is deadline—or action—focused.	Clearly state the end goal of the conversation up front. If the other party is pushing for action before agreement on the problem, meet her halfway by letting her know the goals or next steps will more likely be achieved if everyone agrees on them first.	Count to two before jumping into the conversation to allow a few seconds of silence between thoughts. Let the other parties know it's okay to slow you down or ask questions.
Using intense body language	Large hand movements, banging hands on the desk or waving them around in the air, big gestures.	Keep your own actions subtle and calm to balance the energy in the room.	Look at how others in the room are moving and using space and mirror their behaviors. Find out more about ideal body language and other nonverbal cues during a critical conversation (see Chapter 7).
Talking more than listening	Direct communicators are often so busy expressing their own opinion that they miss the opinion of others. This doesn't mean that they don't care.	Slow down the pace. Step in frequently to make sure all parties have mutual agreements and an understanding of next steps.	Be aware of your pace. Allow others to voice ideas or concerns. Ask for input at the end of each thought. You may practice saying, "Let me take a break from talking and ask for your ideas."

Some people may be intimidated by the intensity of direct communicators and therefore they may not naturally want to speak up during a conversation with them. Direct communicators may benefit from having a trusted peer or coach give them feedback on how their communication style is working or not working, and work together to think of ways to adapt behaviors in the future.

Don't make an assumption. Direct communicators aren't necessarily aggressive or hostile people. Passion, purpose, and drive often fuel this communication style.

Passive communicators

People who are passive communicators resemble introverts; they may speak more slowly and be more careful of how and what they say. Often, they don't voice their own needs and opinions. Passive communicators often avoid expressing their ideas or feelings.

Passive communicators are almost the polar opposite of direct communicators, often using a calm and quiet voice, reserved body gestures, and listening more than talking. All these traits are wonderful in a genuine leader, but because critical conversations focus on mutual agreements that move behaviors and relationships forward, not speaking up for your own point of view can impede a critical conversation.

Although passive communicators may want to work on expressing their ideas, other styles can learn great qualities from this communication style. They're often seen as polite, allowing others to speak and ask many questions. As an expert critical communicator, your goal is to make sure their voices and opinions are heard and not pushed to the side.

Here's what a critical conversation may look like if one party is a passive communicator:

> **Messenger Marvin:** "Hi, Paul. I wanted to talk with you about a potential problem with the project."
>
> **Passive Paul:** "Okay."
>
> **Marvin:** "Based on the numbers from last quarter, we're going to have to cut the spending by 30 percent."
>
> **Paul:** "I understand. What can I do to help you?"
>
> **Marvin:** "I think you'll need to cut all your contractors out of the budget. Can you do that?"
>
> **Paul:** "Of course. Anything to help."

At face value, this conversation looks civilized and really not that critical. After all, no one's emotions get out of hand, and Paul seems to be in complete agreement with Marvin. Unfortunately, Paul never gives an alternative idea, even though he may have better ways to save the money. Passive communicators often feel that their needs aren't as important as the needs of others. Although this approach may be great for avoiding conflict, it doesn't work well for developing mutual agreements that make a difference.

If Paul steps out of his passive style and becomes more assertive (I get into more assertive styles in the next section), here's how the conversation may go:

> **Messenger Marvin:** "Hi, Paul. I wanted to talk with you about a potential problem with the project."
>
> **Passive Paul:** "I'm happy to discuss the problem. What's your concern?"
>
> **Marvin:** "Based on the numbers from last quarter, we're going to have to cut the spending by 30 percent."
>
> **Paul:** "I understand. I have some ideas that may help cut the spending."
>
> **Marvin:** "I'm listening."
>
> **Paul:** "Based on our results, it looks like our project scope has gotten out of control. The team is putting in overtime because we're trying to implement two solutions, when originally we were just doing one . . . ."

Paul still maintains his gentle approach, but with one sentence he speaks up for his ideas and concerns, instead of letting another individual drive the entire conversation.

If you're a passive communicator, or if you're working with a passive communicator, Table 8-2 offers a few tips to make sure that everyone hears the passive voices.

Table 8-2	Behaviors of a Passive Communicator		
Behavior	*What You May Observe*	*How to Adapt If You See This Behavior*	*What to Do If You Behave This Way*
Silence or little active participation	Sitting quietly, not speaking up or chiming in with ideas.	In a group setting, during a break ask for any questions or ideas one on one. In one-on-one situations, let the silence happen because passive communicators often like to process complete thoughts before talking.	Come prepared. If you're leading a conversation, have notes on what message you want to deliver. If you're on the receiving end of a conversation, ask what information you can contribute to the conversation. Perhaps ask, "I'm not sure what to say. Can you let me know what information I can provide?"
Complete agreement, avoiding any conflict	Sometimes passive communicators nod along in agreement instead of speaking up.	Ask probing questions like, "This looks like a good solution. What's missing?" or, "I think this is a great path to take. Can we think of an alternative to compare it to?" Asking for options can be intimidating to a conflict-adverse passive communicator, so try to use the terms *other* or *alternative* rather than *best* or *better*.	Speak up. If you're afraid to voice your opinion, ask others what can be done to strengthen agreements.

If you're working with passive communicators, try to minimize the risk for them to participate. Passive communicators often feel that their needs and ideas aren't as important as others. They may also feel that voicing their concerns will cause conflict. Create a safe environment during the conversation by establishing that the information you discuss stays in the room. You may also want to encourage parties to participate in the conversation by holding a brainstorming session to get ideas rolling.

Watch out for passive-aggressive behavior. Although passive communicators tend to avoid conflict and often go with the good of the group, some passive communicators repress feelings of anger or resentment. The passive-aggressive style may agree in the moment but sabotage the solution later. Gaining agreements throughout the conversation on next steps and clarifying that the message is understood (Chapter 4) can help prevent this sabotage.

Saying Yes to Assertiveness

No matter what communication style you have, trying to use assertiveness and trying to get your employees to use assertiveness is the key to successful communication. During a critical conversation, assertive communication styles deliver the message in a firm yet professional manner. Assertiveness during a critical conversation is about making sure everyone's needs are met rather than getting just one person's point across. Assertive techniques during a critical conversation are geared toward getting other individuals to speak openly and provide ideas and solutions, and then making sure the solutions work for everyone.

Checking out assertive qualities

Assertive communicators have these qualities:

- **They ask questions to spur discussion.** During a critical conversation, assertive communicators ask for the other party's perspective first and then use their own perspective to help generate discussion, instead of simply supplying the ultimate answer.

- **They are flexible with the means, agreeing on the end goal.** Assertive communicators remain flexible with the needs of all the parties and the way to reach agreement. Although assertive styles don't back down from their own needs and values, they can be open to finding new ways to achieve the goals.

- **They take time to build agreement and find solutions that benefit all parties.** Assertive communicators approach conversations as a problem-solving opportunity instead of trying to rush to solutions. They clarify information frequently while they build agreements. For example, an assertive communicator may say, "These three next steps look good. How about making sure we both understand what's on this list. Any items here you would like clarified?"

Here's what an assertive style may look like during a critical conversation:

Situation: Sam has been the product development director at GamesOnline for 23 years. Sam is a passive communicator, sometimes passive-aggressive. A new manager, Alex, was recently hired as the director of Sales and Marketing. He has an assertive style and his goal is to hit the sales targets out of the park and eventually run the company. Alex needs Sam's team to work with Sales and Marketing, but it's not happening. Watch how Alex uses assertive styles to get Sam to come up with ideas to help the team.

Assertive Alex: "Hi, Sam. Thanks for meeting today. As I mentioned to you last week, I want to search for ways that our teams can work together to achieve our company goals for next year. Are you willing to work together on this?"

Passive Sam: "Okay."

Alex: "Great. I noticed last year that both teams were working around the clock to meet our targets, and many people were exhausted after that heroic push. Have you seen or heard of different alternatives to the last-minute rush that have worked in the past?"

Sam: "Not really. We can do whatever you want to."

Alex: "I would love to come up with some ideas together. I would be happy to have you start, or I can put the first one out there."

Sam: "Oh, I'm happy to just help."

Alex: "Okay. One idea may be to ask our teams to sit next to one another in the office, opening up the communication between groups."

Sam: "Sounds great."

Alex: "Finding multiple options could help both teams find even more ways to collaborate. Can we brainstorm an alternative idea?"

Sam: "Sure. You know one thing that we used to do was have quarterly production targets. Not sure why we don't anymore . . ."

Critical communication experts dream about this conversation as an example for everyone to follow. Alex directly states the reason for the discussion and asks for agreement. Asking Sam whether he was willing to work on the issue takes time but builds a key agreement. When Sam responds, "Not really," Alex is flexible in his approach, providing information and then asking more questions to spur discussion. Assertive communicators are more than facilitators or managers — they can be magicians! On the third try, Sam brings up new information, which may never have been discussed if not for Alex's open style.

The goal of a critical conversation is to positively build mutual agreements that solve tough, emotionally charged issues. Using an assertive style helps the other parties provide their points of view to help build a solution everyone can agree on and work toward. Assertive communication may not be your natural style, but practice and feedback from others can help create a balanced assertive style that gets results that everyone can agree to work on the in the future.

Using assertive styles to move to action

If you were a fly on the wall during the conversation in the example between Sam and Alex (see the previous section), you may wonder why Alex tries so hard to get Sam to talk and give ideas. If only one person talks or only one person gives ideas during a critical conversation, chances are good that the idea will never see the light of day after the conversation is over. After all, the parties don't reach an agreement. If a critical conversation is over and nothing changes, you had no consensus and the time was wasted. By probing for ideas and asking for commitment, Alex starts to develop actionable agreements.

Direct or aggressive communicators may get their points across, but later find out find out that everyone was listening but no one agreed. Passive communicators may just let the conversation happen while nodding their heads, but have no commitment to the end goal after the conversation is done.

An assertive communication style advocates the perspective of the speaker and gathers information from other parties. If you make sure the parties discuss all the information and views, you have a higher chance for action after the conversation closes because everyone's views have been heard and incorporated into the final outcome.

Knowing Your Communication Style

Knowing you own communication style helps you create awareness, increase your strengths, and deliver a more productive message that gets results during a conversation. When you enter a conversation, critical or not, do you come with the desire to get a goal accomplished or to get everyone to agree to the goal to be accomplished? Do you use sarcasm and humor to avoid or confront tough issues? Take this eight-question quiz to find out.

Think of the last conversation you had that involved a disagreement or conflict. Did you . . .

- ✔ Feel genuinely concerned about other people's ideas and thoughts?
- ✔ Ask others questions about what they think, feel, or need?
- ✔ Pause for two to three seconds before responding to questions?
- ✔ Avoid confrontation during the conversation?
- ✔ Solve everyone else's problems during the meeting, leaving your own issues for later?
- ✔ Say it like it is?
- ✔ Finish people's conversations?
- ✔ Use sarcasm or clever comments to get your point across?

If you answered "yes" to questions 1, 2, and 3, well done. You use an assertive communication style that facilitates agreements during tough conversations — good for you!

If you answered "yes" to questions 4 and 5, you may be putting your views last. If so, think about how to stop sitting passively during a conversation. Next time you're in a conversation (critical or not), practice stating how you feel and your view of the situation. Don't worry whether your idea is the best one or not — just state that you have another idea or a different opinion. You may be surprised to find that your ideas are the ones that have been missing from the discussion all along.

Did you answer "yes" to 6 and 7? A direct, or even aggressive, style may be standing in the way of getting results. Next time you find yourself in a critical conversation, try to ask others for their opinions and ideas before voicing your own. Try waiting for a few seconds before jumping in to make sure you aren't cutting off another person's thoughts. Aggressive styles can get work done quickly, but assertive styles that build mutual agreements often result in more long-term results everyone can agree on.

Did you answer "yes" to question 8? Humor can help relax a conversation, but too much joking or sarcasm may mean that you're passively pushing your ideas down, leading to passive-aggressive communication styles. Instead of joking about the end result, try using one of the tools in this book — like silence and space in Chapter 7, or the "we" and "us" phrases that I discuss in Chapter 6.

Knowing your own style can help you adapt in nearly all situations, not just critical conversations. If you develop the ability to proactively and assertively facilitate discussions to reach meaningful agreements, you will more easily create action after the conversation ends.

Sharpening Your Communication Style

Even the best communicators can find ways to constantly improve. No matter what style you're most comfortable with during conversations, gaining insight from those around you will improve the way you communicate.

Sharpening your communication style will help make every conversation more productive. To sharpen your style, you have to know what you want to work on. The good news is that these areas aren't that hard to find with a little digging. Three ways to improve your style (outside of reading this book, of course) are to

✔ Ask for feedback.

✔ Manage your style during stressful times.

✔ Learn more about assumptions you making during conversations.

Gaining insight from your peers

Having a little bird that watches every communication and gives feedback in a positive and productive way would be wonderful. In absence of a little bird watching over you, asking for feedback is the best alternative. In Chapter 3, I walk through how to prepare to give feedback to others during a critical conversation. These tools for preparing to give feedback to others and the tools you need to *ask* for feedback from others are almost exactly the same.

Some individuals may not be comfortable providing candid feedback, especially if they've never given feedback before. Keep the process simple by asking these questions:

✔ What am I currently doing well when it comes to communicating?

✔ What do I need to do differently?

✔ What should I prioritize first to keep doing well and to improve on?

After directing these questions to a small group of peers, employees, and managers, you'll probably start seeing key themes and common issues. These themes and issues then become an action plan for your own development. Take each of the themes and turn them into actions by asking yourself the question, "What does this mean I have to deliver?" Spend some time exploring the actions that you need in order to improve your own communication style. Make sure the actions are SMART (specific, measurable, actionable and agreed-on, realistic, and time bound). Check out more on SMART action plans in Chapter 4.

Don't get too stressed out about making sure your conversation style is perfect before holding a critical conversation. Having a good conversation is better than having no conversation. If you still need to work on your tone of voice, work on it during the conversation. Just knowing the areas you can develop will help throughout the conversation. Recognize that it takes commitment and practice to adapt your style, but anytime you open the lines of communication with a genuine desire to help the situation, you help to create a more positive environment.

Here are two of the biggest problems facing communicators:

✔ Being unaware of how others perceive their conversation style

✔ Not fully recognizing their own biases in communication

These problems don't crop up because leaders don't care. They're simply a result of the fact that so few people have been given the opportunity to gather multiple perspectives. Some leaders benefit greatly from a 360-degree communication review. A 360-degree feedback session is when a facilitator asks the leader's employees, managers, and peers for feedback and then provides this information back to the leader. This review is a chance to get feedback from the people you work with most closely, to better understand your conversation style through the eyes of others, and to see what biases you may bring to a conversation.

Managing your style under stress

After reading this entire chapter, you're ready to develop a communication style that can deliver critical conversations perfectly. Yeah! But wait, what's that you hear? Quarterly results aren't as good as expected? A project deadline is moved up a month? Your best employee just quit? Argh — talk about stress. Jump to Chapter 20 to get plenty of tips on how to manage stress during a critical conversation. Read on to discover how each of the three communication styles I discuss in this chapter can deal with stress.

Putting an assertive style to the test

In perfect situations with little stress, using an assertive communication style and remaining patient throughout the critical conversation process is easy. But when push comes to shove, stress can make a conversation turn into a screaming match. Look at the eight-question quiz in the earlier section "Knowing Your Communication Style" and answer the questions while thinking about the last highly stressful conversation you had. The results may be different. This exercise can help you see how your conversation style changes when emotions are high and stress levels are higher.

Challenging direct communicators

Direct communicators may benefit from taking control and directing the process, not the discussion. For example, some direct communicators feel that unless they're being directive and dictating the course of action, they're not being a leader and nothing will happen. Under stress, these leaders may believe that collaborative conversations make them look weak or are just a waste of time. If this is the case, try to direct the process for conversations by exploring, deciding, getting into the action, and evaluating the success of the conversation instead of directing the results. These tools will build actions that all parties are committed to rather than actions that all parties just agree with and ignore after the conversation is done.

Pumping up passive communicators

Passive communicators may withdraw when stressed. This habit can make passive communicators seem indifferent or even uncaring, which is often not the case. Under stress, passive communicators may benefit from actively inviting discussion by first giving their perspective and then inviting dialogue. For example, under stress (or anytime!), a passive communicator could kick off a critical conversation with, "Jim, I feel like our team isn't talking with one another. Our last three meetings seem to have focused on solving the same issue again and again. Do you feel the same way?" Starting with this statement makes sure a passive communicator's feelings and thoughts are heard first.

Passive communicators often have one big advantage they can use during stressful times — they tend to stay calm in the face of high-stress situations. Because these communicators don't jump in and try to fix the conversation while ignoring others, a passive communicator may be a pro at promoting an environment of respect during high-stress times.

Clarifying assumptions

As communicators, leaders are continually observing the actions and interactions of those around them. After a few observations or experiences, you may start seeing patterns emerge. Most people tend to place their own meaning on the behaviors they observe and to make inferences about these patterns. Making assumptions about people's actions or personalities can lead to problems and work against productivity.

Here's an example of someone making an assumption and the consequences that follow:

> *Situation:* David observes Mike talking loudly to employees and often ending calls in a screaming match or with frustration.
>
> *David's assumption:* Mike doesn't know how to control his temper.
>
> *David's conclusion:* David doesn't want to work with Mike.
>
> *David's action:* Never be part of Mike's work teams.

The first problem with this inference of Mike's behavior is that David never initiated a critical conversation to find out why Mike's behavior was happening. You can fix this problem by working through a conversation that's probably long overdue (see Chapter 5). The second — and perhaps more serious — problem with this conclusion is that David may not want to be on teams with anyone who talks loudly because he associates loud talking with Mike's behavior.

A better way for David to approach Mike's loud talking would be to simply ask, "Hey, Mike, I heard some loud voices earlier today when you were on the phone. I'm wondering whether we can have a discussion on how you and I can work together in such a small office space. Would you be able to have a discussion later today?" Critical conversation tools can help avoid assumptions about what is going to happen in the future, and instead gain agreement on what is going to happen in the future.

Interpretations are inevitable, but rather than attribute meaning to behaviors, ask for the meaning.

Part III

Getting Down to Specifics: Creating a Critical Conversation

The 5th Wave   By Rich Tennant

"Maybe scheduling this conversation during lunch was a bad idea. You sent me Mr. Chan's takeout menu instead of an agenda."

In this part...

This is where the rubber hits the road: It's time to start talking. In this part you get all you need to prepare and deliver the critical conversation, keep challenging situations positive, and close the conversation with ease.

Chapter 9

Here's the Warm-Up: Getting Yourself Ready

In This Chapter

▶ Avoiding the four big pitfalls of critical conversations

▶ Becoming physically and emotionally prepared for a conversation

▶ Building rapport and trust

*N*o one expects a tennis player to just pick up a racket and win Wimbledon or a baseball player to pick up a bat for the first time and hit a home run in the World Series. The same goes for a critical conversation: You can't expect to hit the conversation out of the park if you don't prepare and practice. Winging the critical conversation does little to move behavior in a positive direction, and it can potentially make everything worse. This isn't to say that you can't have a critical conversation on the spot if you see an issue that you need to address. You can. Even by reading this book, you're preparing for the conversation.

This chapter gives you the goods to have a great conversation, before you even say a word. In this chapter, you find the four big reasons conversations fail and how your preparation can turn them around. You also discover how to mentally and physically prepare for the conversation so you're ready to make real progress. I also give you ways to keep your hot buttons in check and manage stress, both before and during the conversation. Last, but certainly not least, I provide ideas on how to build rapport and trust — the building blocks of all conversations. By the end of the chapter, you're ready to create a perfect critical conversation with a positive attitude.

Avoiding Pitfalls through Preparation

I see a convincing connection between the success of a critical conversation and the amount of planning that goes into the conversation. Often, I can link critical conversation catastrophes to four big pitfalls. The good news is that you can avoid these pitfalls with the right planning.

- ✓ **Pitfall #1: Unmanaged expectations of the conversation.** A critical conversation isn't just water cooler talk; you have reasons and expectations for the discussion. Critical conversations are complex; spell out the goals up front. Taking the time to write down your expectations of the conversation brings clarity to the conversation and helps you manage the outcome.

- ✓ **Pitfall #2: Badly defined scope of the conversation.** Trying to accomplish too much with a conversation can make the discussion seem overwhelming and unorganized. (Chapter 5 offers recommendations on how to handle multiple issues.) Doing the preparation work up front helps you identify the most important issues to address so that you can create a focused discussion that generates the desired results.

- ✓ **Pitfall #3: Unclear roles.** Knowing who does what in a conversation may seem like a no-brainer — one person talks, the other listens, right? Sometimes. But sometimes you may need to hire a mediation expert or bring in a facilitator (Chapter 15 covers when you may need to use these roles in a conversation). Other times, the initiator of the conversation may need to play two roles — a manager giving feedback and a facilitator keeping a discussion on track. Prep work helps clarify your role and the roles you expect of others.

- ✓ **Pitfall #4: Uncontrolled emotions.** This pitfall often results from a lack of the preparation work I list in pitfalls 1, 2, and 3. When you have confusion about expectations, roles, and the purpose of the conversation, any of the parties involved may quickly feel that they're being attacked or blamed. Focusing on the facts and using the critical conversation process are the best remedies when high emotions take the conversation off track.

With so much at stake during a critical conversation, spending a little more time up front pays off by reducing the risk of these four specific problem areas and helping you to be physically and emotionally prepared for the conversation.

Being Physically Prepared

Of course emotions are high. People aren't in agreement. If they were, it wouldn't be called a critical conversation — it would be called a critical agreement. Managing stress before and during a critical conversation is like having a golden ticket; it can help alleviate almost any emotional situation. Check out *Stress Management For Dummies,* by Allen Elkin, PhD (Wiley), for lots of tips on managing stress. Here are a few proven ways to manage the physical stress associated with a critical conversation.

Schedule so you're not rushed

Calendars are often filled with back-to-back meetings, but try not to make a critical conversation bookended with nonstop meetings. Allow yourself to take a time-out before and after a critical conversation is scheduled. Moving from one meeting to the next and squeezing in a critical conversation can cause stress. If you happen to be scheduled back to back, and you don't have a minute to spare, even 30 seconds to positively focus on the conversation or to go get a glass of water can help you start the conversation calm and collected.

Plan to keep a critical conversation from going off track, but try also to remain flexible to manage the stress. For example, if someone voices a new concern, be flexible enough to leave the topic and address the concern. A conversation should keep a steady pace but not be rushed. If the conversation only gets through half of the agenda in the time allotted, either decide to keep going or schedule a second meeting to create the action plan. Bottom line: Don't veer off course in the discussion, but stay flexible to keep stress at bay.

Eat, rest, exercise

Try to maintain a healthy lifestyle. Although this book isn't about health and fitness, one of the most proven ways to reduce stress in the workplace is to get in shape and take care of your health. Long-term healthy practices are the key to lowering stress, but don't ignore how one day of taking care of your mind and body can positively impact the conversation. Reduce your stress before a big conversation by exercising or simply taking a walk around the block and eating a healthy meal. Relax as much as possible before the conversation; going without adequate sleep or failing to eat prior to a conversation can lead to more stress than the conversation would cause by itself.

Design the questions

Which questions are you going to ask? To make a conversation go smoothly, balance the presentation of your facts and opinions with listening to others' opinions and facts. Don't underestimate the power of planning to ask the right questions to help guide the discussion. Here are a few types of questions you may want to prepare:

- ✔ **Open-ended questions.** Open-ended questions help uncover the information and action plans you need to make change happen after the conversation. For example, encourage discussion by asking how the other individual sees the situation or what information is missing from your point of view.

- ✔ **Leading questions.** Don't let the name fool you into thinking these questions are passive-aggressive or overly direct. Leading questions merely focus the discussion in a specific direction. These questions are good to ask when the other parties are either hiding from the topic or focusing on too many other topics. Leading questions are a great way to lead into action planning. An example is asking, "What are three key actions our team can do better in the future?"

- ✔ **Yes-no questions.** Yes-no questions tend to get a bad reputation during conversations, but they do have their place. Asking an individual whether he wants to share any other information before moving on to problem-solving is a great yes-no question.

- ✔ **Contemplative questions.** Questions that ask for opinions or thoughts on concerns and ideas can be useful, especially if you feel that parties are leaving some ideas or concerns unsaid. Use contemplative questions to clarify whether the other party has any concerns moving forward after you've made a decision. A great way to ensure that you have 100 percent buy-in to moving forward after the conversation ends is to ask, "What concerns do you have about being able to accomplish this action plan?"

Have a clear plan

You don't need to follow a strict agenda, but having an outline of what you want to accomplish and the conversation process can keep the conversation focused. An agenda, like the one in Figure 9-1, is also a great way to take notes during the conversation so that everyone remembers what the next steps are after the discussion. The plan and agenda can also put other parties at ease and reduce stress because they know they're following a process.

Agenda	Date
Conversation topic	
Examine what's happening (facts, data, and perception)	
Decide on options to move forward	
Get moving, action plan	

Figure 9-1: Sample agenda.

Being Emotionally Prepared

Part of preparation is having a clear purpose in mind for the conversation. But preparation doesn't stop there. Remaining calm, open to discussion, and able to step back when emotions get strong increases cooperation and helps you be poised and capable during conversations.

Whether you're on the receiving end of a conversation or the delivering end, being emotionally prepared and mentally ready is no easy task! Here's a critical conversation that Leader Jane has with a small team. She comes into the conversation with data, and she genuinely wants to make the situation better. Note that Jane starts off well with facts and the purpose of the meeting. Then catastrophe strikes.

> **Jane:** "The employee satisfaction surveys came back last week. And my scores were worse than last year. I would love to listen to your thoughts on what I can do to improve."

> **Brave team member Paula:** "I can't speak for everyone, but it seems like you've been in your office more and not out talking to us like you used to."

> **Jane:** "Well, I've been working on the future of the company and just can't be out here all the time. And it's serving us well; we're above our performance numbers, and you know it was the right choice."

> The room falls absolutely silent.

What happened? It all seems so well presented with facts and a purpose for the conversation, and then — *wham!* — the conversation closes down after the first remark. To find out what went wrong with Jane's conversation, and how to fix it, take a look at the following sections that showcase the three main parts to digging in and getting ready: meeting needs, motivations, and beliefs.

Getting to know your motivations

Motivation and attitude before, during, and after the conversation show how different people are. When working with critical conversations, knowing your own motivation and attitude not only prepares you mentally but also allows the discussion time to focus on the motivations and attitudes of the other parties.

What motivates people? Money, respect, recognition, action, making a difference, building relationships . . . the list goes on and on. Sometimes it takes seconds to find out what motivates people; other times it can take years of working together to really find out what makes another person tick. But before diving into knowing what motivates other people (I cover that in the next section), take time to know what's motivating you to have the critical conversation. Think through the list of motivations in Table 9-1 and see which ones you identify with most closely.

Table 9-1	Motivations
Motivation	*Definition*
Action	Getting things done is your number one priority. Why handle it later when you can handle it now? You work quickly and take time lines and milestones seriously.
Money	Being paid fairly for the work done drives your work ethic.
Recognition	Being acknowledged for work done by your team and leadership is important to you. High praise and being admired as an expert drives work and actions.
Respect	You crave a professional work environment, where employees treat you (and one another) with genuine concern, listen to ideas with open ears, and value different opinions.
Teamwork	You value teams working together and can work quickly through conflict. You believe the whole team is much stronger than the sum of its parts.

None of these motivations are right or wrong. However, if you're honest about what motivates you, you'll create an environment that's open, honest, and genuine.

Not sure what's motivating you? Work through this list to find the answers:

- ✔ **Think about what brings you the most satisfaction in life.** Do you love having time to spend with friends and family? If so, flexibility and balance between work and life may motivate you. Do you love being the go-to person for any problem? You may be most happy with recognition in your role.

- ✔ **Find out what energizes you.** What are you doing when you have the most energy? Do you love being part of a group that works together to achieve results? You most likely have a passion for teamwork and action. Do you get the most energy when you get to pore over data and reports or when you're reading a captivating book? You may just love knowledge and research.

- ✔ **Ask others for ideas.** If you have trouble finding out what motivates you, ask peers and close friends where they think your inner drive comes from. Sometimes an external point of view is the answer to discovering your internal drive.

Many people identify with multiple motivators. Knowing your own motivation and even sharing it with the parties involved in the conversation help to create a genuine and safe talking space. You don't have to come in and say, "If this work isn't done, I won't get my bonus!" (You can imagine how many eyes would roll with this comment.) A better option may be, "The work we need to get done impacts the team and me financially. I respect that this may not be what motivates everyone, but can we agree to work together to get this done?" Voicing your motivations in a positive way can help build trust and credibility during a critical conversation.

Meeting the needs of others

If you've studied psychology, you may remember something called Maslow's hierarchy of needs. If you fell asleep during Psychology 101 or if you just need a refresher, here's what you missed: Every human has basic needs that need to be met, including food, shelter, and safety. Humans need relationships and to be part of a group, and they need achievement, and ultimately personal growth. (Some research has shown these needs may not need to be met in an exact hierarchical order and that they aren't mutually exclusive, but the fact stands: People have needs that need to be met.)

Before jumping to the conclusion that humans are one needy group, these needs reveal some clear insights into why people act the way they do. During critical conversations, look at how needs are being met — or aren't being met — to understand different behaviors.

For example, the need for security and safety may cause a number of team and work relationship issues. If a team member doesn't feel safe expressing his views or ideas, thinking about how to be part of a team will be hard for him. If a person does not feel part of a team, he may not be doing much to achieve tough goals for the group. Unmet needs can and do impact the way people act.

Being aware of everyone's motivations and beliefs helps the conversation accomplish personal goals as well as meet the organization's needs. You don't need to go digging for those textbooks to realize that people say and do things for different reasons. People can waste lots of energy by trying to guess what others believe, their motivations, or their intentions. This time and energy can be better used to solve a critical issue during the conversation! Leave out the guesswork, and ask. Just as I recommended finding your own motivations, be prepared to find the needs and motivations of others. Do this by either asking them what they're motivated by, or by coaching them through how to find their own motivations (see the previous section).

Knowing and controlling your hot buttons

Critical conversations are successful when you recognize and address the needs and motivations of others. Ideally, in a critical conversation, you examine the problem you're dealing with, decide on options to solve it, and then gain commitment on what to do next (I cover this model in Chapter 4). But only robots would be able to have that type of conversation without emotions playing a role! Because robots haven't taken over the workplace just yet, address the emotional side of the conversation when you're communicating with individuals who have different motivations, needs, and beliefs. Knowing, controlling, and potentially adapting the emotional side is a fundamental of a successful critical conversation.

Everyone has a *hot button* or something that triggers an emotional reaction. These things drive you crazy; examples may include drivers who don't use their turn signal, having meetings canceled at the last minute, and people who bring onions onto airplanes. (Okay, those hot buttons are mine, but you get the point.) Everyone's hot buttons are different, and knowing your own hot buttons helps keep a critical conversation in check.

By simply knowing your own hot buttons, you're able to start controlling them during an emotional conversation, and you can stop your reaction from getting out of control. As part of the prep work for a critical conversation, think through your hot buttons. You probably know them by heart (if not, ask your spouse, boss, or employees — they can probably tell you when you lose it!). Here are some usual hot buttons in workplaces:

✔ Whining and making excuses

✔ Yelling and patronizing

✔ Pointing fingers

✔ Sarcasm

✔ Overuse of corporate talk (dashboards, bandwidth, touching base) and analogies (often related to marine life and aquatics: think big fish small pond, can't boil the ocean, being in a fishbowl)

✔ Anything to do with cellphones, beeps, or interruptions

 Although you have no easy way to stop these hot buttons, the best way to control your emotions is to physically slow down your reaction. When a cellphone goes off during a meeting with some overplayed song from the 1980s and your blood pressure rises, you have two choices: You can stare at the phone, roll your eyes, and attack the other person with sarcasm, or you can count to five, smile, and ask for the behavior to stop in a calm and rational voice. The latter alternative is much more useful and productive, especially in a critical conversation. Practice controlling your behavior when hot button triggers arise in meetings and around the workplace to set you apart as a composed conversation leader.

Maintaining a positive attitude

I'm trying not to sound like a schoolteacher or mother, but it would be better not to have a critical conversation than to go into one with a poor attitude. Motivation and attitudes are closely linked, and both factor into how people behave. Attitudes that negatively impact a conversation can stem from personal self-interest, misunderstanding, or disagreement on the outcome. During the preparation phase of a critical conversation, take time to understand — and possibly change — your attitude and view of the situation.

You've probably seen a bad attitude in the workplace. It's easy to spot but tough to change. The following positive attitude adjustments are beneficial when you're having a critical conversation:

✔ **Think that change is possible.** If you think all the parties in the conversation can change their behavior or attitude, chances are good that they can. Studies have shown that merely thinking positively can make people more confident, and having positive expectations for someone can actually increase the likelihood of positive change.

✔ **Have patience.** You will always have a learning curve when you're trying to change behaviors, and that takes patience. Knowing that you won't accomplish your action plan in one day can help put everyone at ease with realistic expectations.

✔ **Check your ego at the door.** Yes, you may be the expert, but the person receiving the message probably could do without an ego. Having an answer to everything can lead to a know-it-all attitude. Remember to ask questions, listen to the answers, and be accepting of other ideas and opinions.

✔ **Be genuine.** This mantra bears repeating (and I do repeat it throughout this book!). Having concerns, building trust, and developing ongoing support create an environment and relationship where people see critical conversations as positive rather than negative events. Being genuine shows in what you say and do, so don't just say that you're concerned for someone else; show it by supporting all the parties in the conversation while they work to resolve issues and change behaviors.

In the end, a positive attitude comes down to making sure you want to create open communication and understand the needs of all parties. Whether you're leading your first critical conversation or hundredth, coming to the table with this positive point of view sets the tone for a productive conversation.

Bad attitudes come in many shapes and sizes. Complaining, arguing, and gossiping (otherwise known as examples of bad attitudes) are a few of them, and all bad attitudes are disruptive in a work environment and need to be addressed. A critical conversation probably can't end successfully, however, if it starts with, "You have a bad attitude!" In Chapter 14, I provide plenty of examples on how to work through staff disputes and poor attitudes.

Starting on the Right Track: Rapport and Trust

The final step to preparing for a critical conversation is moving from thought to action. As you get ready to kick off the conversation, building rapport and trust to set the tone can get the conversation on the right track from the start. Everything you've done to this point in preparing for the conversation will give *you,* the deliverer of the message, confidence that the conversation will be successful. Rapport and building trust give the recipient of the message confidence that the conversation will be successful. During the preparation work, your agenda helps you open the conversation with the right words, but the recipient is paying just as much attention to your tone and observing the environment.

Defining rapport and trust

Although not always easy to define, rapport and trust are usually quite easy to see. Most people have been part of a discussion with trust and a good rapport among all the parties in the room; sadly, most people have probably seen the opposite. Although many people have their own definitions of trust and rapport, here's how I define these terms when it comes to critical conversations:

- **Rapport:** Rapport is the environment in the room and the atmosphere during the discussion. When you have good rapport during a critical conversation, the room is free from unnecessary emotions, yelling, and arguing, and it's full of respect and active listening.

- **Trust:** Trust means that everyone believes that all parties will do what they say. You can often see trust by noting how willing individuals are to talk about tough issues.

How do you know you've built a good rapport? Rapport is the building block of cooperation and motivation to do something differently. If one of the parties isn't cooperating or isn't willing to make a change, step back and see whether the environment is safe for all parties and whether all parties are open and willing to trust each other.

Building rapport and trust

So how do you build trust and rapport? Mostly, be prepared, keep a handle on your emotions, and enter the room and relationship with a positive attitude. Outside of these elements, the two make-or-break elements to building trust and rapport are openness and honesty. Both of these behaviors are positive, and they set the stage for how you expect the other parties to act. If you're open with how you feel and what you see, others will follow. If you're honest and do what you say and say what you mean, you build instant credibility.

Trust, honesty, openness, a positive attitude, and being emotionally controlled take time, so while you're being patient with others in the conversation, also practice patience with yourself. You can't build these skills and relationship tools overnight.

How do you begin to build rapport? Here are a few ideas:

- **Let other people talk.** Building rapport is sometimes as easy as asking questions, actively listening, and then reflecting on what was said. In other words, be present in the conversation. When you come to the table with a genuine desire to help, others will see that their concerns and needs are your priority during the conversation. On the other hand, one of the quickest ways to destroy trust and rapport is to dominate the conversation. For more on active listening, check out Chapter 7.

- **Observe body and verbal language, and adapt yours accordingly.** People often trust individuals they feel most comfortable with; try to adapt your style to match, or at least mix well with, other communication styles. If the other party is speaking calmly and making small gestures, observing these behaviors and then mirroring them creates common energy. I'm not recommending mocking the other person — quite the opposite. The goal is to observe and match other styles to put others are ease. Check Chapters 6 and 7 for more on positive verbal and nonverbal skills.

- **Smile.** People often like being around genuine, happy people. If smiling isn't natural for you, practice being authentic and content, and others will soon follow your lead.

- **Get moving.** You can smile all you want, use common language, and listen like a pro, but in the end, people will trust you if you do what you say you're going to do. Actions speak louder than words when you're trying to tell others you can be trusted.

The bottom line: When people feel comfortable with you, they will be more open and trusting.

To show you how all these skills can make a conversation hit the mark, I'm going back to the conversation earlier in the chapter. Jane is trying to find out why her employee satisfaction scores are so poor. When Jane builds trust and openness by demonstrating these behaviors, she quickly gets the information that can help her change, and perhaps even changes some of the thoughts from her employees.

> *Situation:* Before the meeting starts, Jane spends time going through the survey results. She makes notes about what she agrees with and what she disagrees with, as well as creating a

clear purpose for the meeting: What can she and her employees agree will help her become a better leader? At the meeting, Jane starts the conversation.

Jane: "Hi, team. The employee satisfaction surveys came back last week, and I have to be honest, my scores were worse than last year. I want to be a better leader for you. I'd love to walk away with three things I can do differently next year that would make a difference. Would someone like to start the discussion on what I can do to become a better leader?"

Brave team member Paula: "Well, boss, a few years ago you used to walk around every morning and say hi and see how our projects were going. Now it seems like we only talk about that in project meetings. I can only speak for myself, but I miss that casual conversation."

Jane: "Thanks for the information. I know I tend to spend more time responding to e-mails and being on conference calls in the morning than walking around the floor. I didn't realize that was something the team valued, so let me put it down as one idea. Does anyone want to add to that idea or provide another one?"

Team members begin to talk positively and come up with an actionable list for Jane and the entire team to work on in the next year. A year later, when the next employee survey results are completed, Jane gets a five-star rating, and she and her team continue on a productive path to success.

Jane does these three things differently this time:

- ✔ She takes time to think about her own actions and emotions before the conversation starts.

- ✔ She clearly states her own motivations about wanting to be a better manager, instead of talking solely about wanting to improve her score.

- ✔ She keeps a positive attitude. She doesn't say, "Why did everyone think I was so bad this year?" She asks what she can do to become better.

Critical conversations may not create world peace, but by preparing for the critical conversation and managing her own emotions, Jane's team comes together to help create a better organization. Now, that's a critical conversation that rocks!

Chapter 10

Keeping Challenging Situations Productive

In This Chapter

▶ Bouncing back from a bad turn in the conversation

▶ Keeping tough discussions on track

▶ Staying focused when conversations get sidetracked

▶ Dealing with resistance and difficult behaviors

*I*magine a workplace full of happy people who are well versed in critical conversations. The entire workforce gives feedback productively to one another in a timely fashion, no one ever loses her cool, and people sing around a campfire after work. Sounds nice but incredibly unlikely, right? Welcome back to reality. Because you probably don't live in this parallel universe, you have to work through demanding critical conversations. Yes, challenges will threaten the success of a critical conversation at times. Your mission when this threat happens: keep the situation positive. You don't need to move an irate workforce to the dreamland I just described, but you can create an encouraging and optimistic environment in the face of challenge. This chapter shows you how.

In this chapter, I walk you through righting a wrong when a conversation gets derailed. Because maintaining a safe, genuine, and positive environment leads to more productive critical conversations, I also show ways to keep tough situations positive. I go through ways to deal with resistance and difficult behaviors that can surface during tough conversations. And, finally, I show how to maintain focus when conversations go off track.

Righting a Wrong

Mistakes happen, managers lose their cool, and people say things they wish they could take back. Yes, conversations go wrong. The good thing is that with a few essential words, you can turn even the most spoiled conversation into one with a positive outcome. In Chapter 9, I show you plenty of ways to manage stress before a conversation, but when a conversation goes downhill, it's time to recover and rebuild. For more on how to keep your cool when everyone else is losing it, head over to Chapter 20.

Okay, so you lost your cool

You went into the meeting with the best intentions, but you let go of your cool and you lost it. As soon as that happens, do these three things to turn the conversation around:

1. **Acknowledge the comments you made.** If you just keep going after losing your cool, you can be 100 percent certain that the focus will be on what just happened — not on the task at hand. As soon as you lose your cool, take a few deep breaths. And then, before doing anything else, be honest with the group. Here are a few key phrases that will accomplish just that:

   - "I realize I just yelled, and my emotions may be out of control, so do you mind if I take a few minutes to regroup so we can get back on track?"

   - "I realize I yelled/screamed/just let my head pop off. This conversation is important to me, and it's important for me to have a level head. Let me just take a few breaths so I can be more productive for the rest of the meeting."

2. **Summarize what happened.** This step takes attention off your head exploding and moves the attention to the process and what to do next. To demonstrate your commitment to resolving the issue, say, "This issue is important to me, and I felt we were going back on what we just agreed on," or, "We agreed on the ground rules for the discussion and it seems like we weren't following them." These statements let the others in the room know what set you off in the first place.

3. **Reflect on what to do next.** You may not need to completely call off the conversation, but take a moment to resolve the blowup and try to get back on track. Demonstrate your willingness to find a solution in a positive way.

   When you need to take a moment to get the conversation back on track, you can try these methods:

   - **Ask for ideas.** Reopen the conversation if you lose your cool by simply saying you want to create a win-win situation and discuss the other party's ideas on how to keep moving forward. Then use your active listening skills (see Chapter 7) to find a good solution.

- **Say it.** Let the other party know you want to keep the conversation positive and productive by saying exactly that, after acknowledging you lost your cool. Then make a recommendation on what to do next.

- **Work together.** Sometimes both parties may be unsure of how to proceed after a blowup. In these cases, say, "I want to work together to find a good solution. Are you still willing to work together?" Then you may defer the meeting for a while to allow emotions to cool down, or you may be able to pick up right where you left off before you lost your cool. This approach also works when someone else loses her cool.

- **Take a time-out.** If a few breaths and an apology don't seem to be enough, take five to ten minutes to regroup. You probably aren't the first person who has gotten emotional during a conversation, and you won't be the last. Ask the group for a five- to ten-minute break so you can regroup and refocus. I know you may be thinking, "I've never said something like that at work. Won't people think I'm weak?" Quite the opposite is true. Individuals who have a high level of self-awareness and are able to verbally communicate their feelings and their errors are seen as calm, flexible, and focused in the face of crisis and panic.

- **Ask for help.** After acknowledging your outburst, ask the other parties how to move forward. This step takes the pressure off you by giving the other parties input into whether they want to continue the discussion now or reschedule the conversation for later (if that's an option). You can also ask them whether focusing on the issue or concern that sparked the emotion in the first place would be helpful.

- **Reschedule the meeting.** If you happen to lose your cool, you may feel your blood pressure rising even after you acknowledge your behavior. If this happens, be honest with the group members and let them know that you're obviously passionate about the issue but will need more than a few minutes to refocus. This technique works, but if you reschedule the meeting, you can't just pick up where you left off. You'll likely have to solidify the original agreements again, and you may even need to bring in a facilitator to help with the discussion.

If you make a mistake during a conversation, admit it and try to move on. Building trust during a critical conversation and creating a safe environment for the discussion relies heavily on honesty. Admit your faults, and others will be more likely to agree that they may have areas of improvement as well.

Emotional intelligence, commonly known as EQ, is how a person identifies, manages, uses, and productively applies her emotions to positively resolve conflict, communicate, get work done, and do just about anything else. People with a high EQ not only have a high self-awareness of their own emotions, but also can recognize and adapt to the emotions of others. Understanding your own needs and the needs of others is also a big part in being able to control your emotions and adapt when situations and conversations get tough. *Emotional Intelligence For Dummies* by Steven J. Stein (Wiley) is full of ways to develop awareness of your needs and emotions in almost any situation.

Time to ask for support

There's no shame in asking for help. If a critical conversation starts to take a turn for the worse, asking a co-worker or manager to step in and help facilitate the meeting can be a smart move. You're still able to lead and participate in the discussion, but you have another resource to guide the decision-making process to take off some of the stress. Here are some more benefits to asking for help:

- ✔ **Power is distributed around the group.** Asking others to help can shift the balance of power from the leader running the show to a more collaborative effort.

- ✔ **Leaders can focus on content; facilitators can focus on process.** If you're able to ask others to help lead the conversation so that you can participate rather than facilitate, you're then free to contribute to the content of the meeting without having to worry about controlling the process. This refocusing takes a tremendous amount of stress off you as the initiator of the conversation. The stress of trying to participate and facilitate at the same time may be one reason for the blowup in the first place.

- ✔ **The process keeps moving forward.** A facilitator or other neutral party can make process suggestions along the way when the parties in the conversation get stuck during the discussion.

- ✔ **The leader has time to listen.** You already know that you can't communicate without listening, so taking a step back and letting someone else run the meeting frees up your time to listen.

Not every critical conversation needs a facilitator to help get results, but having someone else guide the process can help the conversation bounce back quickly if it has already gone off track. Choosing wisely is key. Here are the two main steps to follow when you enroll others to help make the critical conversation a success:

- ✔ **Find a neutral party.** When a conversation goes south, people often begin to take sides. The best solution is to find a neutral party who can focus on the process of building agreements throughout the conversation, resolve conflicts and diffuse potential conflicts, and keep all parties on track. The facilitator is the chauffeur of the process, making sure the conversation gets from point A to point B safely and efficiently.

- ✔ **Solidify the roles.** One of the first things an outside facilitator should do is be clear about her role. The facilitator can say, "My role will be to serve as facilitator. That means I'm going to be your 'conversation chauffeur.' I'll let you talk about the content, but I'll occasionally intervene to make suggestions to keep the process moving at the right speed." Making sure everyone agrees to the facilitator's role is critical. If the initiator and the receiver in the conversations don't understand or accept the facilitator's role, the facilitator isn't able to function.

One often overlooked way to get help is to ask all the parties *in the conversation* for help. If the critical conversation involves a group of people, rather than just two people talking, the group can be your biggest ally when trying to create a positive outcome. When the conversation goes south, ask the group members how they want to bounce back.

Get help from across the table

An option you can keep up your sleeve is to put the conversation on the other party's shoulders. If you're the initiator of the conversation and nothing is working or if you have had a similar conversation multiple times, ask the other party what she hopes to achieve with her current behavior or performance.

Here's an example:

> "I know this is the third time we've had this meeting to discuss not including teammates in the group decision-making process. I'm not sure what to do next, so I thought I'd ask you to help me better understand your perspective. Do you have time to help me understand what you want to achieve by making these team decisions on your own? What do you recommend I do as the manager of the team to make sure we meet the goals of the company?"

This statement and follow-up question aren't sarcastic. They simply allow the other party to express her perspective and goals. This tactic is never a first line of defense, but it does help a conversation move past the déjà vu stage and into the action stage.

What can you expect from this method? First, the other party may express her views on how the issue needs to be resolved, or whether the issue needs to be resolved at all. Second, if you can find out the process the other party wants to use to solve the issue, you have the opportunity to create a common goal of working toward a resolution of the problem.

This is how the rest of the conversation may flow:

> **Non–team player:** "I don't want to accomplish anything. I like making decisions on my own, and the team simply slows down the decision-making process."
>
> **Manager:** "I see. I understand you want to keep making team decisions on your own, but, as a manager, I need to make sure the entire team is involved in the decision-making process. The fact is, we need to involve the team in the decision-making process, and that is nonnegotiable. I recommend that we do one of two things. First, we can agree that we want to work toward more team collaboration, and we can develop steps that would help us achieve this goal. Or we can ask a third party to come in and help us find a solution. Would you recommend any other ideas?"
>
> **Non–team player:** "No other ideas, but I just can't slow down the process."
>
> **Manager:** "Okay, I understand. So let's find ways to increase collaboration without slowing down the process."

Not only is the manager persistent and direct, but she maintains a positive attitude about the resolution of the problem.

What did you say?! Handling the unexpected

I feel safe saying that if you use the tools in this chapter to work through a tough situation in a positive way, you'll have a successful critical conversation. But sometimes someone says or does something that throws you completely off guard. Literally, you're speechless. If this happens, don't panic. Critical conversations are emotional, and when you hear something completely unexpected or receive personal attacks, the individual is probably speaking from emotion rather than logic.

What is the best course of action when you hear or see the unexpected during a critical conversation? Be honest, of course. If someone swears or gets unexpectedly upset, saying "I don't know what to do with that information" immediately diffuses and neutralizes the incident. At this point, the other party may back down when she realizes you're not reacting emotionally. But, if the other party continues to react unexpectedly, call the conversation off, and enlist a third party (more on that in Chapter 15). Implement this step by restating, "I don't know what to do with this information/statement/behavior. I would like to ask for the help of another party, so let's stop the conversation now and regroup later. Are you okay with that approach?"

No matter the situation, being honest and open is always the best policy. Fighting back with fighting words only makes the situation worse. After you close the conversation, take a break and talk with another manager or mediation expert about the meeting and desired outcomes. When you do regroup, either you or the mediator can specify the consequences of the behavior that happened in the earlier meeting and then start working toward a common goal.

Keeping Tough Discussions Encouraging

You can probably tell that many critical conversations involve delivering less-than-perfect news. Yes, some critical conversations start with wonderful news (see Chapter 12), but for the most part, a critical conversation deals with a highly emotional issue with a goal of turning the issue into a positive solution. That's a tall order. Tough conversations can be an emotional and physical drain. So how in the world do you keep a tough discussion encouraging?

Here are a few straightforward suggestions for keeping a level head and maintaining an encouraging and positive environment when the conversation gets tough:

> ✔ **Separate behaviors from the person.** No matter what has happened in the past, remember to separate the actions and behaviors from the person, and give the other parties the benefit of the doubt. If all else fails, remind yourself that the critical conversation's ultimate goal is to change a behavior or action, and change can be uncomfortable for everyone. Having empathy and understanding the needs and emotions of others will help you do this (see Chapter 9 for more on understanding needs).

✓ **Stay positive, physically and mentally.** Sure, everyone knows that being positive is important, but knowing isn't enough. Your body will tell you a lot about how you feel, so listen to your own body language as a good indicator of your attitude. When asked about the person or the action at the center of the critical conversation, do you immediately cross your arms or do you lean in to discover more? When you're about to walk into the critical conversation, do you feel more energized or just plain exhausted? If you're exhausted or closed off to the process or person, find ways to work through the stress (see Chapter 8).

✓ **Practice, practice, practice.** Critical conversations aren't easy! Find a peer or friend who can help you practice the conversation and practice how you may react to a negative comment or situation. All the practice will pay off, because maintaining a positive environment and flexibility helps keep the conversation moving forward.

✓ **Focus on the purpose and process.** When a discussion starts to become challenging, and maintaining a positive attitude seems next to impossible, remember the message you're sending. If you get upset or even ignore the problem, you're indicating that you have better things to do or that you've potentially given up and thrown in the towel. The other party in the discussion will follow this behavior. But if the purpose is to find a mutually positive outcome, you dramatically change the tone of the meeting. If you come into the meeting working toward a positive outcome, the other party will likely put her best foot forward as well.

With these four ways to keep a tough discussion encouraging, your conversations have a leg up when it comes to positive results. Now you're ready to take a positive attitude and put it on turbo-charge. Warning: The following sections divulge industry know-how. These tools you're about to read aren't for the weak! They take your positive attitude to an entirely new level by motivating you to drive results, be supportive of other's needs, and stop power plays during the conversation. If you're ready, read on.

Motivating people gets results

Although you have many ways to approach a conversation, a critical conversation is most successful when all parties are dedicated to helping make positive change. Because the approach to critical conversation works best when all parties can agree to working on the issue at hand, the more motivated the recipients of the information are, the more likely the behavior or actions are to change.

Even if all parties aren't ready to dive into finding a solution to the problem just yet, the inherent pattern of staying motivating often leads to all parties being ready and willing to take action. And being motivating is more likely to lead to a partnership in the solution; that's always preferable to being told what to do.

You know the saying, "You attract more flies with honey than with vinegar"? Well, the best way to keep all the parties involved and motivated is to act like a coach in the conversation. Which of the following situations would you prefer to be part of?

- ✔ **The motivating coach:** The coach encourages players to do their best and to continue to work toward a goal. When a player doesn't do her best, the coach may give an idea of what went wrong and ask the player to find a different way to address the problem. There is no yelling, no chair throwing. The coach's goal is to make every person on the team excel to the best of her abilities with training, positive coaching, and planning.

- ✔ **The discouraging coach:** A coach yells at players, telling them that they're horrible. When a player makes a mistake, the coach is quick to point it out. The goal of the discouraging coach is to weed out the weak. Yelling, chair throwing, jumping up and down, and acting like a 2-year-old throwing a temper tantrum are encouraged and rewarded.

If you'd rather have or be the discouraging coach, you can probably put down this book and just start telling everyone what to do and where to go since you already know what the answer should be. If you're reading this book, however, I think you agree that the motivating coach is going to get the best results in the long term. Keeping the conversation motivating keeps all parties engaged.

Supporting others' needs

When you're having a critical conversation, you probably know your own motivations and needs (or at least you're thinking of them, and if not, Chapter 9 can help you clarify your own needs). If the conversation focuses on an employee issue, you're probably pretty clear on the needs and expectations of the organization. But what many people forget during a critical conversation is to be supportive of the other party's needs. This means empathy for others by recognizing and accepting what other people need and feel.

Most likely, everyone in this conversation has at least one other thing on her mind outside of the critical conversation. Because very few people will tell you their needs right up front, your job as the initiator of the conversation is to help the other parties identify their needs, and then find ways to be supportive of their needs.

How do you find out other people's needs? Ask. Think of how powerful this message is when asked with a genuine desire to help: "What do you need from me to make this change happen?" This conversation may be the first time any manager has asked the employee this question. After you ask the question, listen to the answer and come up with a game plan to help all the parties involved in the conversation reach the common goal. Head to Chapter 9 for more ideas on how to ask and identify others' needs and motivations.

Missing deadlines agreed to in the conversation or forgetting to identify the successes after the conversation are fairly clear indicators that you don't have a genuine commitment to creating a positive solution. Everyone makes mistakes and gets overloaded. Once is forgivable, but continually canceling meetings, not doing what you say you'll do, or being perpetually late is disrespectful and shows a lack of concern for the needs of others.

You aren't trying to be a therapist; you're just allowing the other parties to voice what they need to help make the situation better for everyone.

Using power wisely

When a conversation gets tough — because individuals start to argue, raise their voices, or simply disagree — you may be tempted to play the power card. That is, you give up finding a collaborative approach to the solution and just say "because I said so" or "because I'm the boss."

At times, a leader can simply say, "You know this solution needs to get done, so we just need to get it done." Deciding on and announcing a solution to a problem is perfectly acceptable in situations where you may not need a long-term commitment, when you have little time to invest in a dialogue, or when the dialogue is merely for show and the boss will ultimately decide, regardless of the feedback. These examples are just a few of the many reasons why a leader deciding on and announcing a solution to a problem may work. But here's an alternative to the power card.

Think of the different reactions a CEO would get to these two statements:

> **Option A:** "I am the CEO and this is what we are doing."
>
> **Option B:** "As the leader of this company, I have a vested interest in exceeding our sales forecast. Can you help me get there?"

I'd much rather be talking with the CEO who uses option B. In option B, the CEO is opening up discussion and asking people whether they can help. The CEO builds an agreement with the audience by asking this question, and now the environment is perfect for exploring options to meeting the sales forecast and then deciding which approach to take. Explore, decide, get moving, and evaluate the impact. Seems like this CEO has the first parts down perfectly and is ready to get her sales force moving.

You have many other options to the power card when you need to use your position of influence to get the critical conversation moving. Here are some alternatives to simply saying, "Because I'm the boss!"

- ✔ **Use your skills and expertise:** Leaders in companies often bring some skill or technical expertise to the table. Acknowledge this skill and then ask for help in other areas. This approach is a no-nonsense tactic because you're not asking for information you may not use. For example, a manager may say, "I have the skill needed to bake the best cupcakes in the world. Now how do we get more customers?" The initiator of the conversation isn't asking for recipes she may later throw in the recycling bin; she's asking for help with getting customers. She's asking for specific information rather than opening up every problem for discussion.

- ✔ **Be informational:** Having important information is often associated with power or position in a company. So rather than tell someone what to do just because of your title, enlist the other party to help create solutions based on this knowledge. A manager may say, "Knowing that our goal is to be number one in our market share, how should we best accomplish this task?" That's a much better collaborative alternative than stating, "I need to get the job done."

- ✔ **Take a relationship-driven approach:** Power, position, and connections to influential people are often related. That doesn't mean it's time to name-drop! Relationship influence is most powerful when you can give insight into how someone else may think. Knowing how another person would respond in a given situation and sharing this information with the other party in the conversation is an example of relationship influence. Using relationship influence, a manager may say, "Last week I spoke with the senior manager in our western division, and she's looking for a new solution for a client. How should we address this need most efficiently and productively?" Notice how differently this discussion would be received if the manager said, "I know Bob, our Most Senior Vice President of the World, and he thinks we need to do something different."

Each of these different levers of influence related to power and position can help create a positive environment for a critical conversation. Avoid the punching power game in a critical conversation! Power is often met with power. Newton's laws of motion state that for every action, there is an equal and opposite reaction. If an initiator of a conversation speaks first about how powerful she is, the recipient of the information will most likely punch right back.

Dealing with Resistance

Okay, I'll say it — some people are just plain difficult to work with! These individuals put up resistance, disagree for fun, and basically just come into work to make your life challenging, to put it nicely. If you work with people who are a little more difficult than you'd like, or if you fear that your next critical conversation may be faced with resistance, this section is for you!

Stay flexible

Balancing focus and flexibility when you're faced with resistance is the name of the game. If you tell someone who's already being difficult that she has to do something or act a certain way, 999 times out of 1,000, she'll put her feet in the ground and do exactly the opposite. But just letting the meeting go astray isn't a good option either. Think of focus and flexibility as the out-of-bounds line in a soccer match. Players, as long as they follow some general rules, have a lot of flexibility to move one way or the other as long as they stay within bounds. In a critical conversation, make those boundaries clear and then let the other parties know where they have flexibility in the discussion.

Here are two easy ways to show flexibility with boundaries:

- ✔ **State what is and isn't acceptable.** Being flexible doesn't mean you need to let someone walk all over you. If someone's behavior is unacceptable — like abusive language — you may say, "I ask that you treat me as a professional and stop using abusive language. I want to work with you, and I'm flexible with how we proceed, but first we need to both talk to one another with respect."

- ✔ **Set ground rules.** If you think boundaries may need to be established during a conversation, set them now, and show flexibility when you set these rules. Before the conversation even starts, you may want to say, "I want to propose some ground rules for our conversation, but I would like to first ask if you have any ground rules you want us to both follow."

Some ground rules may be agreeing to stick with an agenda, speaking the truth, staying on time, or using a professional tone throughout the conversation.

Know when to push and when to stop

A broad range of problems can rear their ugly heads during critical conversations. If the behavior is interrupting the agenda or any progress forward, you have a couple paths to take. First, you may need to assess whether or not all the parties in the room are willing to work toward a common goal. If not, clarify the process and purpose of the conversation and check for agreement.

Here's a good way to approach a person who's starting to show signs of resistance (see Chapter 16):

> "In the beginning of the meeting we agreed to work on finding a solution to why team members aren't comfortable with the language you use in the break room. Are you still willing to work on this issue together, or do you want to find a different way to resolve the issue?"

If this calm and gentle approach doesn't work, be a little more direct in finding a solution. In the previous example, you give the other party the opportunity to decide what to do next. A more direct way of dealing with difficult behaviors is to give two options for what to do next. Acknowledge what the person is saying or doing, validate her opinions, and then either deal with the behavior or defer it until later.

- ✔ **Acknowledge:** Acknowledge the behavior by describing it neutrally. When Mr. Negative makes a comment that the problem isn't solely his problem but rather the team's problem, you may say, "You don't think you're part of this problem, is that right?

- ✔ **Validate:** Without casting judgment, let the other individual know that she can have a different opinion than you have. Continuing with the previous example, you could say, "You may be right. We may need to work on this problem from multiple perspectives." By simply validating opinions, the difficult behavior may stop.

- ✔ **Defer or deal:** To defer the resistance, ask whether dealing with the other opinions later is okay. For example, you may say, "I'll commit to having the same discussion with other team members, if you can commit to working on this side of the problem now."

A last resort is to give even narrower options — stop the behavior or stop the conversation. Be careful not to use this option as a threat, but as a way to move forward. Here you may say, "John, it seems to me that you're placing the blame on other team members, and this is making it difficult to make progress. I see two options. We can work on a solution together, or we can stop the conversation and I can formalize a performance improvement plan." Remember that this statement isn't a threat, but a statement with options.

A gentle reminder or a light push in the right direction often helps to direct resistance more positively or to cool down difficult behaviors. This approach works especially well when the parties in the conversation have worked together successfully in the past, and a particular issue has created a need for a critical conversation. If you need to take a more frank approach, however, remember the golden rule of coming to the conversation with a genuine desire to make the situation better.

Silence is an influential tool. In Chapter 7, I talk about why silence is truly golden during any critical conversation. Don't shy away from using silence as a powerful tool when you're faced with resistance. Listening or simply choosing to be silent allows others to talk and process information.

During difficult critical conversations, sometimes the best option is agreeing to disagree. You don't live in a fantasy world where all critical conversations end up in utopia. Sometimes disagreements are just disagreements. This is okay, as long as the disagreement doesn't significantly impact the outcome of the conversation.

Take two steps forward and one step back

Taking one step back and then two steps forward isn't just a great way to square dance — it's also a necessary tool in critical conversations. One of the easiest ways to keep a critical conversation on track is to continue to build agreement on what to do next, and if the conversation goes astray or if the conversation begins to face resistance, go back to the last agreement and work from there.

Pretend that you're a mountain climber. Most mountain climbers (at least those that tend to make it back down the mountain alive) use anchors to protect them from falling completely down the mountain if they slip or fall. Agreements throughout the discussion are your anchors, preventing the conversation from falling back to square one. During a critical conversation, you may use these types of agreements. When you need to go backward to review a previous agreement, rephrasing or recapping the agreement can help clarify any uncertainties or vagueness.

When you kick off the conversation, ask whether all parties are willing to work on a solution. When exploring and examining what's happening, ask whether all parties agree on what the problem is and why the problem exists. When deciding on options to move forward, make sure all parties agree to the value in solving the issue and know which options everyone can agree to, do, and support.

Ready to see it in action?

> **Leslie:** "Hi, Terry. I'd like to have a discussion with you about how we work together as a team. Are you willing to work with me to find ways we can be most productive?"
>
> **Terry:** "Sure." *This is agreement number one.*
>
> **Leslie:** "Great. Even though we're co–project managers, I feel that you rely on me to do most of the work. For example, I wrote 99 percent of the last report because you were busy, but, in the meeting, you said you wrote it. Do you see how me doing all the work and you taking credit could hurt our working relationship and cause us to be less productive?"
>
> **Terry:** "I see how you think this is a problem." *Agreement number two is agreeing there may be a problem.* "But I told you I would help much more at the end of the project."
>
> **Leslie:** "I'm glad we can agree that this is a problem. I know you offered to help at the end of the project. I think the problem exists because I know I'm going to still manage the team at the end of the project, and I'm not sure whether my involvement will decrease as the project goes on."
>
> **Terry:** "I'm not sure what your problem is. I thought we were co-workers."
>
> **Leslie:** "I understand. I know we agreed to find ways to be most productive, so are you willing to brainstorm some ideas on how we can both feel productive?" *Leslie is recapping and rephrasing agreements number one and two.*

Leslie builds agreements along the way, and when she encounters resistance from Terry, she quickly recaps the previous agreement, while staying positive about how the problem can be solved. If you encounter resistance during a conversation, using this technique can help stop the resistance from getting out of control.

Gaining Focus When Conversations Go Off Track

If you work to develop an actionable consensus among all the parties during a critical conversation and use a positive facilitation approach, then all your conversations will be perfect. Wait, back that up. I mean *many* of your conversations will go smoothly. But conversations can go off track for many reasons. When one does, refocus the conversation.

Refocusing the conversation can be done in three simple steps: clarify the focus, check for agreement, and continue.

1. **Clarify the focus.** When you sense that the discussion is going off track, you may not be the only one who's thinking the same way. Any party involved in the critical conversation can start this clarifying process by opening the dialogue to generate the information needed for discussion. Clarifying sounds like this, "In the beginning of the conversation, we agreed to work through a disagreement on how to productively ask questions during our team meeting. It seems we're now trying to solve the problem of why people are late to meetings."

2. **Check for agreement.** After you clarify the focus of the conversation, develop agreement on the priority of the conversation. To check for agreement, the leader may ask, "Do we want to focus on solving the question of why people are late to meetings first, or should we finish the earlier discussion?"

3. **Continue the conversation.** Finally, help all the parties in the conversation come to closure and move on with the discussion. When the group agrees on what to do next, write down the agreement and continue the conversation. The leader could say, "Great. I've put 'finding out why people are late to meetings' on the discussion board so we don't forget it. Now let's get back to the first concern we were addressing: how to productively ask questions during team meetings."

You may notice that during the agreement process, you're not throwing away the original purpose of the meeting. Sometimes, having flexibility in what the parties will discuss next creates a better environment for tougher discussions and will, most importantly, get the parties in the conversation working together.

Although boundaries and flexibility are important, be cognizant of and respect the hierarchical, cultural, and social norms, values, and rules between parties in the conversation. Ignoring organizational rules or cultural values can cause unnecessary anxiety or anger — neither of which is good for a positive critical conversation.

Chapter 11

Closing the Conversation with Ease

In This Chapter

▶ Discovering why every conversation needs closure

▶ Creating powerful action plans that make the grade

▶ Getting tactical to get results

▶ Evaluating the success of the conversation

The last part — and one of the most essential parts — of critical communication is what happens after the conversation is done. You're done talking, the meeting is over, and all the parties have committed to how to solve the problem. Now you want to make sure these solutions happen. Closing the conversation means finishing the actual discussion and being in agreement about what will happen next. By closing the conversation constructively, you support individuals on their paths to success. And by following up in a timely manner, you help create a positive outcome that lasts.

In this chapter, I tell you why every conversation needs closure. You discover key elements of powerful action plans and how to drive accountability with appropriate follow-up steps. You also walk away with some tactical steps that help all parties get the results they agreed to during the conversation. Finally, you find out how to evaluate the entire conversation so you can discover what worked (and what didn't) to make your next critical conversation even better.

Making the Case for Closure

Closing the conversation is a crucial step in the critical conversation process. In order to make sure this same conversation doesn't happen again in a week, month, or year, you must properly close the conversation with an action plan that makes everyone happy.

If you've done your job well and prepared for the crucial conversation correctly (see Chapter 9 for tips on doing just that), the end of the discussion should bring a positive outlook on next steps. You may even have a sense of relief that everyone involved in the conversation is on the same page, or at least close to it. Closing the conversation is a crucial step in determining whether the conversation was a success.

For most people, a critical conversation is a stressful event. The goal of closure is to make all parties feel valued and motivated to move forward and to accelerate productivity and improve the work relationship in the near term.

The ultimate goal of critical conversations is to turn a high-emotion, high-stakes situation into a positive situation that generates meaningful results and builds a better work relationship.

Creating Powerful Action Plans

Thanks to your prep work, planning, and expert delivery, you aced the conversation. Now you want to make sure all the agreements, ideas, and feedback aren't lost in a post-conversation black hole. Time to create an action plan. Action plans provide goals and time lines that help all parties to be productive immediately and set a positive foundation for future feedback and conversations.

While the action plans may be most applicable in performance discussions, sometimes the action coming out of a conversation is not about performance. For example, if the critical conversation happens between peers who avoid conflict and just talk behind each other's backs, the action plan may simply be an agreement to continue to talk directly with one another when there is a concern or disagreement. In this case, the action plan would be an agreement of what to do if either one of the parties fall back into the old habits of avoiding tough discussions.

Agreeing on next steps

At the end of the discussion, you're ready to agree on clear goals and expectations for the action plan. These goals help all parties involved agree on what success looks like by giving you a clear, measurable way to evaluate, track, and reflect on progress. Gaining agreement is more than just writing down your own thoughts and directives; gaining agreement means all the parties involved in the conversation feel confident in what happens next and are willing and able to make the actions happen.

Gaining agreement is often as simple as asking, "Do I have your agreement that the next step should be to talk with one another immediately if we disagree on what is happening on the project?" By checking for agreement, you continue to build buy-in for how the situation or behaviors will change after the conversation is done.

Even in the most challenging conversations, you can find something that everyone can agree on, especially if you come to the table genuinely wanting to improve the situation. For more on developing agreements during critical conversations, check out Chapter 4.

Determining elements of an action plan

Although you may come across many types of action plans, the basic elements are consistent. The following sections outline the basic elements, telling you what will happen next, who will make it happen and who can help, and when it will be done.

Try to incorporate SMART goals in the action plan: Goals that are **s**pecific, **m**easurable, **a**ction-oriented and **a**greed-on, **r**elevant, and **t**ime-bound. Chapter 4 covers SMART goals in more detail. Try to keep the action plan limited to two or three key SMART goals with action steps to maintain focus on the most important desired results of the conversation.

Figure 11-1 gives you an example of a 30-day action plan that could be used to close a critical conversation between a manager, Anna, and her boss, Kathy, who are focusing on improving team engagement.

What will happen

After a conversation — whether you're delivering performance feedback, dealing with difficult behaviors, or even hiring a new employee — having clear goals and action steps will help all parties involved walk out of the room knowing what needs to happen next.

The action plan makes sure all the parties involved in the conversation are certain about what's going to happen after everyone goes back to his desk. An action plan divides work into achievable steps in the short term, and should be aligned with longer-term goals. In the example shown in Figure 11-1, Anna (the recipient of the feedback) has three main goals to work on, each with action steps that can be achieved in the next 30 days.

What will happen next? Goals and action plans	Actions	Who will make it happen and who can help?
Goal #1: Improve collaboration on the team by September 1st	Action step: Set up monthly one-on-one follow-up meetings with staff. Each staff member will have an individual meeting with Anna. Action step: Launch one-hour weekly discussion meetings with team.	Anna to schedule and lead meetings. Kathy can help facilitate first sessions.
Goal #2: Measure progress of initiatives by September 15th	Action step: Create a scorecard measuring productivity. Action step: Review scorecard with manager and team. Action step: Anna and Kathy meet monthly to review progress.	Anna to create scorecard. Irene in the technical department can help with formatting and data feeds. Kathy will set up one-on-one follow-up meetings with Anna.
Goal #3: Increase employee engagement in the department by September 30th	Action step: Identify and meet with potential mentors within the company. Action step: Work with human resources to deploy employee engagement survey or 360-degree feedback. Action step: Anna and Kathy review feedback about employee engagement and create a 6-month plan of action.	Anna to reach out to mentors. Anna to meet with Jacob in HR. Anna to set up review meeting with Kathy after feedback is gathered.

Figure 11-1: A 30-day action plan.

Drafting the action plan on a piece of paper while you're closing the conversation puts everything in black and white. After the conversation, ask the recipient to summarize the action plan and send it back to you — there is tremendous value in gaining ownership and clarifying the action plan if you do.

To improve your chances of success, try to create immediately achievable "wins." Delivering a critical message and then waiting a year before seeing results is never ideal. Even if your conversation focuses on creating long-term changes on big issues, you can take steps toward achieving the goal in the next one to two weeks. For example, if you're giving a negative performance review to an employee, a few short-term action items may include developing a project plan for a project that's painfully behind schedule and then reviewing it with you. The key is to not overwhelm an individual with goals and plans that are impossible to achieve. The goal of every critical conversation is to make a positive change in behavior, not to destroy morale or put the brakes on someone's career.

A conversation doesn't end when the talking stops; the conversation ends successfully when behaviors, patterns, or situations change; an action plan helps to make these changes happen.

Who will make it happen

Just as conversations aren't one-sided, neither is the action plan. Don't put the entire weight of the world on the shoulders of the other individuals. Instead, make recommendations on who can help make the plan work. In Figure 11-1, while Anna (the receiver of the feedback) is responsible for getting the work done, each action step has at least one more individual who can help in the process. Helpers may include a mentor, an expert in a particular field, or even you. Providing a network of support helps the situation move forward in a positive way. If a conversation is between peers, one agreement may be to agree on who can help if the problem does not seem to get better after the conversation is over.

Before you initiate the conversation, think about who will be able to help make the action plan work.

When will things be done

At the end of the conversation (whether it goes well or not), ideally everyone can agree on what's going to happen next and when these things will happen. If you're asking an employee to change behaviors that are negatively impacting the team, you'll probably want to see some type of change in the next few days to know he heard the message. If he doesn't show that he's working toward change, you may have to deliver the message again.

In the example action plan (see Figure 11-1), the goals have finite dates when the actions should be completed. The action plan also includes a step to review the plan and create next steps for what happens after the first 30 days.

A finite time line is the simplest way to judge whether or not the situation is going to change. For each step in the action plan, include a target date when the action will be complete.

Staggering the time line for actions is a great idea. Put two to three items on the action plan that are due in one to two weeks, and then another two to three items that are due in three to four weeks. Depending on the conversation, a few more action items may be due two to three months after the conversation takes place. Although you may need to alter the time lines for each situation, by balancing short-term action with long-term goals, all the parties will feel confident that they can see progress and know that the messages were heard clearly.

Although things may not change overnight, a good rule of thumb is to agree that changes will begin to happen in the next one to two weeks.

Following Through for Success

After you prepare for the conversation, have the conversation, and write an action plan, you may be exhausted. Take a deep breath and remember that the last step toward closure is following up with the progress of the action plan. Follow-through usually includes

- ✔ Writing a follow-up note to clarify the main points of the meeting
- ✔ Scheduling a follow-up meeting to discuss progress, obstacles, and feedback on the action plan
- ✔ Creating formal documentation when needed
- ✔ Responding to ignored action plans

Writing the perfect follow-up note

A simple note to the parties involved in the conversation reemphasizing the purpose of the initial meeting can do wonders to positively move forward. A follow-up note isn't a legal document (I touch on when you may need a legal document later in this section); a follow-up note is a summary of the main points. Even if you delivered the message flawlessly, some emotion during the meeting will cause both small and large details to be forgotten. Documenting the main points helps alleviate the potential for confusion when the stakes are high.

The perfect follow-up note is simple, positive, and timely.

- ✔ **Simple:** You don't have to revisit every word that was spoken, especially when you have a powerful action plan to follow. Keep the note to the point, and always provide an opening for more discussion to happen.
- ✔ **Positive:** Thank the other party for discussing the issues with you, and reemphasize that the intent of this plan is to make things better (for example, to help the other party be successful in his job or improve his contribution to the department). Mentioning the consequences of performance or behaviors

not changing is acceptable, but remember that the goal is to genuinely want to help the situation improve. At this point in the conversation, focus on an optimistic, productive future rather than everything that could go wrong.

✔ **Timely:** Write the follow-up note before the day is over. Although I give general time lines for action plans earlier in the chapter, the follow-up note has to come before the day is done. The note officially closes the conversation and launches the action plan, and waiting even a day to send the note drags the discussion out too long.

Check out Figure 11-2 for an example of a follow-up note to send when you're sending the action plan.

Dear Employee,

Thank you for engaging in our conversation today about improving your performance and contribution to the team. As I mentioned in our meeting, my goal is to help you be successful so our entire team can be successful.

When you have completed a draft of the action plan we discussed in the meeting, please send it over to me and I will be happy to review it and help if there is any confusion. I will also set up weekly meetings to review the progress. I am looking forward to seeing a draft of the dashboard the next time we meet. Please let me know immediately if you have any questions or concerns about the action plan we discussed during the meeting.

Sincerely,

Your boss

Figure 11-2: A sample follow-up note.

Having the recipient of the conversation create the action plan is a great way to give him accountability for making change.

Scheduling follow-up meetings

The follow-up conversations don't need to be hours long or incredibly detailed; simply agreeing to have weekly check-ins over the next few weeks to make sure that everything is going according to plan will suffice.

You'll get a good reputation as a leader if you're fair with individuals and hold them accountable to delivering on their part of what you just discussed and agreed on. In the end, the follow-up will make your job much easier in the future by establishing clear guidelines for behaviors and performance. This check-in is perhaps one of the most beneficial things for employees receiving feedback or for teams that need intervention, because it gives them extra time and space to process information (much more than any single meeting could give them). Additionally, checking in and making sure you see progress helps people see the importance of the conversation and your commitment to helping the situation change for the better.

During the follow-up session, keep all parties on the same page by documenting in writing what has happened and what is expected to happen next. A shorter version of the original follow-up notes may be a good outline to follow.

Ongoing discussions drive accountability and lasting change. You will most likely need to have more than one follow-up meeting to check on the progress, especially if problems have been occurring for quite some time or are significant (and most issues that lead to critical conversations are!). During each of the check-ins, you can continue to summarize your commitment and expectations to making things change, and ask what the other parties need and can expect of you in the months ahead.

Creating more formal documentation

In some cases, an action plan, a follow-up note, and an ongoing discussion may be all you need to drive accountability and change. Other critical conversations — those that were emotionally heated, or those that are revisiting poor performance and behaviors — may need a little more documentation.

In addition to the action plan, these conversations may need a formal employee letter. In some cases, human resources or your boss may want to have a copy of the follow-up letter. Instead of copying everyone, ask these individuals whether they need a copy of the note and then forward it on as needed.

Formal documentation may include capturing the main points of the critical conversation, confirming what happened during the meeting, summarizing expectations of what happens next, and acknowledging that the summary is accurate. (If your conversation is part of a performance improvement plan, jump on over to Chapter 13 to get more specific information on how to capture the key information.)

As part of the perfect follow-up note (see the previous section), you may want to add statements like the ones shown in Figure 11-3.

When capturing what happened, stick to the facts, just like you did during the conversation. Be careful not to write down your opinions, like, "You had a really bad attitude in the meeting," or, "I am sure you are depressed about the conversation." Instead, capture facts, time lines, and agreements.

Dear Employee:

This letter summarizes our meeting this morning on your conduct in the workplace. This is only a recap of what we discussed.During our meeting I described to you how your language negatively impacts team collaboration and is in violation of our code of conduct policy.

As we discussed in the meeting, written and verbal communication must be professional and appropriate in both language and tone. When your coworkers receive e-mails such as, "I DON'T KNOW WHY YOU CARE ABOUT THIS," or when you tell co-workers they are "idiots and a waste of time," you set a tone that is disrespectful.

In our meeting, we agreed that you will maintain a positive tone and use cooperative language. As we discussed, you need to show improvement in this area immediately. I will schedule weekly meetings to review progress and next steps.

My goal is to help create a positive work environment for everyone in the department. Please let me know of any problems or concerns that arise.

Sincerely,

Your boss

Figure 11-3: An example of documentation following a critical conversation.

Responding to ignored action plans

Even perfect conversations can be quickly forgotten when emotions are high. If action plans or agreements regarding changes in behavior aren't happening immediately, be more assertive before the situation gets out of control. You send action plans and follow-up notes immediately to reinforce that changes need to happen immediately. But if those changes aren't happening, have a follow-up critical conversation using the first three parts of the EDGE model (for more on this model, see Chapter 4).

Following is an example of how to incorporate the steps of the EDGE model to make sure your employees are following action steps and agreements.

- ✔ **Request the follow-up meeting:** "Hi, John. Can you please come to my office for five minutes?"

- ✔ **Examine what happened:** "Two days ago we had a conversation about changing your tone when you communicate with team members. Yesterday afternoon I heard you tell Sally, our new intern, that she is just going to have to find out the answer to her problem on her own. We agreed that all future conversations would be positive and cooperative. Do you agree with what the expectations were?"

- ✔ **Decide on next steps:** "I would like to ask the human resources team to join us in creating a formal plan for expectations to help this behavior change immediately."

✓ **Gain commitment:** "Can we set up this meeting for tomorrow morning at 9 a.m.?"

✓ **Evaluate the impact:** During the meeting with HR, evaluate the impact (the fourth step in the EDGE model).

If behaviors and conduct don't immediately change, the follow-up conversation is more direct than the first conversation. You're still genuine, wanting to turn the situation around, and you're still using facts rather than emotions during the conversation. The difference is that you're leaving no room for misunderstanding or forgetfulness by directing what commitment is made to move forward.

If you don't see an immediate change in behavior, leave no room for misinterpretation about what that change looks like and the consequences of not making the change happen. But keep in mind that mastering critical conversations isn't about being a legal expert or an auditor of company human resources policy. Mastering the art and science of critical conversations is about coming to the table with a genuine desire to help make situations better.

However, if everyone follows the action plan, it is appropriate to thank the other parties for their work. Changing behavior isn't easy, and recognizing the effort will help to reinforce behaviors and create an environment to build off the success of the action plan.

Part IV
Putting It All into Practice

In this part...

In this part I look at different types of conversations that require a little extra attention: conversations in good times and bad, staff disputes, workplace complaints, and customer relationships. You also find out how to resolve difficult behaviors, and I give you tips and tricks to master even the most difficult conversations.

Chapter 12

Conversations in Good Times

· ·

In This Chapter

▶ Using critical conversations to make the good times better

▶ Hiring and developing superstar employees

▶ Providing positive feedback

▶ Creating a conversation-ready organizational culture

· ·

*P*eople love communicating good news. Professional athletic coaches usually aren't that stressed doing a television interview when they're holding a championship trophy above their heads with the crowd cheering. Yes, communicating good news is a lot more fun than giving bad news. However, just because it's fun doesn't mean it's easy. Critical conversation skills can make good conversations great conversations. Using the critical conversation skills in good times makes the good times more likely to continue, especially when you're making hiring decisions and setting goals with employees.

In this chapter, I take a look at the positive side of critical conversations. First, you discover ways to hire superstars by using critical conversation tools. Then I help leaders find ways to accelerate the success of exceptional employees (say that three times fast!) with the critical conversation model. Coaching is a prime way to infuse positive critical conversations into the workplace, so I provide some information on utilizing this great tool. Next, I introduce ways to have critical conversations every day by using positive coaching models and proactive feedback tools. Because critical conversations are only as good as the environment that supports them, I close with ways to create a conversation-ready culture.

Using Critical Conversation Tools to Hire and Develop Superstars

Attracting great employees, developing them, and keeping them are the most likely ways to limit the number of problems in an organization (and to limit cause for subsequent difficult critical conversations). So what's the secret to success when it comes to hiring? Follow the critical conversation method, of course (you saw that coming!). In Chapters 1 and 4 I talk about the EDGE model (E: Examining what is happening; D: Deciding on resolution options; G: Get moving and see the results; and E: Evaluating the impact of the conversation). This model creates a perfect structure for critical conversations. You can use the same model when focusing on more positive conversations as well, like hiring superstars and developing current employees into future superstars.

Hiring the best

Let me back up a bit and walk through how some hiring decisions are made in organizations. First, a job position is open either because an employee left the job or the company is growing or changing. Second, the hiring manager looks for candidates to fill that job. Finally, after a number of interviews, a candidate is offered a job. Not a bad process, and for many organizations this process has worked just fine.

Changing up the hiring process

Think of the outcome if the hiring process operated a bit differently. A leader in a company *examines* how a team is performing and asks other leaders where there may be opportunities for growth and development of current employees. After *discussing* possible options, a team of leaders *decides* on what a great organization looks like and what jobs and roles should be in the organization. Next, the team *gets moving* with promoting employees, putting training and development opportunities in place, and finding the right candidates to fill any gaps the organization may have. Throughout the process, leaders can *evaluate* candidates and the process and make adjustments as needed. This method applies the components of the EDGE model for a critical conversation to the hiring process or for a specific role as well. For example:

- **Explore and examine options:** Find out what work needs to be done and who can do the work. Can current employees be promoted or does the organization need to look externally for the perfect match?

- **Make a decision:** This is where the interviewing takes place and the organization can find the right candidate to fill the position.

- **Gain commitment and get moving:** Once the decision to hire is made, it is time to get to work, make the offer, and get the employee up to speed in his new role.

- **Evaluate:** Once the hire is made, conduct a 30-, 60-, and 90-day review to make sure the new employee is feeling welcome.

During interviews you can look for candidates that have important critical conversation skills as well. If a candidate uses facts and data rather than opinions and rhetoric, you have a good indication that she has substance and is genuine. In fact, all the communication tools necessary to have a critical conversation are great skills to have throughout any organization. Chapters 6 and 7 focus on communication skills that benefit a critical conversation.

Asking interview questions differently

Not only can the hiring process benefit from critical conversation skills, the interview questions can too! Some interviews seem to reuse the same questions again and again and again. The manager asks about the candidate's experience, and then what she can bring to the job, and then her strengths and weaknesses. Yawn, yawn, yawn. If you look at the hiring process and the questions asked from this traditional method, it may not be a surprise that organizations don't always find the perfect employee. Luckily, with a few small adjustments, your typical interview questions will turbocharge the hiring process.

Consider adding a few critical conversation questions into the repertoire of interviewing questions. Here are some examples:

- **Tell me about a time you had to make a decision.** This question asks for data and facts, not rhetoric and opinions.

- **What were the options you explored?** Using the critical conversation model, find out whether the candidate looked at multiple options to solve a problem.

- **How did you decide what to do?** By asking this question, you can find out whether someone used a collaborative approach to decision-making or simply decided and announced what was happening. If your organization values collaboration, this is the type of decision-making you want to hear from a candidate.

- **What did you do?** Everyone wants to see results, and this question's answer demonstrates how the candidate performed.

- **How did you evaluate progress?** Just as you would do after a critical conversation, ask a job candidate how she looked back on an event and decided whether it was successful or not.

The tools most useful to critical conversations and to interviewing are expert verbal skills (Chapter 6) and nonverbal skills, like body language and active listening (Chapter 7).

Conducting an interview that uses the critical conversation questioning technique will help you find out how a candidate may think and act in different situations — that's preferable to hearing her repeat what's on her resume. By using this method for interviewing, you may just find that superstar a little more quickly.

Helping employees soar

To help employees deliver exceptional results, many leaders coach employees as they set goals, check progress along the way, and evaluate the results of their work. Whether you follow a more traditional annual process of employee reviews, or have a culture that's continually reviewing and assessing progress, using critical conversations can provide a consistent structure aimed at results. The performance management process fits perfectly into the last two components of the EDGE model for critical conversations:

✔ **Get moving with goal-setting:** Time to explore and examine options for goals and individual perspectives. Ask what employees want to accomplish and how these goals link into the goals of the company. Decide on the specifics by asking three key questions:

- What are you going to do?

- When are you going to do it?

- What support do you need to accomplish the goals?

These first two questions in the goal-setting process are great opportunities to create SMART action plans (see Chapter 4). These SMART action plans and goals have a clear definition and time line for follow-up because they are Specific, Measurable, Action-oriented, Realistic, and Time-bound.

✔ **Evaluating:** Encourage employees to get moving and then provide continuous feedback and evaluation about how they're doing. Throughout the performance-management process, a leader provides feedback, and the employee should highlight any red flags or changes to goals that come up as goals are accomplished.

When you're ready to start the check-in and evaluation process, Chapter 3 covers how to prepare to give feedback, and the next section of this chapter focuses on how to give feedback as a coach and mentor. For more on performance management, check out *Performance Appraisals & Phrases For Dummies*, by Ken Lloyd (Wiley).

 To use the critical conversation model, examine all the success and why it was successful (more on how to give feedback in Chapter 3), and then decide on next steps and future goals.

Using words that launch exceptional performance

Wouldn't it be nice if you had a list of questions you could ask that would let you discover superstars with exceptional performance potential? Of course it would be. And, yes, I have one for you. Using the critical conversation model, you can help create conversations that generate exceptional performance for your exceptional employees.

During regular meetings with your employees, devote at least half of the discussion to development and growth. Leave the other half for status updates.

To launch a discussion that helps employees excel at their job, start with these questions:

- ✓ **Examine possibilities:** To open up a world of possibilities, ask "What would be a new way of doing this?" Even the most ordinary tasks can be improved. Challenge employees to think of a new way of doing their jobs. Another key question could be "How would you like this to turn out?" Sometimes, working backward from where employees want to go is the best way to find out how to reach their goals. For example, if an employee wants a project she's passionate about to turn into a full-time position, what resources, skills, and leadership support would she need? It is also a good idea to ask what is working and what the individual should continue to do. Building on past success encourages future results.

- ✓ **Decide how to move forward:** After you establish goals, decide what to act on. The perfect question to ask is "How can I support you in achieving your goals?" or "What resources do you need to do your best?" When deciding what to do, even the most talented employees may need to acknowledge some constraints (such as budgets, project time line, or customer needs). Identifying constraints and support systems will put your superstars on the path to success.

- ✓ **Gain commitment and get moving:** Although most high performers don't need to be told to get moving and achieve results, closing the growth-and-development discussion with "Okay, now what's next?" is a great way to set an action plan into motion.

- ✓ **Evaluate success:** Employee and manager conversations that happen regularly are the perfect opportunity for continuous development. Asking a superstar employee "What did you learn and how can you apply that in the future?" may be all she needs to start thinking about ways to make the next challenge at work an even bigger success. Of course, even superstar employees can have setbacks. When that happens, as long as the employee recognizes that things didn't go as planned, ask "How can we set you up for success next time?" Most superstar employees don't need to be told that they made a mistake or didn't hit the mark — they usually know it and are ready to make it work the next time around. Asking how to set them up for success the next time will help them do so.

Coaching with Critical Conversations

Coaching is a developmental process designed to help individuals and teams achieve and sustain top performance in support of the organization's goals.

Coaches provide feedback and encourage discussion that can influence changes in behavior, performance, or even beliefs. Using coaching along with critical conversation methods can turn any positive dialogue into a five-star discussion.

Coaching in organizations isn't a time to show superiority. Starting with "I did it this way" or "I know what to do here" is training and lecturing, not coaching. Coaching starts with "This is what I liked about how you handled . . ." or "Is there anything you want to do differently next time?"

Mentoring is usually defined as an expert sharing information on how to do a task or role better, based on the mentor's experience. Coaches help improve performance by creating a dialogue of what could work — and the ideas could come from the recipient or the coach.

Using coaching methods

Coaching with critical conversation techniques can make your work relationships stronger and improve collaboration within a work group. Here are two ways to approach coaching:

✔ **Navigator of information:** In this case, the coach guides an employee through mountains of information and approaches to solving a problem. A navigator coach is like a search engine on the Internet. Imagine if you had to go through every possible website to find out how to lead business change or deliver a critical message to employees. You may be hunting for years! A coach would be able to direct you to the information that meets your needs in an efficient manner.

✔ **Giver of feedback:** Provide feedback on the areas the person being coached identifies. This identification is the difference between having a critical conversation to improve performance, behavior, or actions and using critical conversation skills to coach the growth and development of an individual. In coaching, the person being coached identifies what she wants to improve. In critical conversations, the manager or initiator usually identifies the areas of improvement.

Coaching gives you the opportunity to encourage an employee's ambitions or goals. During a regular critical conversation to improve performance, the initiator has a specific goal in mind for the conversation. On the other hand, during a coaching conversation, the person being coached can identify areas she wants to improve. Kick off this discussion by asking "What issues are you facing that have you stuck? What do you want to achieve through our discussion today?"

Even though the focus comes from different perspectives, the conversation and process still follow the same steps: examine what options are out there, decide what to do next, go and do it, and then evaluate how it went.

Coaching with critical conversations is different than a traditional manager-to-employee discussion, and even different than one-way feedback. Table 12-1 shows some of these differences.

Table 12-1	Managing Employees versus Coaching with Critical Conversations	
	Managing employees traditionally	*Coaching with critical conversation skills*
Solving problems	Manager tells employee what to do. Can control solutions and next steps	Coach explores & brainstorm options with employees, and together they create a plan of action.
Feedback	Manager lets an employee know what she did wrong or right.	Coach asks the employee what she felt she did well and what she would do differently.
Development and training	Manager informs employee of what she needs to improve. Focus on results and bottom-line fiscal improvement.	Coach encourages the employee to explore options for doing things differently; coach and employee reflect on the results and make adjustments.

A coaching conversation is a partnership, not a lecture. In a manager-to-employee discussion, the manager is usually in control and communicates to the employee. In a coaching conversation, the manager and employee engage in two-way conversation; you encourage the employee to share ideas, concerns, and experiences. The coach may share ideas to help steer a discussion, and the person being coached will process this information and apply it to her day-to-day work. For example, the coach may say, "Your way of handling customer complaints is a great strength. What do you think? How do you want to use this strength as you move into a leadership role in the company?" In this case, the coach helps guide the discussion. If the person being coached asks for feedback or ideas, the coach steps in to provide options for improvement or continued growth.

Although not all situations are right for coaching, you can see how coaching can create a positive partnership, rather than a hierarchical relationship.

Here are the two different approaches to conversation in action. Burt, the boss, just promoted Arnie, the employee, to be the head of compensation and benefits. Everyone is happy,at least for now. Burt walks into Arnie's new office and says, "Congratulations, Arnie," and then . . .

> **The approach: Managing the employee.** Burt says, "I would like to walk through your action plan for the next few months. As the manager, I would like you to make sure you do all the weekly employee reports and production reports. I would also like you to fill out this incentive compensation report 42 times between now and the next board meeting; you can find it on the shared drive. If you have any questions, let me know. Once again, congratulations on your promotion."

> **The approach: Coaching the employee with critical conversations.** Burt says, "I would like to spend some time exploring what you think needs to happen in this role." Arnie replies, "Thanks, Burt. I am so happy to have this opportunity. You know, I do have some ideas. Oscar was in this role for 20 years before he retired; he had some great methods, but there are a few things I'd like to do differently. I would love to share some ideas with you and get your feedback."

Asking Arnie what he wants to accomplish and how he wants to approach a problem generates a number of ideas and discussion opportunities. It also creates a partnership and a shared responsibility for getting things done.

Using the "management tells you what to do" strategy often does little to drive long-term performance. Can anyone expect others to embrace solutions and ideas if they had little or no input? On the other hand, a partnership, using critical conversation skills, opens up the flow of information and helps create ownership. The latter option is usually the preferred choice when an organization values innovation and teamwork.

You may notice a theme in the coaching model: the coach starts with exploring what's possible and the options available. This is the same first step of development in a successful critical conversation.

Finding coachable moments

Many of the examples in this book are those moments that are fairly big deals: landing a client, behavior that's stopping team productivity, and recurrent performance issues. When using critical conversations, however, the event doesn't need to be monumental — almost anything can be a coachable moment. *Coachable moments* are simply times when you observe a behavior or action and can either tie that action or behavior to consequences or potential growth. Here are some examples of coachable moments that can help keep a top performer motivated:

- **Coachable moment: Results.** An employee accomplished a task that helped the organization meet its goals. This moment is the most common for positive feedback. Keep the energy flowing by providing specific details on the outcomes and tying them to specific organizational goals. These coachable moments are great chances to link the big picture or the big organizational goals to the work that your high performers are doing every day.

- **Coachable moment: Innovation.** Did an employee use resources creatively or reengineer a process? If an organization values innovation, provide positive feedback when an employee creates a better and more effective way to do something.

- **Coachable moment: Commitment and motivation.** Although results are important, don't forget to provide feedback on the process and commitment an employee has to the organization. If the team came together to solve a tough issue during a tight deadline, thank the employees for showing commitment to the goals.

Finding coachable moments isn't just a tool to help employees keep performing like superstars; it's also a way to give attention and support to high performers. Often, the low performers can take the majority of your time and energy. Using critical conversations in a positive way makes sure you give high and low performers consistent guidance and input.

Making Everyday Conversations Count

Delivering tough messages in a critical conversation takes planning and organization. But if you want to avoid those tough conversations in the first place, it's the day-to-day conversations that matter most. Day-to-day discussions with employees and peers can solve many difficulties before they become problems that need a critical conversation and catch employees when they do something right.

Changing day-to-day talks into motivating moments

Everyday moments like a morning greeting or walking back to your office after a meeting can be moments for positive critical conversations. Simply add a specific example, why you thought it was positive, and then ask for the other person's perspective to turn a casual hello into a coachable moment.

For example, in the morning you may say, "Hi, John. I just wanted to let you know you handled that customer call perfectly yesterday. You kept calm and asked how you could help a number of times. I am so thrilled you are excelling in this role. How did you feel after the discussion?"

This simple hello has now opened the conversation and has reinforced desired behaviors. In this example, John now knows that asking a number of questions on how to help the customer is something he should repeat again. He also knows you feel he is doing well in his role. And finally, now John has the opportunity to talk about what went well and create a positive development opportunity, and even ask for feedback on another topic.

Using feedback to create results

Many people hear the word *feedback* and immediately think: oh no, I did something wrong. This view of feedback is just plain wrong. Feedback is a powerful tool employees can use with one another, managers can use with employees, and employees can use with their managers. But feedback must first be positioned as information an employee can use to develop. And it must also become part of everyday conversations. If you give feedback only when something goes wrong, well, yes, feedback will probably be seen as a negative event. However, if you can give feedback when things go right, well, you guessed it — feedback can create a productive and motivated workforce.

A mistake many managers make is providing positive feedback with little substance. Saying "good job" or sending an employee his favorite bottle of scotch for landing a dream client is nice. Really nice. But it does little to support ongoing development and continued success. Rewards and recognition are important, but when an employee does something great, make the connection between specific actions and how to replicate the success again in the future.

Using positive feedback to create results is just as important as giving developmental feedback when things go wrong. Luckily, feedback is feedback. To master the art of feedback, you can follow the same rules in any situation:

- ✔ **Rule #1: Always be specific.** Talk about tangible behaviors that the employee can control — not general feelings or impressions. Instead of just saying, "You built a good relationship with the client," say, "I see that you're always spending extra time to understand the client's needs." Another specific form of feedback is "I know many employees just e-mail clients or call them. I can see that you go the extra mile and make that professional connection face-to-face."

- ✔ **Rule #2: Draw connections.** Describing what happened as a result of the actions can help your employees repeat the specific action in the future. In the case of landing that dream client, the manager may tell the employee, "Visibly letting the client know you're there for them was a key part of us getting the contract."

- ✔ **Rule #3: Focus on the most important behaviors.** Even if your employee is perfect, to the extent that she can walk on water while juggling everything the client asks for, overloading the feedback can be overwhelming. Try to group the positive aspects into themes. Going into the smallest detail of everything an employee did right can dilute the message just as much as it does when giving an employee negative feedback.

- ✔ **Rule #4: Check for understanding.** Yes, of course people just love hearing how great they are — but as you close the conversation, give the most amazing employee in the world a chance to ask for clarification and respond with other ideas. Asking "Is there anything else you need from me?" can open the discussion for clarifying anything. Asking "Do you have any ideas about how we can spread this type of behavior out to the rest of the organization?" demonstrates that you value opinions and ideas, and that you have an understanding of the exact behavior that was simply awesome.

✔ **Rule #5: Make feedback a two-way street.** Even great employees may feel a bit awkward giving feedback to a boss or peer. When giving positive feedback, ask the other person whether she has any feedback you can use. And of course, if someone gives you feedback, go through the critical communication steps to create a plan to act on it! This two-way street creates a positive and open environment and mutual respect.

Opening Your Culture to Conversation

Organizational culture is simply the personality of the organization. But culture is perhaps one of the most complex challenges and greatest resources an organization has. Culture is seen, felt, and heard, and an organizational culture that supports critical conversations is as close as you may find to organizational Shangri-la.

Often organizational culture experts talk about norms, values, and artifacts when describing an organizational culture. But you have a much more straightforward way of looking at how cultures value conversation. Look at how knowledge is shared, what values employees have in common, how decisions are made, and what behavior is rewarded. These essentials are central parts of an organizational culture. All these elements can influence conversation skills.

If leaders can create a culture of conversation in the good times, handling tough situations or difficult news in the bad times becomes much easier. To create a culture that's open to critical conversations rather than one that's closed to any exchange of ideas or information, ask these questions (and note the ideal answers):

✔ **How is knowledge shared?** Information and knowledge, and how they're shared, influence a culture of communication. Are individuals slow to share information or only hoard it, or do individuals ask and provide information to help the team reach its goals? In a culture open to conversation, information is free flowing.

✔ **What values are shared?** In a conversation-ready culture, trust and honesty are encouraged, accepted, and rewarded. Employees and leaders in conversation-ready cultures open their doors to people if they have differing opinions or questions and give the attention they expect to receive.

✔ **How are decisions made?** In conversation-ready cultures, employees and leaders decide together. Although leadership may give constraints to what can and can't be done (especially when it comes to budgets and other resources), decision-making happens at all levels of the organization.

✔ **What behaviors are rewards?** Conversation-ready environments not only have a culture of rewarding what people say they will do, but also make sure everyone knows what type of behaviors will be rewarded. And these rewards are consistently applied. Conversation-ready environments expect and reward managers who spend time giving feedback to employees, and these cultures reward employees who listen and use the feedback to improve performance. Finally, rewards in conversation-ready environments value both what is done and how it is done. That means it isn't enough just to complete a project or meet the numbers. In conversation-ready environments, a project team is rewarded for completing the project under budget if the team also worked together and valued different opinions.

For more on how to change your organizational culture or create an even more open one, pick up a copy of the expertly written, *Leading Business Change for Dummies,* by yours truly and Terry H. Hildebrandt (Wiley).

Table 12-2 provides a quick reference of the conversation-resistant and conversation-ready cultures discussed in this chapter.

Table 12-2	Conversation-Resistant versus Conversation-Ready Cultures	
	Conversation-resistant cultures	*Conversation-ready cultures*
Knowledge	Information is stored as data.	Information is shared through discussion and supported with open technology.
Values	Values what work is done, like meeting sales targets or a project coming in on budget.	Values what is done and how it is done. Employees need to get the work done, and do so in a collaborative and genuine manner.
Rewards	Employees are rewarded for working their way up the ranks by doing what they are told to do.	People are rewarded for creating and discovering new ways of doing things.
Decisions	Decisions are made by leaders deciding and announcing a decision or by leaders gathering opinions and then deciding what to do.	Leaders work with teams to gather information before making a decision or let teams make decisions based on information.

Chapter 13

Conversations in Bad Times

. . . .

In This Chapter

▶ Giving effective feedback when performance is suffering

▶ Creating clear action plans to support the conversation

▶ Firing employees with compassion

. . . .

*W*hen an employee just isn't living up to expectations, you have two options: have a performance discussion to see whether the employee can improve, or decide to part ways if the situation is irresolvable. One option that you should steer clear of is ignoring the situation and hoping that it goes away or corrects itself.

In this chapter, you get the lowdown on how to let employees know that they're just not cutting it. I start at the most logical place to begin: preparing for the performance discussion. I then jump into how to make sure the conversation changes behaviors with a clear action plan. Although some conversations end with a turnaround in performance, some end with the employee and organization parting ways. To help you through this process, I give you ways to fire an employee with empathy and compassion. Finally, I touch on how to make sure everything stays confidential during a critical conversation.

Preparing for a Performance Conversation

To conduct a meaningful performance conversation, be prepared to explain why the conversation is happening in a clear way. State the purpose of the discussion to set the tone and focus, and briefly define why the conversation is important to the employee and the organization. The purpose portion of the conversation should include a compelling reason why performance is important to the organization and to their career. For example, you may balance how completing tasks leads to higher productivity in the organization, and completing tasks on time demonstrates the individual is valuable to the company and has career potential.

The key to a good performance conversation is to have the sender of the information be crystal clear on the message. To do this, ask yourself (the sender), "What message do I want to send to my employee and why?" Is it that the employee needs to be on time to work, or is it that when the employee comes into work late the rest of the team feels disrespected because the team is picking up the employee's work? Once you know the message and why the message needs to be delivered in a critical conversation, you can create an agenda that gets the message across clearly but with compassion.

The next preparation step is to define the desired outcomes in advance. During the critical conversation, both the initiator and the receiver of the information work on action plans (which I discuss in the later section, "Moving toward action") to change behaviors and work styles. But you don't need to come into the discussion with a completely blank sheet of paper when it comes to what you want to get out of the discussion. Write down the goals that *you* want to achieve. These goals could be focused on the conversation, like delivering feedback effectively, and overall performance goals, like improving an employee's performance in the next two weeks, making a team operate more effectively during the next project, or knowing that when work is given to an employee, it will get done. The goals that you come into the conversation with will be the benchmarks for the action plan that you create together during the discussion.

Having Conversations When Performance Is Suffering

Giving an unfavorable performance review is right up there with getting a cavity filled at the dentist. It's something you know you need to do but really wish you just didn't have to do. But just like that cavity, the quicker you get the performance review done, the quicker you can go on with your life. And, just like that nasty cavity, you really want it done the right way the first time so you don't have to go back again and again.

Before I show you how to do the conversation right, here's an example of a performance review that went horribly wrong:

> **Manager Maggie:** "Hi, Joe. Thanks for meeting with me. [The conversation then turns into 15 minutes of small talk or status updates.] So, Joe, I know it's been a while since we've had a meeting. I'm really sorry about that. [Nervous laughter.] But the real reason I asked for this meeting is to let you know that you aren't performing well. Your numbers are bad. I expect much more from a senior manager. I just need you to do a better job."
>
> **Joe:** "Okay. Yes, it has been a few months since we talked. I didn't expect the conversation to go like this. I didn't know my performance was that bad."
>
> **Maggie:** [Cutting Joe off.] "Don't you read your e-mail? I sent you your numbers last week."
>
> **Joe:** "Um, yes, but . . ."
>
> **Maggie:** [Cutting Joe off again.] "Well, listen, you need to improve it. Can you do that ASAP?"
>
> **Joe:** "Of course. I'll get right on it."

I always like to start a critique with the positive, so the positive part of the conversation is that Maggie had a conversation with Joe in the first place. Well, at least she scheduled it and kicked the conversation off. Unfortunately, Maggie fell into the trap that many managers fall into when they have to give a critical conversation around poor performance. They may have the intent to make a change, but managers tend to dance around the issues and never help the employee develop an action plan that creates better results. There is a better way to get results. Critical conversations can improve if you **e**xamine the facts, **d**ecide how to move forward, **g**ain commitment to get employees moving in the right productive direction, and then **e**valuate the performance after the conversation ends (the components of the EDGE model; see Chapter 4 for details).

Clarifying what's not working

During a critical conversation focused on performance, start with the facts and avoid dillydallying around the issue. Simply put the facts out there. In Chapter 4, I lay out how to use the EDGE method in critical conversations. Step 1 of the EDGE model is to examine the facts.

You don't need to dive into the conversation without any human interaction, but making excuses or being unclear about what the real problem is doesn't serve anyone. In fact, it can make everyone a bit more nervous.

Being held accountable

Holding employees accountable is a clear way to make all the parties in the conversation answerable to a common and clear definition of success. Sometimes employees aren't aware of their own roles or what effects their performance may have. Asking the following questions can help guide the agenda and message of a critical conversation, and may even help prevent a poor performance critical conversation in the future:

✔ **Does the employee have a defined role?** So many performance issues begin with employees having absolutely no idea what they're supposed to be doing. Make sure each employee has a clearly defined job description. You can't hold someone accountable for something he doesn't know he's responsible for doing. Give the employee the opportunity to ask for clarification about your expectations for the role.

✔ **Are expectations in writing?** You don't need to document every minute of an employee's day, but you should have a working plan or written job description for an employee. At the very least, write down and share with an employee the expected skills he should have and the competencies he should exhibit as he does his job.

✔ **Does the employee have clear consequences?** Consequences for doing or not doing the job need to be clear. No, don't threaten an employee's job the second he mistypes an e-mail or has a bad day, but let the employee know that if expectations aren't met within a certain time frame, you may need to consider whether he's the right fit for the job.

Giving clear and consistent feedback on how well an employee is performing is preferably done on a regular basis (biweekly or monthly is ideal). But even if you haven't been providing feedback on a regular basis, talk specifically about how the employee's performance is not meeting standards and expected outcomes. As you discuss the issues, state the facts in a clear and coherent way.

In Maggie's case, a better conversation may have gone like this:

> **Manager Maggie:** "Hi, Joe. Thanks for meeting with me. I know it's been a while since we've had a meeting, but I wanted us to start a conversation about your contributions to the team. I see by the numbers over the past few months that your performance has been decreasing. A specific and recent example is last week's sales numbers . . ."

In this case, even though Maggie hadn't been meeting with her employee, she talks about a trend in downward performance and then goes right into a relevant example.

Bringing up issues from months earlier can put an employee off guard. The employee may wonder why you didn't bring up the issue earlier. This is not to say you cannot bring up issues from the past, but, if you do, be aware it may put the employee off guard and potentially make the employee defensive or question why you were hiding this information for so long. To counter this reaction, start with the most recent examples and then say, "This may potentially be a trend. Four months ago I recall a similar example (and then state the example). I don't want to bring up things from so long ago, but I do want to make sure we can resolve any concerns so we can start focusing on the future."

Here are a few other situations in which you may find yourself. Use these tips to present negative feedback in a positive, fact-focused way:

- ✔ **When you don't have hard numbers:** "Last month you committed to doing and you did." This statement is an efficient way to introduce poor performance when you don't have any hard data like sales targets or customer service ratings. Use this statement when working with individuals who haven't met deadlines or who aren't doing what they say they'll do.

- ✔ **When performance disrupts a team environment:** "Our organizational goal for this year is. In the beginning of the year, we set your goal as. You're not on target to meet that goal." This setup is a good way to introduce goals and how they impact a team environment. If an employee's performance is just starting to go off track, making him aware of the consequences to the team and organization can help turn performance around.

- ✔ **When performance spirals downward quickly:** "Our minimum standard is. Based on the past month, you're performing below that. These are the benchmarks needed for your role." This is a constructive way of letting employees know that they need to focus on their individual performance or their job could be at risk. Don't threaten an employee with job loss. Simply put the information out there and let the employee know the expectations for his role.

Never come to a performance discussion reading a laundry list of poor performances. Imagine the employee's reaction if a manager started a conversation with "I'm not sure I've made your role on this team clear. Let's go over your job description and I'll rate your performance on a scale of 1 to 10 on each item." A leader has every right to have an opinion, but opinions need to be backed up with facts. Letting an employee know he's a 1 out of 10 on everything he's supposed to be doing is simply demoralizing. Keep the conversation focused on the most important areas to improve and the areas for which you have the most relevant facts.

Coming to the conversation with a genuine desire to help, even when performance is poor, can be hard. Sometimes you may be shocked by just how little an employee does or how much an employee expects from the organization with little in return. But this isn't the time for lecturing and finger pointing. A critical conversation is the time to present facts and then create action plans to turn around behavior.

Looking for options

Step 2 of the EDGE model (see Chapter 4) is to decide on options and find ways to move forward. Use the following questions as ways to prompt positive actions:

- ✔ **"What do you think about approaching the problem from this angle?"** Deciding on the plan of action may be hard for an employee who hasn't been stepping up to the plate. Giving him a few options to consider may help, especially if you'll accept only one or two ways of approaching an issue. For example, if a software engineer is not completing user testing on time, you may ask him to approach the issue from one of two angles, both which will help complete their action plan. You may say, "What do you think about working with the senior engineer to review the user testing plan or presenting your time line to the team in the next meeting?" You aren't trying to back the employee into a forced answer; you're simply giving him the two options he has to do his job.

- ✔ **"What have you tried in the past? What worked and what didn't?"** The best teacher is always experience. Even though an employee may be getting a less than stellar grade right now, chances are good that this employee once was successful at something. Try your best to find out what experience may have been successful in the past and then tie it to how the employee can improve his current performance. For example, if a team member is having trouble with the quality of work, you may ask, "Can we talk about a time when you were most satisfied with the quality of work you did on another project?"

- ✔ **"What is your first step? What is your next step?"** Critical conversations should create a culture of independence, not dependence. Balance between telling employees exactly what to do and letting them think for themselves. Asking about the first step and the step after that will help the employee start thinking of what he should do to improve his performance. You can do this most simply by asking, "What do you think is the first step?" and when the employee develops the first step, add in another question, "And what do you think should happen next?" And that's better for long-term success than just telling him what to do to improve his performance.

The "deciding what to do next" phase sets the stage for employee improvement to start happening right after the critical conversation. Setting goals that are specific, measurable, actionable, realistic, and time-bound (SMART; see Chapter 4) helps to reinforce the critical conversation message and gives an employee work he can immediately start accomplishing. Coming up with ideas for the action plan together, rather than having the employee create the plan alone or the manager handing over a detailed to-do list, also shows the support necessary to turn around performance. A critical conversation must end with a clear action plan if a positive change in behavior is expected to happen. With no action plan, the conversation may as well have been just a bunch of words.

Moving toward action

Time for action. Step 3 of the EDGE model (see Chapter 4) is to get moving. Put the action plan into place so the receiver of the information can get his performance back on track.

Although some critical conversations solve the problem then and there, performance issues aren't as easy or quick to solve. That doesn't mean you need to keep the critical conversation cycle going on forever — especially if you don't see results in the first few weeks. Action plans should include items that can be accomplished in the short term (within two weeks) and longer term (within four to six weeks).

Figure 13-1 shows what an action plan may look like with two-week, six-week, and twelve-week goals for a manager who isn't making the grade. Notice how all the items are specific, measurable, actionable, realistic, and time-bound, even when you don't have hard numbers to measure performance against.

2 weeks	6 weeks	12 weeks
• Develop a list of recommended metrics to measure team performance. • Develop plans to address concerns from employee satisfaction surveys. • Set up regular one-on-one meetings with staff.	• Begin tracking measurements for team improvement. • Meet with region partners to review goals. • Deploy at least three improvements that are tied back to the employee engagement survey.	• Track measures against goals, reviewed regularly. • Review employee engagement progress with regional director.

Figure 13-1: Two-week, six-week, and twelve-week action plans.

After you create and agree upon an action plan, you can further help an employee succeed by asking the following two questions:

✔ **"What are the barriers to accomplishing the goals on the action plan?"** Even the best intentions can get side-tracked by unexpected obstacles. Encourage poor performers to think about what to do if something gets in the way of being able to accomplish the goal. For example, ask your employee to think about where he could find information if his first source isn't available or doesn't have all the answers.

- ✓ **"How will you let me know if things are going well or if you need help removing additional barriers?"** This question is the perfect closing question after you develop SMART goals. Asking an employee how he will update you outside of these meetings puts responsibility in the hands of the employee. It makes the employee accountable for the success of the action plan and encourages him to speak up when he may have a problem. Also establish regular check-ins as status updates, but this question takes status updates to the next level.

Creating the action plan together is more effective than dictating the plan because the employee has contributed, feels valued, and is more likely to follow through with the plan. This collaboration also helps the manager understand the employee's perception of what is required to get the job done. This give-and-take discussion can result in new and better ideas. Plus, during follow-up coaching sessions, the manager can remind the employee of their contribution to the solution.

Assessing the conversation's impact

Critical conversations that generate positive results do more than just create healthy dialogue during the meeting — these conversations have immediate and lasting impact after the talking is done. Although this book is all about the conversation, the real change happens after the conversation ends. So now is the time to measure how marvelously the conversation went by using Step 4 of the EDGE model, evaluating the impact of the conversation. (See Chapter 4 for details on the EDGE model.)

After the initial critical conversation, schedule another meeting for two or three days later. That gives the employee time to think through the what he needs to deliver to be successful.

After these two conversations end, and the action plan is being carried out (Step 3 of EDGE: Get moving), check-ins with the employee (using an abbreviated critical conversation model) ensure that the conversation has a positive and lasting impact.

Regular check-ins assess the conversation and adjust course as necessary. Assessing progress along the way also gives managers an opportunity to reward improvement in real time. If an employee does want to turn around his performance and the critical conversation kicks off that turnaround, giving acknowledgement of the effort can go a long way toward making the new behaviors stick.

During the post–critical conversation assessments, look for three key things: an ability to do the job, willingness to improve, and improvement. The following sections take a deeper dive into each of these areas.

Ability

During the critical conversation, employees may agree to complete an action plan, but as the employee starts to work on the plan, it may become obvious to all parties that the poor performer simply doesn't have the ability to complete the task. Even when the desire to improve and the work ethic are solid, some tasks are just beyond an individual's ability or knowledge. If this scenario happens, you have two options:

- ✔ Give the employee training on the task that needs to be completed. Some of these skills gaps may have been highlighted in the action plan during the critical conversation, but others may not be known until the work gets underway.

- ✔ Stop the action plan and determine if there are tasks that the employee can complete. If an employee cannot complete the tasks necessary for the job, one option is to terminate (see how to fire employees with compassion later in this chapter). The other option is to try to find a job that the employee can do. If the employee is willing to improve, you may want to consider if there are other jobs in the organization the employee can perform. This may not always be an option, but doing so does show a genuine desire to help the employee rather than just firing them.

Willingness to improve

Willingness to improve and actual improvement are both needed to turn an employee's performance around, but the willingness to improve comes first. If, after the critical conversation, an employee does nothing on the action plan, be open and honest with the employee by saying, "What you said you would do and what you are doing don't match. What is going to happen differently in the next week?" Willingness to help is a commitment to making a difference. If an employee isn't willing to do whatever it takes to hit or exceed the goals, it may be time for the employee to find another job. (See "Firing Employees with Compassion" later in this chapter.)

Improvement

If the results are improving with time, and the employee is performing what he's capable of, you can almost guarantee that you aced that first critical conversation. Luckily, measuring improvement against a critical conversation action plan is one of the easiest parts of the conversation. Here are a few questions to ask as you evaluate progress after the critical conversation:

- ✔ "Were the tasks on the action plan completed?"

- ✔ "What is the progress?"

- ✔ "When will this action be finished?"

- ✔ "How can we keep the discussion going between now and next week to make sure the goals are accomplished?"

- ✔ You may also want to focus on how work will be different when the action plan is done by asking, "What will it feel like to have this completed? What's going to happen if you do not take this action?"

- ✔ You may follow up with asking the employee, "Were there any areas of concern when working through the plan?"

This list of questions opens up the critical conversation cycle again: Examine what happened, decide what to do next, and then get commitment to get moving. Here are the three questions critical conversations repeat again and again: "What happened?" "What are we going to do?" "How are you doing?" When performance goes off track, getting back to what happened and what is going to happen next quickly redirects performance.

Turning Poor Performers into Productive Performers

Don't miss out on a great opportunity for harnessing the positive energy of improved performance. Instead, use it to find ways to help the employee continually learn and develop. Yes, fix the problem of performance first, but don't end on a negative note.

To keep the discussion going, first make sure the employee knows this specific performance improvement is complete, and your intent with kicking off development is to help the employee excel in the future. Your job is to be more of a sounding board, rather than a manager of performance. During the performance improvement process, you may have taken a heavy hand in directing what needed to be done to help the employee get up to an expected level of performance. Now you can turn the tables and ask challenging and provocative questions, while you ask the employee to help focus the discussion.

After the employee has completed the initial action plans to improve performance, offer to sit down with him and find ways to help him develop in the future. This is where coaching fits in (head to Chapter 12 for more on how to coach with the critical conversation method). To help a once-poor performer to start thinking of what's possible now that his performance has improved, ask the following questions:

✔ "What opportunities exist for our organization that we haven't yet thought about? What opportunities exist for your career that you haven't yet explored?"

✔ "What changes could make a big impact on the organization? On your career?"

These questions show a leader's commitment to an employee who has successfully moved from being a bad apple to working his way up to the top of the tree. If the initial critical conversation did what it was supposed to do, the action plan will have created continued momentum toward getting the job done. With all the focus on an action plan, it can be refreshing to invite the employee to step back and see what's possible in the current role and in future roles, rather than jumping straight into action again and again.

Firing Employees with Compassion

It would be nice to think that critical conversations, followed up with action plans and evaluations, would turn even the worst performers on a team into at least good employees. Sadly, this isn't the case. Sometimes an employee doesn't have the ability or willingness to get the job done. If you take all appropriate steps to maintain an employee's employment, with no success, it may be time to part ways and move on.

Don't go it alone. Firing someone without working through an organization's human resources department and within the constraints of company policy is like taking a big cruise ship through the northern Atlantic Ocean and forgetting to watch out for icebergs. After you work with your HR department, use these critical conversation skills to make sure everyone walks away from the employee termination in one piece.

Why should you care about letting an employee leave with respect? Employees talk. Employees post things on the Internet. Employees talk more. Letting an employee leave with respect makes the final interaction with the company as positive as possible considering the circumstances.

Be professional and empathetic

Firing isn't fun. Being fired isn't fun. But you can fire someone with compassion. Even if you're trying to improve your reality TV show's ratings, simply dismissing an employee is rude. If all else fails and your human resources department supports the termination, stick to the facts and actions when going into the conversation.

Using the basics of the EDGE model, check out the following list to navigate your way through a firing critical conversation:

- **Examine the data:** The performer has not completed the action plan or continues to not meet the expectations of the job.

- **Develop options:** In this circumstance, developing options takes on a different meaning by informing how termination is the option that must be used.

- **Get moving:** Detail the termination process, what steps will happen next.

- **Evaluate the impact:** Find out how managers can learn from what led to the firing and perhaps how to spot potential performance issues earlier. Evaluation can also be personal reflection on how the critical conversation steps were used effectively.

Here are two examples of fact–action messages that help people leave with respect:

Fact: "John, four weeks ago we developed an action plan to improve your performance on the team. In every meeting we've had, we've discussed that none of the actions have been complete."

Action: "We've worked together to try to support you in achieving your goals, but because they haven't been met, I'm going to be terminating your employment. I'd like to use this meeting to walk you through the termination process."

Fact: "Janice, your sales performance hasn't met the expectations of our plan or of the team. After six weeks, your sales numbers continue to fall."

Action: "Based on these facts, it's time to terminate your employment. I want to assure you that I'll do everything I can to support you through this time and transition. I'd like to walk you through the process now."

Venting

Sure, employees need to let off steam sometimes. But, in the case of critical conversations, it's probably best not to have every detail divulged to other members of the company. Promote open communication, but tell employees that aspects of performance reviews or other important discussions should be kept confidential.

Although the termination may seem like just the final straw in a long series of conversations, it deserves as much attention and planning as all the previous conversations.

No apologies necessary

Try to resist the urge to apologize profusely or soften the message too much when you're firing someone. Saying "I'm sorry I have to let you go, I really don't want to do this," puts all the responsibility on you, rather than simply stating the fact that this is the action that's being taken because an employee's performance wasn't up to par (even after many attempts to help). Up to the point of firing an employee, a manager should take the time to create collaborative plans that inspire performance. When the decision is made to fire someone because of continued poor performance, the action shouldn't be a surprise. Simply state the facts and action clearly, and then move on to what's happening next.

Keeping It Close to the Chest: Confidentiality Is Critical

Confidentiality is an issue in almost every performance-focused critical conversation. This isn't just for legal reasons (although those are quite important too). Confidentiality during tough conversations helps to create an environment of trust between the receiver of the information and the initiator. At the start of any conversation, especially those dealing with difficult behavior, discuss and agree on what is and isn't confidential. If you plan on sharing any of the information with your boss or the human resources department, make sure the employee knows (and agrees to) it before information is shared. That way the receiver of the discussion doesn't feel that you went behind his back.

Questions you may want to pose, especially if a performance issue is large or the work an individual is performing impacts multiple departments, include:

✔ **"What information stays within the walls of the conversation?"** Both sides should agree on what should remain confidential.

✔ **"What information needs to be shared with others, such as the human resources department?"** Part of this answer may be dictated by company policy. For example, if your company has a policy to let HR know every time someone needs to improve his performance, it would be good to make sure everyone knows that policy exists.

Chapter 14

Dealing with Staff Disputes

●●

In This Chapter

▶ Figuring out what to do when employees don't get along

▶ Finding expert tactics for handling staff disputes

▶ Resolving five of the most common staff clashes

▶ Discovering how critical conversations reduce workplace stress

●●

*S*taff disputes need extra care — and that's where critical conversations come to the rescue. Staff disputes can cover anything from different personalities having to work together to employees who think their co-workers talk too loudly or are just plain obnoxious, and everything in between. This chapter looks at how to use critical conversations to help employees solve their own problems and how and when a facilitator should step in when a resolution doesn't seem to be anywhere in sight. I also discuss expert tactics for handling disagreements with the critical conversation model. And I give you examples of how to use critical conversations to resolve five of the biggest workplace disputes.

Getting Results When Employees Aren't Getting Along

So you thought you dropped off your screaming kids at school this morning and would get to spend the rest of the day with adults only to come into the office and find that your employees are having their own version of sibling rivalry. Different personalities at work will, at some time or another, lead to a staff dispute. Just like kids, sometimes employees need to work it out on their own. However, sometimes, a responsible adult needs to step in.

As the initiator of the conversation (also known as the responsible adult), your job is to know when to intervene and when to step aside. I can't give you a perfect formula for when you should step in and help diffuse — and perhaps even solve — the staff dispute and when you should let the employees work it out on their own.

But if the arguments are escalating and getting in the way of productivity, initiate a critical conversation.

Knowing how to step aside

Before jumping in, taking time away from valuable work, and having to play referee, it may be a good idea to ask the employees to solve problems themselves.

Asking employees to identify the type of conflict they're having is a great way to help encourage them to begin to solve the issue on their own. With a little guidance, by helping the employee identify the real problem, you can help set the scene for how to diffuse the issue.

Unnecessary conflicts

When an employee or co-worker starts complaining about another employee, use those active listening skills from Chapter 7, state your observation, and then ask the employee what she wants to do next. This is a good way to help coach the employee on how to solve the conflict.

Often mannerisms cause the most stress for people. For example, someone may not like the way another person dresses or talks, or even presents ideas in the meeting. Often this conflict is unnecessary and a complete time drain (Does it really matter that Mary happens to chew her gum a bit too loudly in the office?). However, this type of conflict is common and if it isn't handled directly, it will cause stress and productivity loss for those involved.

In each of these next examples, the manager takes two important steps by stating her observations and then asking the employee what she wants to do next:

> **Employee:** "Sally keeps talking too loudly on the phone."
>
> **Manager:** "Sounds like you and Sally may have different opinions about how to communicate. Why don't you talk with her and try to work something out?"
>
> **Employee:** "Billy is just so rude in meetings. He is just so annoying."
>
> **Manager:** "Sounds like you and Billy may have different ideas on how to work together in a meeting. Why don't you talk with him and try to work something out that you both agree with for next week's meeting?"

Employee: "Tommy can never keep his ideas to himself, can he? He's always jumping in and cutting off other people."

Manager: "Sounds like you and Tommy may have different ideas on how to present ideas to the team. Why don't you talk with him and try to work something out you both agree with for next week's meeting?"

Does this sound like a broken record? Yes. Why? Because the first step is asking employees to work it out themselves (by using critical conversations of course, so make sure you buy them a copy of this book). The one thing that was common in all the reactions, and is sometimes overlooked, is stating what's happening. In each example, the manager states what she heard to be the problem and then proposed an action to encourage the employee to solve the problem directly with the individual they are having the conflict.

The response from the manager always examines what's happening by stating the fact, and then making a recommendation on what to do next. Although the manager responded with a simple sentence, she's using a light treatment of the EDGE model by **e**xamining and **d**eciding. (See Chapter 4 for details on the EDGE model.)

Necessary conflicts

In the previous section's examples, the staff disputes weren't about content. They were about the mannerisms of another employee, not what work is done. So what happens when people disagree on the work that needs to get done? Ah, that's the beauty of critical conversations. The same model can be applied again and again.

Note the manager's responses in the following two examples:

Employee: "Sally doesn't agree on the time line for the project."

Manager: "Sounds like you and Sally may have different opinions about what resources the project needs. Why don't you talk with her and try to map out the different resources you both think are needed for the project and collaborate on a project plan?"

Employee: "Tommy doesn't seem to agree on the problem statement."

Manager: "Sounds like you and Tommy may have different ideas on what you're trying to solve. Do you both agree there is a problem?"

Employee: "Yes, we do."

Manager: "Great. Why don't you try to agree on why the problem exists and then go back to working on the problem statement?"

You may notice that the manager seems a bit less like a recorder when the dispute focuses on content. Before stepping aside to let the parties resolve the situation on their own, you can help by pinpointing the source of the problem. Content disputes can often be resolved once the source of the problem is identified.

Realizing when to intervene

When your staff is in the midst of a dispute, intervene for any of these three reasons: when issues are being ignored, when working it out on their own doesn't solve the problem, and when you have a safety or danger concern.

Issues are being ignored

Sometimes, employees really don't feel comfortable addressing a staff dispute. You may sense this in their body language or tone of voice, or you may notice that they simply avoid at all costs the conversation that needs to happen. If you see this discomfort, offer to step in as a facilitator to get the discussion and agreements on the right track. If team members are so angry or upset that they can't focus on tasks, having a critical conversation will make great strides in getting a team back on track. Chapter 3 gives you all the guidelines for facilitating a critical conversation like a pro.

If you do agree to facilitate a discussion, let all the parties know that you're happy to fill this role to resolve an issue and that you'd also be happy to help teach each of the parties how do it on their own in the future.

The goal of intervening when you see a problem is helping others to resolve the problem *and* helping others discover how to resolve their own issues in the future. Jumping in to help is fine, but being a permanent lifeboat isn't.

Working it out isn't working

If an issue has gotten so far out of control or if it's been there for so long, a facilitator can calm all the parties involved so the issue can be resolved once and for all. Whether the issue is focused on content or mannerisms, step in only when all parties have tried to work it out in the past and everyone understands your role is as a facilitator, rather than the person with the right answer. (Of course you can step in earlier if you're asked for help directly; see the previous section for details.)

While you can be both a facilitator and leader, the two roles are different. A facilitator is the process chauffeur, so to speak, the individual who protects ideas and helps steer the process. On the other hand, a leader is the individual who can direct the content within a conversation or discussion and make decisions about next steps. Be clear which role you're playing so all parties have clear expectations.

Safety is an issue

There are two types of safety concerns: one that is inherent to the job, like wearing safety goggles when working with chemicals or machinery, and one that stems from concerns about workplace violence. Workplace violence concerns need to immediately be raised to emergency professionals, no critical conversation needed. However, when someone is breaking a safety policy of the company, a critical conversation may help the individual understand the importance of following the rules. Two approaches to asking people to follow policy are to tell them they have to do it, which often lasts about one or two weeks until they go back to their old behaviors, or approach it as a critical conversation to make sure all parties understand the importance of the issue and how to resolve it in the future. I would recommend the latter.

 If you have a safety concern or dangerous situation, follow your company policy on violence in the workplace or get emergency professionals involved right away. No critical conversation can or should resolve violent behavior or threats, period.

Getting Expert Tactics for Handling Staff Disputes

When you step in to help resolve a staff conflict, you have three goals for the process: resolve the conflict, make the conversation positive for all parties, and help teach all the parties how to resolve the conflict on their own in the future.

Yes, these are some pretty lofty goals, but consider for a minute the alternatives. If the conflict isn't resolved, the emotional drain will continue and the time spent trying to resolve the issue may be seen as wasted time. If all parties don't walk away from the conversation feeling positive about the result, one party may feel like they lost or both parties may feel like they compromised too much, and the conflict will start all over again. When people walk away from a critical conversation, they need to feel respected and valued. Finally, if you always solve employee's problems, you (or another responsible adult) may always need to spend time fixing their problems. With all those alternatives in mind, the three goals seem like pretty good options.

Using five steps to resolve conflict

Like any good critical conversation, this conversation should follow a common process: examine the issue, options, and ideas; decide on solutions; and then get moving and evaluate the results of the conversation. During staff disputes, the parties involved often need to spend more time appreciating others' points of view. Although appreciating others' feelings is part of other critical conversations, when you're dealing with conflict, this step can't be ignored or hidden within other agreements during conflict resolution. The five steps you need to follow are highlighted in Figure 14-1.

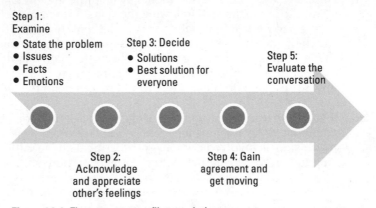

Step 1:
Examine
● State the problem
● Issues
● Facts
● Emotions

Step 3: Decide
● Solutions
● Best solution for everyone

Step 5:
Evaluate the conversation

Step 2:
Acknowledge and appreciate other's feelings

Step 4: Gain agreement and get moving

Figure 14-1: Five steps to conflict resolution.

Here's how the five steps break down:

1. **Examine and identify the source or root cause of the conflict.** As the discussion begins, clearly state your reason for the meeting. Stating the purpose of the discussion helps set the tone for the rest of the conversation. Additionally, all the parties may be able to reduce some of the stress of the conversation by stating how they feel to one another. Just getting things off your chest can take away some of the pressure and stress, as long as it's done in a professional manner. Stating your own feeling is also a more neutral way to begin the conversation.

   During staff disputes, stating "I feel" in the beginning helps to frame the critical conversation in a constructive tone, instead of being accusatory. Right after stating your own feelings, use an objective, non-confrontational statement to state why you feel this way. Just as in other critical conversations, this links a fact (what the other person is doing or saying), to a consequence (how it is making you feel).

   While you're clarifying how you feel and why you feel that way, keep the following tips in mind:

- Always use a friendly, polite tone. Even if there are water-works in the room or someone is yelling or swearing like a sailor, stay professional.

- Keep your emotional statements short and to the point. Going on and on about how you're just so confused or how your dog died just muddies the water. Be clear and concise.

2. **Appreciate the other person's point of view.** Often, conflict arises when people feel that their feelings and ideas aren't being heard. Whether you're the facilitator, initiator, or a party having the critical conversation, when parties disagree, that disagreement is often tied to another person's ego. If no one is acknowledging how other people feel during the conversation, the quality of the critical conversation and the results of the conversation most likely are going to be poor. By appreciating another person's point of view, you're legitimizing that what you see or hear has value. "I hear your complaint," or, "I can understand why you may feel betrayed," acknowledges that the individual's feeling is real. Note that appreciating another party's point of view and agreeing with it aren't the same thing.

   Before moving on to the next step, ask whether everyone is willing to work together to resolve the issue. This question may seem obvious (who's going to say no?), but gaining this agreement before diving into solutions creates a mutual agreement in even the most hostile environments. Think of this mutual agreement as a baby step toward solving the problem.

3. **Decide on possible solutions and then decide on the solution most acceptable to everyone.** If a staff dispute is out of control or if the parties have significant disagreements that may never be fully resolved, an alternative to 100 percent agreement is 100 percent acceptance. Although the conversation may not end with everyone going off into the sunset and working happily ever after together, the conflict can end with all parties being able to live with and support the decision and next steps. If the conversation is about an employee talking loudly on their cellphone (even for work purposes), the conversations may never stop, but all parties may agree to live with having cellphone conversations in a designated area.

4. **Gain commitment to get moving.** When you're resolving conflict, especially staff conflict, action needs to be quick after the conversation ends. Because most staff conflicts are based on emotions, you want to see an immediate change (within 24 to 48 hours) in behavior. If you don't see change that quickly, the parties in the conversation may start wondering if change will ever happen, which can start an entirely new set of emotions and conflict in the workplace.

If actions need to take place, put together an action plan (see more on action plans in Chapter 11) to make sure the decisions made during the conversation happen.

5. **Evaluate results after the conversation.** Evaluating the results of whether or not Sally and Jim like each other more or can agree to work together may not be as clear as asking an employee to improve sales performance or client retention, but it can and should be done. Simply say, "Let's check in next week and see how these decisions are working," and then check in a week later.

Starting with facts and feelings

When you're describing personal feelings, always start with "I" to make it clear that you're describing your own perspective. Try to avoid using a critical "you"; instead, ask a question or pose a statement that helps resolve how you're feeling.

Here are a few examples of how to express both fact and opinion when kicking off a critical conversation:

✔ When you feel frustrated when a discussion continues to go round and round without any resolution, you may say: "I feel frustrated. I understand that we've been talking about this issue for a few months now, but I'm still unclear about how we're solving the quality problem in the future."

✔ Emotions often focus on expressing personal opinions and ideas that aren't being heard. If this is the case, you may start with: "I feel undervalued when my opinions are not part of the discussion."

Of course there are wrong ways to express emotions during a critical conversation, so to avoid those, here are some ideas on how to revise what first comes into your head so you remain calm during the discussion:

Instead of saying: "I can't believe you need so much handholding!"

You may say: "I feel exhausted from having the same discussion about our project. It seems like we end up having two meetings to discuss ideas, one with the team during the weekly web meeting, and another face-to-face when we see one another the next day."

Instead of saying: "You are annoying."

You may say: "I feel anxious when we go into client meetings together. I think we have different communication styles. I have noticed you tend to talk loudly when you're passionate about a subject, and I think our client has a more reserved communication style."

Instead of saying, "You smell bad."

You may say: "I feel uncomfortable telling you this, but I think I may be a bit sensitive to your perfume or lotion."

Turning a conflict into a positive experience

Making the critical conversation a positive experience for everyone involved makes great strides in keeping the team productive. Critical conversations are both an art and a science. The science is following the steps of the EDGE model (see Chapter 4): **ex**amining what's happening, **d**eciding on the next steps, and then **g**aining commitment and getting moving and **e**valuating the success. The art is finding the most effective way to get information and using the information to make productive and positive change. The art of conversations during conflict takes time to perfect, but the benefits are tremendous.

Here are some do's and don'ts when making the critical conversation a positive experience for everyone:

- ✔ **Do** remain patient and relaxed. Be patient and try not to interrupt someone midsentence or midthought. Unless the other party is going on and on about information that isn't relevant, let everyone speak their minds. A facilitator can help make sure all ideas are heard; if you don't have a facilitator in the meeting, pause before stating a comment or asking a question.

- ✔ **Don't** assume silence is a bad thing. Give the other parties in the conversation time to listen and respond to questions.

- ✔ **Do** use neutral questions and speak for yourself. Use "I" statements and facts to probe for the root of the problem. Say something like, "I feel you are ignoring my recommendations on the project. I have given a number of ideas on how to improve our quality, but none of them have been discussed at team meetings."

- ✔ **Do** give space to other parties when negative emotions arise during the conversation. If a person is angry or unresponsive, acknowledge the feelings in the room and either come back to the issue at another time or try to get all parties to agree to work together to resolve the issue. You may say, "I hear you're raising your voice when we talk about the issue. Do you want to take a break before we continue the conversation?" Or, "I hear you're raising your voice when we talk about the issue. Can you and I agree to work together before we try to solve the problem?"

- ✔ **Do** acknowledge how the other parties may be feeling. But **don't** say you know how the other parties feel. Saying, "I can understand why you might be angry about the project being delayed," shows empathy. Saying, "I know you're upset about how the project is intruding on your other responsibilities," makes you seem like you know it all, which isn't a good position to be seen in during conflict.

✔ **Don't** get angry, irritated, or annoyed. Even if the other individual is irate, try to remain neutral. If anger and other negative emotions aren't returned, the behavior tends to diffuse itself.

✔ **Don't** give unsolicited advice. After reading this book, you may know exactly what the other party should be doing or needs to do. Even with the best of intentions, saying, "I can see you're ready to rip up my *Critical Conversations For Dummies* book, but you really need to think about how to present facts and work on a mutually positive outcome," will most likely be met with negative feelings (and the book flying across the room). Instead, state how you feel and end it there. In this case, it may be better to say, "I see you're upset with my comments. Are you willing to work together to find a positive outcome?" You aren't in the conversation to solve the problem *by yourself.* All parties need to work together to resolve the issue at hand.

Talking today to solve tomorrow

A critical conversation takes people through agreements to solve the current dispute; those same agreements can be a reboot button for how the parties work together in the future. Use the following four questions to gain agreement regarding how to fix the dispute, and then use them again to resolve any future obstacles:

✔ **"What are the problems, and why do they exist?"** Solving a problem before the problem is defined is often quite hard. In the examination phase of a critical conversation, the parties discuss opinions, facts, and ideas. Approaching problems with the facts rather than accusatory opinion is a great way to kick off solving any problem in the future. *Use in step: Examine and identify the source or root cause of the conflict.*

✔ **"Is everyone willing to work together?"** Before jumping into problems and solutions, everyone needs to agree to be in the same room and talk. During a staff conflict, this could be the first time the parties agree on anything; going forward, this agreement is a great way to unite everyone toward one goal. *Use in step: Appreciate and acknowledge the other person's point of view.*

✔ **"What potential solutions will resolve the problem?"** During the deciding phase of a critical conversation, solutions are discussed and agreed on to fix the dispute. In future problem-solving discussions on a team or one-on-one, use the same process to identify all possible solutions before deciding on which solution is the best. *Use in step: Decide on possible solutions and then decide on the solution most acceptable to everyone.*

✔ **"Is everyone willing to support the decision?"** In a critical conversation, there may not be one solution that creates world peace. Because you need collaboration, ask the staff members whether they can support and live with the outcome. To use this to avoid conflict in the future, during future team discussions, rather than simply asking whether everyone agrees with a solution, ask whether everyone can (and will) support it. Agreement is easy to say and then ignore after the conversation is done; living with something and supporting it makes the solution more likely to stick in the long term. *Use in step: Gain commitment and get moving.*

Resolving the Five Biggest Staff Disputes

I can only scratch the tip of the iceberg with all the possible staff disputes that could happen in the workplace. Because this book doesn't have enough pages for me to list every issue I've seen, researched, or experienced, these five big disputes — and how to solve them — give you a well-rounded look at organizational dysfunction. Don't forget to check out other examples in the book as you tackle those critical conversations for performance management (see Chapter 13), workforce complaints (see Chapter 15), and difficult behaviors (see Chapter 16).

Fight or flight — or a critical conversation

Conflict can make people feel anxious, stressed, and frustrated that the situation is out of their control. Biologists know a thing or two about stress, and it's not just because they're hanging out with rats and germs all day. Biologists have long known that organisms under stress will take actions to get out of the stressful situation. Many behavioral psychologists refer to the same fight-or-flight reaction when discussing how a lot of animals deal with stress; fight-or-flight reactions mean that under stress, animals either attack the source of stress or run away from it.

Employees and organizations react similarly. Although humans still have that fight-or-flight genetic makeup, as a species we have refined these responses to gossiping, ignoring, yelling, juvenile quarreling, sarcasm, bickering, and on and on. Critical conversations introduce new ways to eliminate stress in the workplace. You don't have to fight, and you don't have to run. Just share information and feelings and acknowledge how people feel.

Ending offensive comments from a co-worker

Even in the most professional workplaces, employees can tell jokes or make rude comments that cross the line from bad taste and poor judgment to offensive behavior that could be seen as harassment. Chapter 15 talks about harassment claims in the workforce, but my goal is to help you stop the offensive behavior before it gets to the level of a legal complaint.

What is an offensive behavior? Offensive comments in the workplace include (but aren't limited to) name-calling, swearing, gossiping, and being argumentative with the sole intention of starting an argument.

Whatever the offensive comments, the tactics shown in the following example can help put an end to them.

> **Adam, the offensive employee:** "Hey, Little Miss, how was that board meeting last week?"
>
> **"Little Miss" Linda:** "Adam, I'm happy we're good colleagues and team members. However, referring to me as 'Little Miss' makes me feel like we don't have mutual respect for one another, and I feel it's condescending. I'd like to ask you to call me by my name so we can remain professional and respectful. Can you begin calling me by my first name?"
>
> **Adam:** "I didn't realize you were offended by the comment. I thought I was being cute. I will use your name from now on."
>
> **Linda:** "Thanks for understanding."

Linda followed the components of critical conversations perfectly. First, she examined the situation by starting with how she felt ("Referring to me as 'Little Miss' makes me feel like we don't have mutual respect"). Second, she helped direct a decision that could resolve the conflict ("I'd like to ask you to call me by my name so we can remain professional and respectful"). And third, she asked whether her colleague could support the recommendation she made as they gained agreement to move forward ("Can you begin calling me by my first name?").

Dealing with an obnoxious co-worker

Obnoxious co-workers somehow find their way into many workplaces. A co-worker blasting her iPod, slamming drawers or doors, never replacing supplies in the common area, talking loudly on the phone, "forgetting" to give credit to team members that do the work, or simply ignoring what other team members say . . . these are just a few of the obnoxious behaviors I heard about before lunch today. These types of co-workers usually are behaving unattractively for one of two reasons. They may be completely oblivious to their own behavior. I call these "blind spots," and even the best employees have them. Or they may not realize how their behavior impacts others. Regardless of why they act the way they do, a critical conversation can stop the behavior and perhaps stop other obnoxious behavior in the future.

Here is a positive and professional way to help resolve conflict with an obnoxious co-worker.

> **Jane:** "George, I find your loud music is disruptive to my concentration. Are you willing to talk about how we both can be productive?"
>
> **Obnoxious co-worker George listening to his music on the highest setting:** "That music must be in your imagination — my music is on my headphones. I would never think of being obnoxious."
>
> **Jane:** "I understand you like your music at work, and I understand how you may think the music is at a low volume. Are you willing to work with me to find a volume that allows everyone to be productive at work?"

Now George has the option of saying yes or no. If he says no, Jane may have a valid workplace complaint that she needs to bring to a manager's attention. However, if George has any common sense, he will probably say yes, and then George and Jane can begin to brainstorm solutions and come to a mutual agreement.

Jane mastered the critical conversation elements in this discussion. First, she examined and presented the problem without threat or negative tone. George really may have a genuine lack of understanding of what makes a respectful workplace, and with Jane's help, he can see how a workplace needs to work for everyone. Second, Jane helped decide what to do next by making a recommendation to change behavior that would work for everyone. And third, she asked whether George would be willing to work together to create a solution (appreciate and acknowledge feelings) and get moving forward. This trifecta of critical conversation talking points avoids an autocrat "I'll tell you what to do . . ." and creates solutions everyone can live with and support in the future.

Putting away grudges

Putting away anger or pride is never easy, but settling a grudge, whether you have it or someone else has it against you, will make for a better workplace, even if it means putting ego aside. Of course, critical conversations can help (but you knew that already, right?).

Simply examine and present the problem without threats or negativity, make a recommendation to help decide on next steps while acknowledging the other persons feelings, and gain agreement on how to get moving forward.

Suppose your boss decides to buy an island in the middle of nowhere. The $20 million price tag on the island is a bit of a hit to his checking account, so the boss decides to cut all bonuses for his employees for the next 100 years. Some of the employees (okay, all of the employees) are a bit mad and are holding on to some pretty strong grudges. If a critical conversation can solve this one, a critical conversation can probably solve just about anything.

> **Cameron, the employee, during a one-on-one meeting with the boss:** "Dennis, I'm still feeling angry about your decision last year to cut bonuses. I know we can't go back in time, but I'd like to be able to move on and make our relationship and company stronger."
>
> **The boss, Dennis:** "I had no idea you felt so strongly."
>
> **Cameron:** "I want to be up front about what I want from this conversation. It would be nice to find a way to reinstate the bonuses in the future. Are you willing to work together to find a solution?"
>
> **Dennis:** "Well, we just don't have the funds now."
>
> **Cameron:** "I understand that we're under financial pressure. Are you willing to work toward a solution all employees can live with?"
>
> **Dennis:** "Of course. I didn't realize this had such a negative impact on the company."

Now Dennis and Cameron can have a discussion about solutions to truly dropping the grudge and moving forward. Although it may be hard to put your feelings out there as honestly as Cameron does in this conversation, if you truly want to resolve the grudge, both parties have to be willing to put everything out on the table. Because grudges by definition have been going on for a while, coming to the conversation with a genuine desire to help make the situation better and being clear about intentions helps everyone to forgive and forget.

If either party doesn't want to work together, the only option for resolution is for the initiator of the conversation to move on and let go of the grudge. No critical conversation can force another person to change — the conversation can only create an environment that makes change likely and possible.

Handling waterworks in the office

When an individual gets a bad review, is under stress, or is dealing with personal issues, one reaction may be crying in the workplace. Many people perceive crying as a weakness, when it's really just a reaction, much like anger, sarcasm, or silence. However, if you tend to react differently, seeing someone cry in the office may catch you off guard.

What is an expert communicator to do? First and foremost, try to keep the crying in perspective, and don't judge the other person. Second, if the person isn't already in a private office when the crying starts, offer to go to one right away. The next step is to get the critical conversation going as soon as possible to help manage emotions. Many managers either quickly back down from a comment that made the other person cry or just do whatever it takes to make the crying stop. Neither of these options is a long-term solution. Use the critical conversation method to get to the real problem and allow everyone to maintain dignity.

During a critical conversation about poor performance, Alex starts to cry. Having just read *Critical Conversations For Dummies,* manager Maggie refocuses the conversation.

> **Maggie:** "I can see that you're upset about the feedback. I've found that everyone reacts differently to performance reviews. Would you like some time to yourself?"
>
> **Alex:** "No, just a tissue. I just can't believe I'm doing so poorly. I can't lose my job. My kids are in college, my mom is sick, and I have a mortgage."
>
> **Maggie (after a short pause):** "I can understand how you'd feel overwhelmed by everything going on in your life. My goal is to help you excel at your job, not to fire you. I've found that having a clear action plan makes doing a great job easier when you're trying to fulfill many responsibilities. Are you willing to continue the conversation now and find ways to boost your performance?"

At this time, Maggie and Alex can agree to continue the discussion, or, if needed, postpone it. Crying is no different from any other reaction employees may have during a critical conversation or leading up to one. State the problem or situation, acknowledge and appreciate other's feelings, and then decide what to do next (in this case, either work on the performance feedback or postpone the meeting).

Note that Maggie didn't apologize for Alex's feelings or back down from the issue they were originally discussing. And she kept the conversation going in a humane and respectful way. Critical conversations allow everyone to have feelings and express their feelings, but still get work done. Marvelous, if I may say so. Of course, I'm not saying that critical conversations can solve world hunger or create world peace, but they could get the conversation started.

Discussing differing values and personal styles

It's a fairly well-accepted fact that people have different views on what is and isn't right. These views permeate through what you say, how you act, what you wear, and nearly everything else that happens from the time the alarm clock rings until bedtime. You and your staff are likely to have different opinions on what's right and what's wrong in the workplace. Luckily, company policies can help dictate appropriate behavior and dress code, but when the policy's line is blurry, a critical conversation can clear up the difference.

To help any workplace value diversity more effectively, teach employees to value differences and better understand their own communication, conflict, and leadership styles and the impact of their styles. Although leadership assessments and trainings that help to increase self-awareness and emotional intelligence are a great ways to make meaningful change, the conversation about these activities can start with a critical conversation. For more on Emotional Intelligence, check out *Emotional Intelligence For Dummies* by Steven Stein (Wiley).

Here's how the conversation may start:

> **Manager Max:** "I think diversity is the best way to generate new ideas. Over the past few months, I feel there have been a number of conflicts and differences in opinions within our team that seem to be inhibiting innovation rather than helping it. Do I have your commitment to work together to find out what's happening and then try to resolve it?"

Now Max can introduce training, assessments, or a group activity that can create a better understanding of differences with the team's support.

Chapter 15

Identifying and Working through Workplace Complaints

In This Chapter

▶ Resolving workplace complaints

▶ Recognizing when critical conversations aren't the best option

▶ Evaluating when an outside mediator can help

▶ Becoming familiar with special workplace and ethical concerns

*A*lmost every manager has an employee who voices a concern about behaviors or actions in the workplace. These concerns aren't just personality differences or performance matters (see Chapter 13 and 16 for those); these concerns are workplace complaints that could potentially lead to legal or ethical problems.

Don't take these concerns lightly. A critical conversation isn't the only tool you need to solve them, but the critical conversation approach can help you through these problems. If you hear about a workplace concern, or if you have one you need to voice to a leader in your company, the recommendations in this chapter can help.

This chapter defines what a workplace complaint is, and what to do when you hear or have one. I present ideas on how to address the complaint and how (and when) to involve human resources or other outside professional mediators. Because workplace concerns aren't limited to the nonmanagement ranks, I also discuss what to do when you have a legitimate complaint about a leader in the company. Although these kinds of workplace concerns are often considered from a legal point of view, they can be seen as ethical concerns as well. Ethics is a big topic in today's corporate culture, so I cover ethical concerns from two angles: cultural differences that can be perceived as ethical issues and the difference between ethical and legal concerns. Finally, I cover two important aspects of conversations that address workplace complaints: how to maintain confidentiality and how to move forward after the issue is resolved.

This chapter doesn't replace the need for legal counsel, working with your internal human resources department, or involving government agencies that safeguard workers' rights. Using critical conversations can help focus the discussion, but they don't replace the need for legal expertise.

Addressing Workplace Complaints

When considering whether or not to use a critical conversation to rectify a workplace complaint, there are three things to take into consideration.

First, for how long has the issue been present? If the issue has been going on for some time, even if it has just recently surfaced, heading to HR to help resolve the complaint may be a better option. However, if the workplace complaint is new, a critical conversation can help make the employee aware of the behavior and change it.

The second consideration is the severity and risk of the workplace complaint. If a workplace complaint is about an employee using foul language, a critical conversation can help turn the behavior around. However, if the employee is making employees feel threatened, unable to work, or putting them under extreme stress, the first step should be working with HR.

Finally, if an employee breaks the law, most organizations have steps in place to handle legal concerns, and a critical conversation should not take the place of a legal discussion. If a workplace complaint involves discrimination in the workplace or other violations of the law, work with your human resources team to keep things legal.

Defining a workplace complaint

A workplace complaint is a problem that disrupts the productivity of employees. Workplace complaints can range from the temperature of conference rooms or the noise level in an office, to harassment or legal concerns. In the next two sections, I walk through some of the more common issues that need to go directly to the legal or HR team and other concerns that may be able to be resolved with a critical conversation.

Legal concerns shouldn't be taken lightly, but sometimes it's difficult to tell the difference between a legal concern and a staff dispute or personality difference. The steps during a critical conversation can help managers and employees, as well as HR teams and, if needed, legal or outside mediators, find out what's really happening.

Figuring out when critical conversations aren't enough

Critical conversations aren't the only tool you need to work through workplace concerns. I'll say it: Critical conversations sometimes aren't enough (my fingers just hurt typing those words). A conversation isn't going to fix a legal issue. Verbal and nonverbal cues in a critical conversation can help steer discussions, but if someone is breaking the law, or potentially breaking the law, you can be charged with a violation if you do nothing or if you don't follow the appropriate regulation or law.

I don't want to scare you into referring everything to the human resources or employee relations departments, but if you're unsure of or find yourself questioning what to do next, ask. That's always better than finding out later that you didn't do enough. Here are some of the most common workplace complaints that should not rely on a critical conversation:

- ✔ **Breaking the law:** If the name "Enron" rings a bell, it should, because it sent an alarm through corporate America. Break the law, and the company could disappear almost overnight. Whether you have an employee stealing from the company, or an entire company being made up on a balance sheet, concerns about breaking the law should sound the alarms.

- ✔ **Discrimination:** It's next to impossible for any professional outside of the legal profession to know every regulation that governs the workplace, but most boil down to not treating employees fairly. Treating employees equally — from the hiring process to the termination process — is covered by workplace regulations. If you don't follow those regulations properly, it could be considered illegal.

 It's good to handle an initial discrimination discussion with a critical conversation, but when someone says he feels that he's been discriminated against, convey this information to the legal or human resources department immediately to make sure you're doing what's legally required to find out the truth.

- ✔ **Workers' compensation benefits:** In the U.S., if an employee is hurt on the job, the specific states regulate what the company must do and what a company can't do. These regulations vary widely state by state, but if someone is hurt on the job and complains that he wasn't treated fairly, alert human resources immediately.

✔ **Personal safety concerns:** Critical conversations also can't solve serious concerns of safety or a highly hostile environment. If the participants have restraining orders against each other, or feel their safety is at risk, a critical conversation isn't recommended without a mediator or another third party being involved. I cover more on mediators later in this chapter. If there is any threat to or concern for safety, immediately bring in professional counsel to help keep the situation safe for all employees.

✔ **Harassment:** Workplace harassment is a big concern in many organizations, and it should be. But because the name can make companies fear the worst (a lawsuit and horrible PR), it may be easy to overreact if an employment law specialist isn't involved. Employee relations professionals can help decipher what's harassment and what's just poor behavior. Critical conversations *can* help uncover some of the facts when a potential harassment issue is brought up and, if the issue is minor, can often be used to help stop the behavior. Critical conversations can help you understand what's happening, but if an employee feels that he's being harassed — or even says the word "harassment" — it's best to advise your human resources or employee relations department. If you don't have one of these departments, confidentially bring up the issue to your boss and document the critical conversations you already had. If you need it, seek out legal advice. When dealing with any potential harassment issue, or any legal issue for that matter, document and raise the concern. The worst thing to do is to keep the information secret and do nothing.

✔ **Ethical concerns that also break the law:** Laws governing ethics in business seem to change almost daily. In the past, it may have been unethical for a financial services company in the United States to give money to a political party and then bid on government work (with the same politicians the executives may have just given money to), but today the Dodd-Frank Act makes that explicitly illegal. However, some issues aren't that black and white. If an act is deemed unethical, but isn't illegal, what should you do?

If an ethical concern breaks the law, treat it as breaking the law (see the first bullet in this list). Corporations have created ethics hotlines, governance boards, codes of conduct, and social responsibility offices to lay the foundation for what the organization feels is ethically and morally right and to direct employees on how to respond when an unethical act is discovered.

These areas are by no means a complete list of when to use extra caution when considering a critical conversation. Anytime you're in doubt about what to do next, talk with an employment law expert or your human resources or employee relations department.

 I'm not a lawyer or employment law expert, nor is this book a replacement for such counsel. If you find yourself wondering what's ethical or legal when a concern is voiced or you have such a concern yourself, corporate human resources departments, outside legal counsel, local business chambers, or even the United States Labor Department are resources that can help.

Complaints that benefit from a critical conversation

Now that you know what you probably should not try to resolve with a critical conversation, you may be wondering if a critical conversation can help rectify any workplace complaints at all. The answer is yes. Here are a few complaints you may hear that can benefit from a critical conversation:

- ✔ **Employee morale issues:** Many employee morale issues may tie back to staff disputes (see Chapter 14), but some may focus more on a larger group or team, or even the organization itself. Someone may complain that they don't feel valued, or are unhappy with co-workers' attitudes, or they are just plain old burnt out. A critical conversation can help get to the bottom of the complaint and resolve the issue.

- ✔ **Issues that mask real concerns:** Some workplace concerns are not really concerns at all. They are personal grudges or cries of panic when the complaining employee knows they are underperforming. If an employee gets a poor performance rating, they may say they are being discriminated against. Of course, this could be true, but it also may be that the employee is blaming others for their poor performances.

- ✔ **Some ethical concerns:** Most employers have rules in place that govern ethical issues, like surfing the Internet on a company computer and using a company-issued cellphone to make personal calls. Of course, you've probably heard of an employee checking his personal e-mail or shopping for that last-minute birthday gift over his lunch hour. These ethical concerns can often be resolved by kicking off a critical conversation. Of course, if the behavior does not change with a conversation, then a manager may have to consider more severe options (like firing the employee or putting them on a performance plan).

✔ **Off-the-wall inquiries:** Yes, there will be some complaints that may leave you speechless (at least until you kick off the critical conversation). These can include anything from the size of someone's office, when the trash is or is not picked up from the cubicles, and so on. While these issues may not seem like issues at all, the individual raising them could potentially be emotional about the outcome, and therefore a critical conversation could help.

The rest of this chapter focuses on what to do when these types of workplace complaints are raised and how to use critical conversations to help dig into these types of workplace concerns.

Using Critical Conversations When an Issue Is Raised

What do you do when an employee comes and lets you know that he has a concern that potentially can be resolved with a critical conversation? In most cases, you can follow the steps for handling a staff dispute (see Chapter 14). But, as you are digging into what is really happening, the best thing to do is to listen before you act. Make sure you focus on finding out all the facts and maintaining a positive environment. Ask what happened, take notes, and then agree on what should happen next.

Here's an example of how to follow the critical conversation steps when an issue is raised. Suppose Sally comes into the office obviously distraught. She tells you that Frank, her co-worker, just commented on how cute she looks and makes inappropriate comments about other women in the workplace. As the receiver of this information, you should follow many of the main critical conversation elements of a staff dispute:

✔ **Examine and acknowledge the other person's feelings:** Because these types of conversations usually aren't planned, take a minute to let the other party know that you're here to listen and to help resolve the issue. In this case, you may say, "Thanks, Sally, for coming to me. I want to help resolve this issue so we can all work together in a positive environment."

✔ **Examine what happened:** Ask what specifically happened and whether the other person feels comfortable telling you more specifics. Often these conversations are emotional, so try to stick to the facts, but be sure to acknowledge feelings along the way. In this case, ask, "Can you give me a few examples of what happened so I can best understand the issue?"

Examining what's happening can help you uncover what the facts really are before you make a decision about what to do next. Try to avoid leading questions that sound like you're putting the spotlight on a person in an investigation room. For example, don't ask, "Since you didn't try to ask Mike to stop making comments, was there anything else you couldn't do?" A better option for uncovering the facts would be, "Did you think about talking to Mike about how his behavior made you feel?" Asking leading questions could lead to defensiveness and add to an already emotional situation.

- ✔ **Examine and acknowledge feelings and perspectives (once again):** Let the other person know she did the right thing by coming to you even if it may have been tough. This acknowledgment keeps the communication channel open for any future discussions. "I can understand why you would be upset, and I appreciate your courage to come to me."

- ✔ **Decide what to do next:** If you recognize you're dealing with a potential legal workplace complaint or an ethical concern, bring in your human resources or employee relations resource to help with the process quickly. Balance this action with an agreement to do so, and with what you or the initiator of the conversation may or may not do in the interim. You may say, "This does sound like something we should involve HR in. Would you be comfortable talking with them, or would you like me to talk to them first?" Also ask the other party to do two things between now and the next step: first, maintain confidentiality (more on that later in the chapter), and second, to come to you if the situation gets worse.

- ✔ **Gain commitment and get moving:** Now you do what you agreed to do and then work with the parties involved to solve the problem.

- ✔ **Evaluate the discussion:** Once the issue is resolved, or in some cases passed on to the legal or HR department, follow up with the individual that voiced the complaint. You may say something along these lines: "Thanks for voicing your concern. Is there anything I could have done differently to help rectify the situation? I want to make sure you feel I have done my job well."

Digging into Workplace Complaints

An employee complaint can be resolved with a critical conversation, like those I listed earlier in the chapter, and you can follow the same critical conversations model outlined in Chapter 4 (examine what is happening, decide on next steps, put the plan in motion to gain commitment and get moving, and evaluate results).

However, workplace complaints that can be resolved by (or at least started with) a critical conversation tend to have even higher emotions. Therefore it is a good idea to spend a decent amount of time repeating the steps of examining what is happening and acknowledging emotions before decisions on next steps are made. This might also involve bringing in other parties to find out a bit more about what is really happening. The bottom line: You will be doing a bit more analysis on what the real problem is before you can work with the other parties on ideas of how to fix it.

Let's say an employee comes to a senior manager soon after having a poor performance review with their manager and begins to complain that they feel discriminated against because the manager does not like her. The senior manager can effectively handle the situation by examining what is happening and acknowledging feelings, and then deciding what happens in the next phases of a critical conversation.

> **Employee Bob:** "Terry is a horrible manager. He just does not like me and gave me a bad review."
>
> **Senior Manager Mike:** "Thanks, Bob, for coming to me with your concern. Can you tell me a little more about the parts of your review that make you feel this way?"
>
> **Bob:** "Well, he said I never contribute to the project. I work so hard. I am here every day and stay late. I work harder than any other person on that team. Terry just does not like me. He is just discriminating against me. I heard everyone else got great reviews and giant bonuses."
>
> **Mike:** "I can understand how you might feel by putting in so many hours and not getting the review you expected. If we can try to keep the discussion focused on your performance and expectations, I would be happy to talk with Terry and get his perspective. Would you think that would help clarify parts of your review or would you like to recommend a different solution?"

Mike examined what was happening, acknowledged how Bob felt about what was happening, and then proposed one next step to continue identifying what is really happening. Now Bob has a choice of including his manager in the conversation or continuing to complain. If everyone agrees to talk about the review, they can follow the steps in Chapter 13 on how to deliver a negative performance review and create next steps to resolve performance issues.

And, yes, Bob's manager, Terry, should have read Chapter 13 before he gave a poor performance review in the first place.

Of course, if Bob chooses to not involve his manager in a performance discussion, the conversation may continue like this:

> **Bob:** "I really don't think that will work. He is discriminating against me every day because he does not like me."

> **Mike:** "I hear your concerns and I know tough reviews are often difficult to give and hear. If you feel you are being discriminated against and it is not just a misunderstanding, you may want to talk with human resources about your complaint."

Mike diffused a potentially emotional situation by listening to Bob, and recommending approaches to moving forward to find out more facts. He did not place blame or disregard the employee's comments. Instead, he used empathy and honesty to help resolve the situation — the pillars of any critical conversation.

Outside of moving gracefully between examining what is happening, acknowledging the other's feelings, and involving others as needed, there are a few other expert tips to keep in mind while trying to identify why the complaint surfaced while maintaining confidentially and respect: maintaining confidentiality, not placing blame, and separating personal issues from real grievances.

Maintaining confidentiality during communications

Whether the situation can be resolved with a conversation or series of conversations, or if the issue has to be referred to higher sources, confidentiality is key. Keeping conversations behind closed doors can be a legal requirement, but it also helps to maintain productivity and a positive work environment. If people are talking about the workplace issue around the water cooler, they probably aren't spending as much time doing their jobs.

Confidentiality is the responsibility of all parties. If you do have to escalate issues to a third party, be it HR or a more senior leader, make sure all the parties know how the issue will be handled so there are no surprises. Confidentiality also helps to maintain the dignity of everyone involved, regardless of the outcome. You can imagine how difficult it would be for the accused individual to regain credibility if the complaint turns out not to be accurate.

Closing the rumor mill

Sometimes a workplace issue is just blatantly obvious to anyone within a three-mile radius. People start asking questions and the rumor is at full speed. So how do you get the word out about the issue without discussing the issue? It is simply best not to say anything about the issue itself. Instead, focus on why confidentiality is important for everyone by saying, "I know there may be a desire to learn more about the issue, but for the sake of everyone involved, I ask that you respect my request for confidentiality." For more on how to use a critical conversation to quiet a gossiper, jump ahead to Chapter 16.

Not placing blame

It's hard not to have prejudged conclusions about people's behavior. If someone is in your office complaining about a potential law being broken by a colleague and you've always thought that colleague was a bit deceptive, do your best to maintain a clear head and not judge the colleague guilty before the facts are in. If you feel that you can't be objective, ask another manager or professional to work on finding the facts. That helps you maintain an innocent-until-proven-guilty perspective.

Your role is to gather information so you can help decide who needs to be involved. Your role is not to interrogate a suspect at a crime scene. Be careful not to turn into a special investigator, because holding something of a Spanish Inquisition could prevent the employee from feeling comfortable bringing any issues to you in the future. Instead, simply ask what happened and what he's comfortable telling you. If you need to involve anyone else, let the employee know what steps you think you should take as well.

Separating the personal issues from valid grievances

Employees are smart — they read the paper or listen to the news and may hear of harassment lawsuits that resulted in millions of dollars for some employee being unfairly treated. Laws are in place to protect employees, but not every workplace issue is a legal issue. Some people may cry wolf — either intentionally or not — when they feel they've been wronged.

You don't need to be an expert in employment law, but in many cases (with the exception of violence or gross misconduct), a critical conversation facilitated by a neutral party can help separate personal issues from potential legal concerns.

Bringing in a Mediator

Ideally, individual employees or groups of employees and managers will be able to resolve many complaints in an atmosphere of mutual respect by using the critical conversation fundamentals. People make mistakes, and sometimes they say things that they shouldn't say. And, in most cases, when these things are brought to their attention, the offending parties respond by changing their behavior. When that doesn't happen or when additional conversations aren't probable, you may choose to bring in a third party to facilitate the resolution.

What is a mediation expert?

Mediation is a process that allows individual opinions, emotions, and points of view to be heard when a direct conversation doesn't work. A mediator facilitates communication and negotiation between people experiencing conflict to assist them in reaching a voluntary agreement regarding their dispute. A representative from HR or the legal department may also act as a mediator.

Although many good mediators are attorneys, a good mediator doesn't have to be an attorney. HR professionals, internal legal experts, or ombudsmen in the company are great resources to tap into when looking for help with the critical conversations.

Mediators may be internal or external to the organization. In any case, first determine whether the mediator has any conflicts of interest that would cause a participant or the mediator to feel that the mediator can't be impartial.

When to bring in a professional

Deciding when to work with a third party is often a judgment call based on the history of resolving issues between the parties and the state of the relationship before the issue happened. A mediator can make your job easier and prevent workplace concerns from turning into crises in situations like these:

- ✔ **Emotions are at an all-time high:** High emotions are part of critical conversations, but if one person gets defensive or cries when the other speaks forcefully, and the parties can't move past this behavior, a mediator may be a good option. If emotions prevent either party from focusing on the real problems, a mediator may be a good option.

- ✔ **When the conversation is at an impasse:** You can use mediators not only for workplace or ethical concerns but also when a conversation is at an impasse, when multiple and complex issues continue to surface, or when multiple parties are involved in the conflict.

✔ **The boss is in question:** A critical conversation with a boss who's behaving poorly may need to involve a third party to solve the issue Critical conversations are tough enough when the concern *isn't* about your boss or another superior in the organization. If your boss is the one in question, a critical conversation isn't necessarily futile, but you may need to take a different approach. In some organizational cultures, questioning the boss and giving feedback is acceptable and encouraged. In these organizations, you may feel comfortable examining behaviors or actions with your boss. For example, you may mention that you didn't understand a certain accounting change or agreement with a customer. If you come to the table with a genuine desire to help and understand, the ethical or workplace issue may simply be a misunderstanding.

But not all cultures are this open, and it does take a tremendous amount of nerve and self-confidence to talk about workplace issues with leaders. Therefore, it may make sense to go to your human resources manager to talk through the issue. If you're still uncertain whether or not the issue can be resolved after speaking with HR, you may consider talking with a mediator to solve the problem.

In these situations, having a conversation mediated by a third party can help resolve a seemingly irresolvable issue.

If no legal precedent is set, mediation is a cost-effective alternative to a lengthy lawsuit. Of course, if legal issues are at stake or one party is screaming "I want my lawyer," a mediator may need to step aside and allow for an even more formal legal process.

How a mediator can make your life easier

Because mediators are experts in conversation, your job in the conversation is to focus on what's happening instead of the process to resolve it. A skilled mediator can also help coach the participants about ways to improve their communication so that after the issue is resolved, all the parties can continue in civil working relationships.

If you're the boss facing a workplace or ethical concern, or if you feel the need to involve a third party, professional mediation can make the process easier. Mediation is simply a critical conversation with the added benefit of an expert in conversations and more formal documentation. If you find the conversation at an impasse, shifting to the mediation process should be relatively simple, albeit emotional, as it follows many of the same steps as a direct critical conversation.

Here are the steps involved in a professionally mediated conversation:

1. **Preparation.** Depending on the complexity of the issues and the number of participants, the mediator may request to review relevant documents, speak with participants individually, and ask that the participants sign a mediation agreement describing the role of the mediator, the process, and confidentiality.

2. **Setting expectations and establishing ground rules.** The mediator works with the parties to establish guidelines for respectful communication and confidentiality.

3. **Exploring opinions, data, and feelings.** Just like in a critical conversation, the mediator asks participants to describe their perspectives of the events giving rise to the conflict. This step may also include identifying the underlying interests or unmet needs that are driving the conflict.

4. **Identifying issues and setting an agenda.** The mediator helps the participants identify the issues or problems they want to address during the course of the mediation.

5. **Generating, evaluating, and choosing options.** The mediator encourages the participants to brainstorm all possible options for resolutions and then guides the participants in choosing what to do next.

6. **Developing final agreements.** The mediator usually prepares a formal document on what was agreed to and what should happen next.

Do these steps sound familiar? They should. The steps a mediator uses are almost identical to the steps of a critical conversation. The main difference is that someone else is in the room to keep emotions at bay and to help enable seemingly impossible conversations to occur.

Moving Forward after Tough Workplace Conversations

Workplace complaints and ethical issues can cause a tremendous amount of stress on the parties involved and in many cases on an entire organization or team. In order to move forward, it's helpful to have a critical conversation that conveys your interest in keeping open communication and getting everyone back on track — whether the issue was found to be invalid or valid.

The alternative to having a direct yet critical conversation to close a workplace complaint is to say nothing. But by saying nothing, the void will be filled with rumor or assumptions. As with most critical conversations, be genuine, focus on the facts, and make sure you have a clear plan of action for what's happening next.

Remember that confidentiality is not just a legal matter — when you're dealing with sensitive workplace complaints or ethical issues, it's essential to protect all parties and get employees back to work after the issue is resolved.

Part of moving forward after a complaint is resolved is to make sure that people feel they can get back to work. If the individuals in the conversation have maintained confidentiality throughout the process, even if the complaint was not valid, all parties may agree the issue was a misunderstanding and go on with work. This is the easiest solution and the reason that confidentiality is key.

However, if someone has said something to someone (and this does happen), the best way to handle invalid complaints is to ask the person wrongly accused how he wants to address the situation. Some may just want to move on, but others may want to bring closure to the event more publicly. Work with your employee relations or human resources expert to determine what is and isn't appropriate to say. You may even have another critical conversation to close out the complaint like this one:

- ✔ First, *examine* what's happening and state the facts, keeping them short and simple. For example, you may say: "Over the past month, there have been concerns about our conflict of interest policy." Make sure all the parties know that you've been listening. You can do this by saying, "I know this process hasn't been easy for anyone, and I thank you for your patience and honest discussions."

- ✔ Then, state that the issue was looked at, and that a *decision has been made*. Using the same example as above, this could be: "I've worked with all the parties involved, and I've found that the issue was a misunderstanding. We can support one another by getting back to focusing on what's most important: serving our customers."

> ✔ Finally, allow others to provide confidential feedback (*a way of evaluating how the process was handled*). This will help everyone get back to work while helping all the parties involved maintain respect and dignity. A conclusion may be: "I also want to thank you again for feeling comfortable voicing concerns, and I'd like you to know that if you ever have concerns in the future, my door is always open."

If you find an issue is not valid, or not resolved the way an employee hoped, this is a good time to use those critical conversation skills again. If the employee is upset or angry, you may want to jump ahead to Chapter 16 to learn how to handle these situations.

Chapter 16

Resolving Difficult Behaviors with Critical Conversations

In This Chapter

▶ Exploring behaviors that push buttons

▶ Discovering how to focus on behaviors, not labels

▶ Building a difficult behavior toolbox

▶ Finding four approaches that resolve difficult behaviors

Although I'd hate to label anyone as difficult, almost everyone in an organization (or on Earth) can acknowledge that some personalities are just a little more challenging than others. A simple conversation won't solve the challenging behaviors — oh, if only it were that simple. But critical conversations can get the ball rolling in the right direction — right toward a productive working relationship.

Relationships based on trust and credibility take time to develop — there's no way to get around it. One of the best ways to develop these relationships is to give meaningful and timely feedback, with the intent of improving the situation for all parties involved. So if you want to just tell that annoying co-worker to take his loud gum snapping somewhere else, a critical conversation probably won't help. But if you're interested in building solid relationships, where you work though disagreements professionally, and everyone comes out ahead of the game, start working through these challenging behaviors with a critical conversation.

In this chapter, I walk through how to recognize the behaviors that push your buttons and how to separate these hot buttons from the person pushing them. Next, I load up your toolbox with different approaches to address the challenging behavior, using the critical conversation formula (examine, decide, gain commitment and get moving, evaluate = successful conversations). Finally, I uncover some real-life examples of challenging workplace behaviors, and I give you the exact script to start with as you take on any challenge outside of your cubicle.

Defining Difficult Behaviors

In Chapter 9, I walk through how to work through behaviors that push your buttons. Some of these behaviors include whining, pointing fingers, sarcasm, never picking up a phone call, always insisting on e-mail, and on and on. Although hot buttons can create a tremendous amount of stress in the workplace, difficult behaviors are a little different. Difficult behaviors almost always stop or greatly impede performance in an organization.

Difficult behaviors, similar to staff disputes discussed in Chapter 14, are issues that are negatively impacting the performance of a team or organization and will worsen over time if left alone.

What are difficult behaviors that some people display? Here are a few:

- ✔ **Constant complainers:** These individuals think everything will fail and are constantly pointing out what is wrong to other employees or supervisors.

- ✔ **Solo workers:** These individuals will often exclude certain people or groups from decisions or projects.

- ✔ **Controllers:** Controllers may undermine others' abilities or just try to dominate or take charge of everyone's work.

- ✔ **Know-it-all's:** They may use sarcasm to degrade other people's ideas and often must have the final say.

- ✔ **Indecisive participants:** These types may just want everyone to like them, but are unable to manage making even seemingly easy decisions.

- ✔ **Too busy for anything:** The types of behaviors are often driven by a mix of a number of difficult behaviors. They need to be involved or have some control in everything and have difficulty delegating or making decisions. They may want to take on all the work because they refuse to work with others. They are difficult because they cannot give the time needed to the work that matters, and therefore they often stall progress in an organization.

Difficult behaviors can also include blaming others for everything, frequent shouting or yelling, constant rudeness, or gossiping.

Difficult behaviors can, and often do, impact performance. These behaviors need attention with a critical conversation and plenty of critical follow-up.

Difficult behaviors are different from personal hot buttons or simple annoyances. Sure, it may annoy you that someone stands too close to you or chews her food with her mouth open in the cube next to you, but in the bigger scheme of things, these behaviors really shouldn't make or break the performance of an organization. If you're faced with an annoying hot button that you just can't get over (why can't that person just close her lips when she eats!?!?!), having a critical conversation is perfectly fine. Start with how you're feeling and how it impacts your performance. Just don't be surprised if the other individual tells you that heating your food in the microwave has been annoying her for some time now, too. There's something annoying about everyone; your choice is whether or not you address the little things and knowing when to address big things (also known as difficult behaviors).

Keying in on Difficult Behaviors

As hard as it may be, when you're working with difficult behaviors, you need to separate the behavior from the person. Remember: Your observation of the behavior may differ from what the person's motivations actually are. Yes, you (and most likely many others) think the individual is incompetent, but she may actually think she's trying to help the situation.

Looking at intentions

In the workplace, I often see employees who are persistently pessimistic. The difficult behavior is that the person in question complains about everything, but rarely offers ways to fix the situation. In her defense, the person may want to make sure all the risks are identified before moving forward with any decision, or the individual may just be fearful of doing anything different. The behavior may be difficult, but what the person is trying to achieve may be worthwhile (in this case, pointing out risks to avoid problems in the future).

When separating the behavior from the person, you can use either the gentle nudge approach or a more direct approach to examine what is happening:

> ✔ **Gentle nudge:** A gentle nudge is just a subtle, yet genuine, way to state how you feel and what you observe, without the risk of creating too much conflict. If you're using this approach, you may say, "Hi, Julia. I noticed that you bring up many ideas about what could go wrong with the project during the meeting, but it does not seem like we have time to discuss any possible solutions before you bring up another potential problem. Are you willing to work together to find a

way for us to talk about both the problems *and* possible solutions during the meeting with the group?" In this case, gently letting another employee see a different point of view can show how their way may have been counterproductive.

If the other individual is more direct in their own communication, you have a strong work relationship with the other individual, or if the behavior has been going on for a while, you may choose to use a more direct style of examining what is happening. Additionally, if you tried to use a gentle nudge and it did not work, you may need to use a more direct approach to separate the behavior from the person.

✔ **Direct approach:** If you're using this approach, you may say, "Hi, Julia. I realize you have many ideas on what could go wrong with the project. I noticed that you bring up many problems during the meeting. Can we talk about what you would like to achieve in the meetings and then find a way to focus on solutions to these problems?" Directly asking the intent of actions may put the person on the spot if done in an accusing manner. Therefore, it's critical to follow golden rule #1: Come to the table with a genuine desire to help make the situation better (not a desire to tell someone she's an idiot and a time drain).

Be careful in your choice of words when using a more direct approach. When you're looking for the intent of the behavior, asking, "What are you trying to achieve?" can be perceived as a sign that the person is failing at what she wants to do. Asking "What would you like to achieve?" tends to be a bit more positive and goal oriented. A few words can make a world of difference.

If you find the intent or reason for a behavior, it will be much easier to find a resolution. In the case in the previous list, just telling Julia to stop discussing risks and problems could make Julia feel that her ideas are no longer valued. However, if you can find ways for Julia to voice her opinions during the meeting or even help put the agenda together, her desired goal may be achieved in a more productive way. Sometimes the simplest solutions, like making a point to ask for Julia's opinion, will resolve the problem. You might do this by being proactive and asking for her ideas and thoughts during the meeting.

A conversation with a gossiper isn't going to be the easiest conversation, but difficult behaviors call for strong leaders and team members to stand up and talk about what's happening. If the conversation seems a bit too hard to say for the first time, you can preface the statement with how you feel by saying, "I don't want to be too pushy, but can you tell me what you want to achieve by having conversations that counter the agreements we had just made?" To stay aware of your attitude and nonverbal communication during this conversation, check Chapters 6 and 7.

And sometimes the only way to find out the other person's intentions is to state the obvious problem in a non-accusatory voice, say how you feel, and ask what the purpose of the behavior is. And remember, you may need to have these conversations more than once to resolve the issue. And of course, remember to stay genuine.

Difficult behavior may just be different perspectives and views on the world. A behavior you find odd or difficult may just be a person trying to do her job in the best way she sees appropriate.

Focusing on behaviors, not labels

As with all critical conversations, start with facts (I see), opinions (I think), or feelings (I feel). When working with difficult behaviors, it's more important than ever to base the conversation on what's really happening — not on the perception of the person or behavior or what you heard through the grapevine.

Asking for the meaning of the behavior is simply finding out the intention (like the example in the previous section). This approach not only takes the guesswork out of determining what's going on, but also helps to prevent labeling someone as a bad employee, an annoying boss, or a disruptive co-worker.

The easiest way to focus on behaviors rather than labels is to be as specific as possible, without feeling like you're nit-picking every little step.

You can imagine how differently these two conversations would be perceived by an employee who never answers her phone and only replies to anyone via e-mail, even in highly charged discussions:

A labeling conversation (not a good approach): "You have been so difficult to work with lately (labeling). You don't answer your phone at work; I have to e-mail you to get any answer. And you're causing us to lose clients because I can't speak with you directly." Telling someone they are difficult, or any other label, can immediately put them on the defensive.

The behavior-focused critical conversation (a much better approach): "I feel like I'm not communicating with you efficiently. Last week, I was working with a deadline on a client contract, and we weren't able to talk on the phone about a specific policy. I want to have a conversation about how we can avoid some of the back-and-forth clarifications over e-mail in the future. Are you willing work on this with me?"

Staying away from labels isn't easy. People observe the actions of individuals and the interactions of individuals over time, and patterns of behavior start emerging. These patterns often prompt a critical conversation.

It's perfectly fine, and even preferable, to have two or three recent and specific examples of the behavior that's causing concern. When preparing for the conversation, list the most relevant examples of a behavior and share those observations. However, even if you think the person you're talking with is a horrible, difficult employee who yells, backstabs, and gossips, check your emotions at the door and be specific about the observed behaviors that are exhibited in the workplace.

If an employee comes to you and starts to label another employee, your job is to refocus the issue on the behavior (with a critical conversation) and then, when possible, ask the employees to resolve the issue on their own.

For example, if an employee comes into your office and says, "Boss, I'm totally fed up with Bill; he's such a slow worker!" You may refocus the conversation on behaviors (not labels) by saying, "Thanks, Jane, for coming to me with your concern. I know we are all working long hours these days. Have you had a chance to talk with Bob about your concern?"

If Jane says no, your response could be to examine what is happening by saying, "Well, it may make sense to try and talk with Bill. We are all part of the same team. Would it be helpful for us to talk about what you see as 'slow'? When you talk with Bill, it may be more productive to talk about specific actions rather than general descriptions."

If Jane says yes, and Bill is still slow, your response will be quite similar to the one above. "We do need to work as a team. If you are willing to try and talk with him one more time, I would be happy to help you better define what you see as 'slow.' When you talk with Bill, it may be more productive to talk about specific actions rather than general descriptions."

In both cases, you (the manager in this example), examined what is happening and acknowledged Jane's concerns and you have started to replace a label with behaviors. Now Jane can have a constructive critical conversation with her co-worker, all thanks to your brilliance. For more on dealing with staff disputes and how to earn a nice label of "Boss of the Year," head over to Chapter 14.

Using a Critical Conversation to Turn Around Difficult Behaviors

If you know it is time to stop a difficult behavior that has a negative impact on productivity, and start finding better ways to work, it's time for a critical conversation.

The goals of a critical conversation, whether the discussion is delivering bad news or working through difficult behaviors, remain the same: use honesty and empathy to create a positive solution for everyone involved. When you are trying to create a more positive future when dealing with some pretty negative behaviors, you'll want to first pay special attention to your own emotions and perspectives. Then put the critical conversation into play by examining what is happening, deciding on next steps, and beginning to get moving on a more productive path.

Paying attention to your own opinions and perspectives

There are a few ways to get a grip on your emotions: stop assuming and start breathing. In Chapter 5, you can find out more about how to control your own emotions. Here are a few more ways to make sure your own emotions don't cloud the conversation.

Stop assuming

When trying to work with individuals who have more difficult personalities, it can be easy to jump to conclusions that their sole purpose is just to make your life more difficult. Even if it is not your immediate reaction, take the time to stop assuming the worst, and examine what is really happening without judgment. If you don't know what the other person is trying to achieve, ask and then find ways to create a resolution that will work for everyone (more on finding out about intentions earlier in this chapter).

Start breathing

In Chapter 5, I walk through ways to calm your own emotions as you prepare for a conversation. Having any critical conversation is difficult enough, but when you add in even higher emotions and personal behaviors, it is easy to get overwhelmed and nervous.

Putting the critical conversation into play

Starting a critical conversation to change or modify difficult behaviors in the workplace is tough, but the ultimate goal is to make the workplace more productive for everyone. You may want to head back to Chapter 4 for more on the critical conversation elements, but following is what they may sound like when working through difficult behaviors.

Examine what is happening

Honesty is the best policy when examining what is happening that leads up the conversation in the first place. When examining what is happening, it is often useful to make statements that balance facts and feelings. For example, say: "I feel our conversations end with arguments (fact), and this is preventing you and me from working together more effectively (feeling)."

Identifying feelings, even your own feelings, can be a challenge. If emotions are getting the best of you or the situation, say what behavior you see. With empathy you may say something like this: "I feel it is difficult for me to voice my opinion and be taken seriously in our discussions. When we talk, I often hear sarcasm. For example, when I recommended we hire an intern to help with our reports, you said, 'Is number crunching beneath Your Highness?'"

You may end this by acknowledging how the other individual feels, asking, "Do you understand my perspective?" You aren't asking the person with a difficult behavior to agree with you, you are just asking if they understand why you feel the way you do.

Decide what to do next

After calmly examining what is happening, find out if the other person is willing to find a mutual solution. If someone has been using sarcasm to avoid talking directly with co-workers for their entire career, one conversation may not resolve the issue, but it can be a start. Ask, "Are you willing to work with me to try and find a solution to create a more productive workplace?" It may take time for someone to unlearn old, difficult behaviors, but that is where the plan of action can help.

Focusing on building relationships and creating an open environment to work together is the ultimate goal when deciding what to do next. This is much different than coming into the conversation saying someone needs to change his behavior. Of course, there still needs to be agreement on what is going to happen after the conversation ends, and that is where a plan of action comes into the conversation.

Building a Toolbox: Action Plans for Difficult Behaviors

When you're moving through the critical conversation process (also known as the EDGE model — examining behaviors while acknowledging others' perspectives, deciding on actions, getting moving, and then evaluating performance), some actions to change behaviors may be incredibly obvious and others, well, not so much. If a person is losing it because she's working 24 hours a day, 7 days a week, and hasn't slept in about 3 months, find a way to give the person a break and get her help so that she can sleep and return to her normal self. But few difficult behaviors are caused by a lack of sleep; most run much deeper. You need an action plan to change difficult behaviors.

 Answers aren't always obvious. Some individuals don't realize that they actually need to change. If an individual doesn't acknowledge that her behavior has a negative impact on her career or on her team, action plans may scratch the surface, but in the end no real change in behavior will happen.

Before jumping into action planning, the individual needs to accept that she must change. The critical conversation brings awareness of a difficult style or behavior, and the next step is to gain acceptance of the consequences of the behavior. When you kick off the critical conversation about difficult behavior, you may ask what goal the behavior is going to accomplish. This question is a good first step in identifying the root cause of behaviors.

After you start the identifying process, dive into the following three areas to help change the behavior:

- ✔ Coaching and support
- ✔ Education and mentoring
- ✔ Rewarding

The following sections offer a how-to approach to each of these areas.

Coaching and support

Think about this unfortunately common workplace example: A manager never gives credit to employees for their work (behavior) because he wants to get more face time with the big boss (intention). Until the manager accepts how this behavior negatively impacts the team, he will always be looking for another way (potentially more damaging) to get the face time he craves.

Coaching is providing ongoing support and guidance to employees and leaders faced with personal and professional challenges. Coaching a difficult behavior helps the individual see her current level of performance, style, and behaviors through another pair of eyes. Essentially, the coach is continuously providing critical conversations to explore what's happening and can help the employee work on new, more productive behaviors.

After the initial meetings and agreements, the coach begins the process of collecting objective data, reflection, experiences, and feelings from the individual, and sometimes from her peers. Then as the individual is made aware of her style and how it impacts others, she has a choice of becoming more proficient and competent in her role or continuing along her current path. Then the coach and individual work to create ways to communicate better, delegate more effectively, involve employees in decision-making and problem-solving, resolve conflicts, motivate employees, manage time, and the list goes on.

In addition to support and an outside perspective and feedback, coaching is about helping a person clarify what they want and guiding them to get there through powerful questions, active listening, and straight talk to help them align their thinking and behaviors to get what they want. During this process, the attitudes and behaviors that get in the way become undesirable and they want to change.

This coaching stuff sounds great, right? Yes, it can be — but it takes time, and a person has to want to be coached. Even the best coach cannot force someone to change, the individual needs to know and want to change. Accepting one's own behaviors and acknowledging that a change needs to happen may take time, but you can predict how successfully a person will be coached by how she answers these questions:

> "Imagine that this behavior we've been talking about is resolved. What would be possible?" "How will it feel when this outcome is achieved? How will it impact you and others?"

With these simple questions, you can find out whether the person is wants and desires to change. If the answer sounds something like, "Well, I'm not really sure I need to change anything. Everything will be the same," you probably can place a bet that no matter what you do, change is going to be a long, long process. In this situation, if the behavior is stalling progress, it may be best to think about whether the employee is a good fit for the organization (Chapter 13 talks a bit more about firing an employee with compassion).

If a person is pushed into action planning before she accepts that her behavior is real, before she accepts its negative impact on others and on herself, and before she identifies what different goals she wants to achieve, the difficult behavior will surface again, and again, and again.

Education and mentoring

Changing behaviors means discovering a new way of working. If an individual has always pitted one employee against another to try to remain in power, that employee is going to have to learn that collaboration can generate much better results. Education can come in a number of ways.

Progress occurs when the difficult behavior is replaced with a positive behavior. After the conversation, one of the action items may be to attend a class on conflict styles or enrolling in How To Be a Decent Manager 101 so the individual learns about other ways to achieve her goals (ways that don't involve the difficult behavior). The training may also come from mentoring. A coach or mentor can help deliver personalized learning to a specific situation, the unique qualities of the leader, and the exact behavior that needs to change.

Although external coaches are often great, objective teachers, don't underestimate the power of role models and mentors in helping to change behavior. Encourage individuals to broaden their base of support by finding people who challenge them and provide constructive input on a regular basis. Mentors are people who have experience and knowledge to share that will help the individual do his job in a more effective and efficient manner. In other words, they have been down the same road and have firsthand experience.

Rewarding the right behaviors

So often, action plans focus on what was done wrong and what needs to be done to correct the situation. These steps are necessary, but don't forget the value of praise and rewarding the right behaviors. I'm not suggesting giving the difficult person a giant raise or a bonus because she stopped back-stabbing people. Recognition can range from a simple "thanks" for a job well done to publicly recognizing the employee for high performance.

When an employee exhibits the desired behaviors, recognition should be:

- ✔ **Timely:** Don't wait until the next team meeting or performance review to say thanks — just say it.

- ✔ **Sincere and specific:** Be specific about what the reward is for, and make sure you're genuine in why you're recognizing the person in the first place.

- ✔ **Positive:** When trying to change behavior, remember to keep the message positive. Saying, "Congratulations, you didn't screw up that one," isn't a good recognition. Saying, "Congratulations, you really made the team come together to solve the problem," is a good recognition.

Recognition is one of the simplest forms of performance feedback that behavior is changing. It delivers consistent messages about what's important, both to the recipient and to everyone on your team.

Some leaders love to talk about what the recognition is (cash, a team lunch, a pat on the back); try to focus more on why you're giving the recognition — to reinforce the behaviors you want to see continue.

Rewards are not the same for all individuals. It all depends on what motivates the individual. Some may prefer to be given a more flexible schedule, or a written note of appreciation, or public recognition. Check out Chapter 9 for more on what motivates individuals.

Finding the Words for Special Circumstances

When you have all the tools in your toolbox and a solid understanding of how a critical conversation flows (see the previous sections in this chapter for more information), it's time to roll up your sleeves and have conversations! That cheer may not be as powerful as "One small step for man, one giant leap for mankind," but the result of the conversations can be just as powerful. If people can't work together, work can't get done. Not everyone on your team will want to be friends with one another, but by resolving difficult behaviors, teams can focus on what matters most: getting the work done right.

The following sections cover how to handle some of the more popular (er, not so popular) difficult behaviors. While I outline specific ways to work with each type of behavior, most of the approaches can be used with almost any difficult behavior you may face.

None of the upcoming examples or critical conversation tactics is a quick fix that will turn a grumpy old gossiper into a star employee and team member. Reinforce the message through multiple conversations, and follow up to find out how the change is going. You may need to talk with a screamer, gossiper, or angry hostile type after seeing her in action and give critical and timely feedback on performance. Persistence and a genuine attitude does pay off with difficult behaviors, but the first step is having that first conversation.

Defusing a screamer

ARGH!!! SCREAMERS CAN NOW YELL OUT LOUD OR SIMPLY PUT EVERYTHING IN CAPTIAL LETTERS WHEN THEY RUTHLESSLY REPLY ALL (and then some) TO E-MAILS.

Some screamers really scream; others choose to use technology to scream for them. You can address the problem behavior in the same way — just don't do it over e-mail. Here's how:

- ✔ **Examine what's happening:** When the screamer is screaming, you can say, "I notice you're raising your voice when someone else presents their ideas. What is the goal of your communication?" That's a good way to present the facts and then ask why the behavior is happening. Or if you're talking with an employee after the meeting, say, "In last week's meeting, I noticed that you yelled at the team members when they didn't complete a task on time. What was the goal of your communication?" If you're dealing with an e-mail screamer, pick up the phone or walk over to her office, and state the same thing, "I noticed that you tend to use capital letters in your responses. I feel that these capital letters are the same as screaming at another individual. What message do you want to send with the e-mail?" This is the right place to acknowledge the other person's feelings and opinions. For example, "I understand you want people to know that this topic is important to you."

- ✔ **Decide on options:** I like to listen to the entire conversation before replying. I've also found that asking for clarification helps in these circumstances. Say, "Are you willing to work together to find another way to let people know that you're passionate about a topic?" If necessary, you may need to take a break and specify the consequences of the behavior on the group. Say, "People stop listening to you when you scream," or, "People delete your e-mails."

Very few people just yell for the sake of yelling. Find out what's driving the behavior and then focus on that intention.

Quieting the back-stabbing gossiper

Oh, if only high-school behavior ended in high school. But that little back-stabbing gossiper somehow found her way into your company. What do you do? Just like in high school, the gossiper may feel that her opinions aren't being listened to, she may be insecure about her abilities, or she may just be looking for attention. Some things never change. But unlike high school, addressing this behavior by focusing on the intention is a much better option than writing something nasty on her locker.

The first step: *examine what is happening.* The challenge with gossipers is that they often don't have a specific action that you can observe (hence it's back-stabbing, not front-stabbing). They may sit quietly, smile, and just agree. Ten minutes after the meeting, they're telling anyone who will listen how horrible the meeting was, how dismal the project is, or how much they don't like their teammates (or you).

Here's how a team member may *examine what is happening* with the back-stabbing gossiper:

> Team member: "I know we agreed in the meeting to all go back to our teams and ask for their input on the type of learning and development they want to see next year to help meet the company goals. I noticed that you told your employees that learning and development is unnecessary and an added cost to the company. Could I help clarify any of the agreements we made in the meeting?"

Next up: *deciding what to do next.* What happens next (the decision point) depends on how the information is received. If the recipient of the information replies with, "Oh, no, that isn't right. I would never say anything like that," your response could be, "Great. Do you want to schedule a meeting tomorrow to walk through the ideas the team may have?"

Of course, one day the back-stabbing gossiper may say something like this:

> **Back-stabbing gossiper:** "I don't agree. This whole project is nonsense."
>
> **Team member:** "Let's go back to last week's meeting. We agreed on the goal, the problem, and the time line. Did something happen to change that agreement?"

In both examples, the examining what is happening focuses on the facts and trying to find out why the back-stabbing gossiper isn't voicing her concerns in front of other people. Of course, the gossiper may continue with the difficult behavior; in that case, it is time to go back to examining what is happening by stating the problem and then asking for the intention:

> **Team member:** "We've been working through this project for six months, and I feel we've had some great success with our team discussions. I noticed that you voice your opinions to others after the meeting, and I feel this is going around the process we agreed on. What do you want to accomplish by having conversations that counter the agreements we had just made?"

Using the examine and decide steps should help the recipient of the information understand the impact of their behavior and provides a productive and positive way to help move forward.

Cooling down the angry hostile types

If you've ever been in a meeting with one of those angry hostile types, you know how difficult it can be to get any work done. These people are mad at the world, and they want you to know about it. Some angry hostile types start off as people with bad attitudes — they complain about everything, blame others, and never take responsibility for anything, ever. It's always someone else's fault. You may use some of the techniques described earlier in the chapter to have a conversation with an angry hostile type after the situation occurs, but here are a few ways to use critical conversation as the behavior is happening.

If you're in a meeting with an angry hostile type who has her arms crossed, taps her foot, and shoots down any possible positive comment before you can say "annoying," try this approach:

> **Examine what's happening.** Say, "I'm really confused by your behavior, John. I thought we agreed to talk about the possible solutions, not all the reasons the solutions won't work. Does the group want to talk about problems or solutions?"

In this example, the team member examines what's happening, states how she feels about the problem, and then proposes a way to go forward. The beauty of this approach in a meeting is that the group can help solve the problem — it's not up to just one person.

Another tried-and-true tactic for working with an angry hostile type is to state the behavior you see, validate it, and then either defer the problem to another meeting (perhaps a one-on-one critical conversation) or deal with it.

✔ **Examine the situation by stating what you see:** Continue examining what is happening by saying what the person is doing as neutrally as possible. If John is shooting down every idea in the book, you may say, "You don't think this solution will ever work, right?"

✔ **Validate the comment:** After you state the problem, validate that whatever John is saying may be true. You may simply say, "You may be right. We're facing a really challenging issue."

✔ **Decide what to do next by dealing with or deferring the comment:** Talk about the issue now or work it out later. If you chose to defer dealing with the behavior until later, you may say, "Would anybody disagree with brainstorming the possibilities that might work first? Then we can look at the risks and challenges." Use the group to help with this discussion. The other option is to deal with the problem right then and there. Remember to stay genuine. You want to solve the problem instead of telling John that he's just the most negative person in the world and you wish he wasn't there. Say, "Thanks, John, for your comments. Does anyone else want to talk about the solutions?" If that doesn't work, you may want to take a break and confront the person with, "John, I feel that you're interrupting the discussion quite frequently. What would you like to achieve with this behavior?"

One of the big challenges when working with the angry hostile type is that often a number of other difficult behaviors are under that mean shell. These individuals may polarize teams or just argue with any new ideas for the fun of it. They may also be angry or moody by habit, even if they have nothing to argue about. They may also be critics, where nothing other than their own ideas is adequate.

Although all these difficult behaviors may have an impact on performance, try not to overcommunicate during any conversation. Doing so can muddy the waters, detracting from the real behavior that needs to change. When preparing to have a critical conversation with the angry hostile type, or if you find yourself needing to deal with them at a moment's notice, remember to have a core message. The core message addresses the single most important behavioral change you need this individual to address. For more on preparing for a critical conversation, look back at Chapter 9.

Stepping in When Bad Behavior Becomes a Pattern

Sometimes a behavior can work itself out. People have bad days and, rather than jump to conclusions, you may want to give them the benefit of the doubt. If an employee who otherwise is calm and collected becomes a monster during a meeting, it could be because of something completely unrelated. Exhibiting the behavior once or twice is just an incident — three times is a pattern. Having the empathy and trust to give a person the benefit of the doubt also helps to build relationships.

Although three times may not seem like enough to have a critical conversation, think of it this way: Because no one knows what the other person is trying to achieve with the difficult behavior, it can often just be ignored. Soon, the moderately annoying behavior becomes such a giant issue that no one wants to work with the individual anymore.

 In a genuine, otherwise healthy relationship, abrupt changes in behavior are a matter of concern. In this case, the conversation might be about the well-being of the person and have little to do with work.

 Intervening when a pattern emerges doesn't need to be difficult. For example, you may have the following conversation:

> **Boss:** "Josh, I noticed you cut the discussion short when the team was brainstorming different solutions earlier today. It seems like the project setbacks are making this project frustrating."

> **Josh:** "No, the project isn't frustrating! It's been a long complex project with no breaks, team members keep being pulled off the project, the software has bugs, and I'm exhausted."

Now you have a reason for the behavior in the meeting, and you can start working on a solution. If you don't say something by using critical conversation principles, more people are likely to leave the team to avoid working with a monster for a project manager — barely recognizable as the composed employee he used to be. Letting some behaviors work themselves out is okay, but don't wait too long to explore what's happening.

Chapter 17

Customer Conversations

. . . .

In This Chapter

▶ Having critical conversations with customers

▶ Talking with customers when they break the rules

▶ Using critical conversations as part of a public relations strategy

. . . .

"The customer is always right!" Or, so they say, but I'd like to propose a different view: "The customer may not be exactly right, but the customer has a right to complain, go somewhere else for service, or accept the solution and continue being a loyal customer until the end of time." I bet you can guess what I'm about to write: Yes, critical conversations can turn even the worst customer nightmare into a positive solution.

In this chapter, I start with uncovering what customers tend to want when they have a complaint. Then I get into applying critical conversation skills to start creating a solution everyone can agree to. I also tell you how to let customers know they may be breaking the rules of professionalism — or that they're just plain being rude. Next, I give some advice on using critical conversation skills as a public relations tool. Keeping customers happy is always better than having to find new clients, so I end the chapter with ideas on how to open a discussion with customers when it's time to renegotiate the future of a business relationship.

Helping Customer Relationships

Unless your company is in a bubble with little or no contact with the outside world, at some point you need to talk with customers. Yes, really talk — and not just with some pretend agent wearing a headset on a customer service web page. It's nice to think that customers will just happily call you to say how great you are, but most likely these talks will be highly emotional because something has gone wrong. That's where critical conversations can help.

I would be generalizing if I said customer critical conversations can always help resolve complaints or concerns, but they can make a huge difference in maintaining a positive customer relationship. Here's an example to show you just how easy it is:

> A customer storms into the store with a complaint about the new phone that he waited 26 weeks in line to get — he's probably still a little upset about not showering for half a year. Using critical conversation skills, the genius customer service agent says, "I can understand how you would be upset that the battery lasts only 12 minutes. There could be a few reasons why this problem may be happening." This statement examines what's happening by stating the problem and acknowledging feelings. "Would you be willing to let me take a look at it and we can try to solve the problem?" Asking whether the customer is willing to work together to decide how to solve the issue is a positive step.

And here's another example:

> A client paid lots of money to a consulting firm to help the client solve all its problems. The problems still exist. Thank goodness the head of consulting read this book before the client called. He says, "Thanks for sharing your perspective with me. I've heard what you said about expectations and want to work with you to resolve the issue." This statement acknowledges how the customer feels and examines what just happened. "Are you willing to work together to make sure we're all in agreement with what happens next?" Deciding to agree on the next course of action is a step in the right direction.

These two examples are just the first few sentences of a bigger conversation, but it's clear that examining issues, acknowledging feelings, and getting that initial agreement to work together to solve the problem are much better than rolling your eyes behind the counter or just giving in and giving the customer everything. Giving the customer something to make him happy may seem easier, but taking the extra step to work with the customer to resolve a specific issue and to find out what the customer really wants and needs will set the stage for a long-term relationship with the customer.

Giving in to anything the customer says may set a precedent that as long as the customer complains loudly enough, he gets anything and everything for free. This approach usually isn't a good business model.

Customer discussions that use the critical conversation format usually involve a type of customer service complaint, a customer who breaks the rules, a company giving bad news to a client, or a preemptive conversation on how the customer and company plan to work together in the future. I devote most of this chapter to these four main topics. But even if your conversation falls outside the lines of these topics, keep reading, because you can likely transfer these approaches to almost any customer interaction.

Providing Exceptional Customer Service

I love customers. Most businesses do. But loving your customers doesn't mean that the company has to bend over backward to fix any problem a customer may have and break the bank doing it. Customer service and customer satisfaction are two different things. Both need to be positive in order to avoid that horrible review on Google, Yelp, Twitter, or Facebook (or any one of the million other review sites out there). *Customer service* is how the company reacts and what the company does when a customer has a problem. *Customer satisfaction* is how the customer perceives the situation was resolved. Critical conversations can help both customer service and customer satisfaction.

 Suppose your flight was delayed for hours and eventually the flight was canceled. At this point in time, as a customer you are unsatisfied with the result (canceled flight) and probably think the service was pretty shabby, too (sitting through one delay after another, only then to have the flight canceled). Here is how a typical conversation may go in this situation:

> **Customer:** "I can't believe I paid $500 for a ticket to see my friend's wedding and now I can't get there!"
>
> **Agent [typing about 20 letters a second]:** "I can get you on a connecting flight tonight."
>
> **Customer:** "I am so upset!"
>
> **Agent [still typing]:** "Here is your new boarding pass."

With this situation, the customer is still upset with just being handed a new boarding pass, and who knows if they are satisfied or not since there was barely any interaction or acknowledgment from the customer service agent that there was even a problem. While even the best customer service agent can't control the planes or weather, a customer-focused critical conversation can turn a bad situation into a positive outcome. Here is how the previous example could create a better result using the critical conversation model:

Customer: "I can't believe I paid $500 for a ticket to see my friend's wedding and now I can't get there!"

Agent: "I understand how frustrated you must be. It is really hard to have no control over the delays in air travel, but a weather front over the region has made it unsafe to fly. Are you willing to give me a few minutes so I can try and find another option for you?"

Customer: "I guess I don't have any other option, do I?"

Agent (with empathy): "I would be happy to refund your ticket, but I bet you want to get to that wedding, right? Are you willing to give me a few minutes so I can try and find another option for you?"

Customer: "Sure, I guess that is fine."

Agent: "I have been able to find a connecting flight later tonight that gets you in at 8 a.m. tomorrow morning. Or, I can book you on the first direct flight out tomorrow morning. The flight in the morning can get you there by 10 a.m. tomorrow. Would either of these solutions work for you?"

Customer: "Well, the wedding is not until 2 p.m., so the 10 a.m. flight is fine. Thank you."

This critical conversation delivered results by first acknowledging how the customer was feeling and then gaining commitment in regard to how to handle the situation. In the end, even the most irate customer would have to be satisfied with how the situation was resolved since the customer chose the outcome.

I'd be a billionaire if I could solve all the airline complaints that surface during every takeoff and landing, but I will tell you this: Critical conversations can help diffuse many of the situations that arise every day in every business around the globe. The following sections go through some examples, actions, and key phrases that can help you be a superhero when it comes to delivering exceptional customer service.

Using key elements to work through complaints

Using a critical conversation with a customer can help in any situation, regardless of the level of the complaint. If a customer simply needs a different size shoe shipped to him and that's what your company's promise says it will do, well, just ship it. Do what you promised and move on. If, however, the customer is ready to throw a shoe at you (whether the customer's complaint is valid or not), a critical conversation can help calm the situation. Critical conversations also work well if the issue is a little bigger than a pair of $100 shoes. Perhaps a consulting contract didn't meet expectations or you're having a business-to-business problem that can impact revenue targets of the customer.

In these situations, the best way to resolve a customer complaint is to solve it before it needs a referee to prevent it from getting out of control. Examining what is happening, acknowledging feelings, and then deciding together what the right solution may be gives you control of the situation quickly and efficiently so you can get moving to solve the problem and rebuild the relationship. (See Chapter 4 for details on the EDGE model, which is the basis for this conversation.) Here's what to do:

- ✔ **Examine what is happening.** Taking this step during a customer complaint may seem obvious, but when a customer complains, you need to examine what is happening. What you observe helps to make sure all parties understand the problem. Examining what's happening may be as simple as stating, "I can see that your computer is broken. Can you tell me a little more about when this problem started?" Or, "I understand that our billing process is incredibly stressful on your account payables department. Can you tell me about some of the information that seems incorrect from your perspective?" When you have multiple problems or when the problem isn't exactly clear, it may be helpful to ask, "Do you agree that this is the problem, or am I missing something?"

  When you examine what's happening with a customer service complaint, always try to state what's happening or what you hear. Often, customer complaints, especially those in the service industry, result from the customer wanting to know that you're listening to his problem.

- ✔ **Acknowledge what the customer is feeling.** A simple "I understand that you're upset about [having to wait on the phone/not getting the right shipment/missing a deadline]".

- ✔ **Decide what to do next.** If a customer has a valid complaint and you have a no-questions-asked return policy or fix-it policy, the decision is pretty clear — follow the policy. But when the answer isn't black and white, a critical conversation looks at the problem from both the company's view and the customer's view. Usually the individual trying to resolve a customer's problem will make a recommendation.

Critical conversations take deciding what to do next to the next level — working together to come up with a solution. Here's how it works. The employee asks, "Are you willing to work with me to find a solution?" If the customer says yes, continue with, "I have an idea on how we can fix the problem. I can ask one of our service team members to fix the broken dishwasher today or tomorrow. Would that solution work for you?" And if the customer says no, he doesn't want to come up with a solution together (and yes, that does happen when customers are quite upset), then reply with, "How would you recommend we solve the problem?" Either way, the question and answer keep you in control of the situation and provide the opportunity for the customer to make the situation positive.

✔ **Gain commitment and get moving.** If you say you're going to do, do it. Did you agree to get a new team of engineers on a plane to fix the power system? Get them on the flight. Agree to fix an order that went terribly wrong? Fix it.

✔ **Evaluate the results.** Almost every company — from a mom-and-pop flower shop to the Fortune 100, from government agencies to nonprofits — has online customer service tools available to them, and following up with a customer complaint is easier than ever before. Ask for feedback, and if the problem isn't resolved, keep working at it until the customer and you agree that the solution has fixed the complaint. If you see a trend, make a plan of action to examine and decide how to fix the trend.

For more on customer service, I recommend reading *Customer Service For Dummies,* 3rd Edition, by Karen Leland and Keith Bailey (Wiley).

Noting the differences and similarities between internal and external issues

There are two big differences between dealing with issues of external customers compared to issues of internal employees. Take a look:

✔ **Most companies don't fire their customers for poor behavior.** Of course some companies don't do business with one another after a disagreement, and that drunk who wears cut-up t-shirts and punches the bartender is no longer accepted in the local pub. For the most part, however, most companies want to keep customers coming back.

✔ **Business isn't Vegas.** What happens between a company and a customer doesn't stay between the company and customer. Whether you're an individual selling an old Star Wars set on eBay, or a giant corporation selling multimillion-dollar power generators, opinions on service and quality, and how complaints are managed, are somewhere out there on the Internet. Just search customer service complaints for any company you're thinking of using, and you'll find opinions, often lots of them. Of course, not all the opinions are fair, true, or even legible, but they're out there and can make or break a buying decision.

Although these two differences are important — some may even say critical — there are two similarities between customers and employees within a company that make using critical conversations a logical, and perhaps even easy, approach to problems. Here are the similarities:

✔ **Customers and employees both have personal opinions, perspectives, and ideas on how a problem should be solved.** If everyone is happy and in agreement, well, a critical conversation is probably overkill. When one person — a customer or an employee — is upset or has a disagreement on how to go forward, a critical conversation can help.

✔ **Just like it does with its employees, a company often has a long-term relationship with its customers.** (When I say "relationship," I mean the business kind, not an OMG high-school romance.) A critical conversation can preserve a relationship and even grow one in the face of conflict.

Knowing what upset customers want

When a customer is upset, he may tell you that he wants to talk to your manager, and your manager's manager. He may tell you that he wants to bring the company down or call his best friend who just happens to also be the CEO of the company (a bit of an exaggeration). But in the end, if a customer is upset, he wants to be heard, to be treated with respect, and to know that his problem is going to be resolved. Your job is to use a critical conversation to talk an upset customer down from calling the Supreme Allied Commander to fly the right shipment out the door within seconds, to agreeing that a delivery person in a brown or blue suit can deliver a replacement in a more reasonable amount of time.

Although it may seem like Customer Service 101, finding out what the real problem is and then resolving it is the name of the game in

customer service and customer satisfaction. A big problem companies make is to just hand over solutions or products for free anytime a customer gets mad. But customer satisfaction comes from
a good relationship with the customer, and that's often best built
with a critical conversation, not a 10-percent-off coupon on your
next order.

If you can't find a mutually agreeable solution as you decide what
to do next, use one of the most straightforward and often overlooked
plans of action: go to the source (the customer, that is) and ask
how he would solve the problem. Ask the customer what he thinks
a fair solution is — it's one of those win-win solutions. A customer
tells you a reasonable solution *and* you have the option of responding, "Yes, we can do that," or, "That's different from how we usually
resolve these types of issues. Let's work together to see what's
possible."

Some people fall into the trap of asking, "What do you want to
resolve this issue?" The problem with this question is that giving
the customer anything other than what he says will result in poor
customer satisfaction, even if customer service is exceptional.

Handling a Customer Who Crosses the Line

When leaders talk about customer service, there's an assumption
that a customer is complaining about the service or performance.
But what happens when a customer breaks the rules? If a customer
lies, stretches the truth, or acts unethically, a company doesn't
need to just accept that behavior.

Managing "I want to talk to the manager"

One of the most frequent unethical behaviors is when a customer
treats an employee with disrespect by yelling, calling him names,
or making threats to call headquarters, the boss, or the President
of the United States to complain. Some customer service courses
tell you to smile and say okay or to ignore it. But I present another
alternative: create a conversation that not only finds a solution,
but also creates a foundation for the customer-company relationship to continue in the future.

I walk through the following example to show you how a few simple sentences can take a customer interaction from producing a solution or finding a solution to creating a better relationship in the future.

> An irate customer is on the other line of the phone, threatening to call everyone he knows to 1) get the employee fired, and 2) put the company out of business. The customer service representative could say, "Yes, you can talk to my supervisor. I'm putting her on the phone now." Nothing is wrong with this statement, but you can guess that the customer now knows that if he starts complaining, he doesn't have to go through the process that everyone else has to go through; he can get to whoever is in charge if he yells loudly enough. Think of how this slightly modified reaction may work better:

> "I can understand how you'd be upset. If you want to talk to my manager, I can provide you with her e-mail address or phone number. I suggest working through the returns process because that works for many of our customers. Would you like to continue our conversation about how I can help you, or would you like to talk to someone else?"

This critical conversation examines what's happening and acknowledges feelings by restating the customer's desire to talk to the boss and understanding how the customer could be upset. Then, the customer service agent (well versed in critical conversations, of course) gives options about how the customer could decide to move forward. Instead of just handing over the call to the boss (of course, the customer could still very well want to talk to the boss, and that's a perfectly acceptable option), asking the question helps the customer slow down and evaluate what the right decision may be and helps the customer save face if he realizes that he may have been a little over the top with his complaints and yelling.

Facing a hostile customer

Yelling customers making threats face customer service agents in almost every company on any given day. Sometimes customers break rules or cross the line from being upset and irate to being hostile to an employee or group of employees.

The following critical conversation sounds and feels like a critical conversation you'd have when an employee's behavior is disrupting work. In this case, a customer manager or leader in the company presents the facts, examines what's happening, and works with the customer to decide on what to do next.

Suppose an employee who works for one of your clients repeatedly ignores your e-mails and phone calls and frequently reschedules meetings at the last minute. When they do return calls or meet with you, it is often at the last minute and very rushed. This results in you having to stay until midnight to get work done on time, or not having sufficient time to incorporate their feedback when you have to deliver documents to their boss. The options are to ignore the behavior since the customer is, well, the customer, or to confront the problem in as positive a way as possible. As hard as it is, confronting a customer who breaks the rules is the right solution in the end, whether the customer is misrepresenting facts, not doing their job, or howling like a wolf under a full moon. How do you do it? The same way you do with any other critical conversation. Here's how:

Employee: "Mr. Customer, thanks for agreeing to meet with me. We appreciate your business and want to make sure we can give you the best customer service possible. Over the past year, I feel my ability to serve you has gone down because I don't have all the critical information I need to serve you in a timely manner. Before our meeting with the VP, you said you reviewed the presentation and had no comments, but then in the meeting, you said that you had never seen the presentation before. This also happened in our meeting with the directors last week, and with your team the week before. I know you're busy, and I'm hoping we can find a way to be more productive."

Customer: "Oh, no, that was just a mistake."

Employee: "I understand. Are you willing to work together to find a solution that helps us both be more productive?"

Customer: "Well, of course."

With this decision to work together in place, if the same behavior happens again, the employee can go back to this agreement to work together. The key to this discussion, as with all critical conversations, is to come to the discussion with a genuine desire to make things better. Luckily, most people are, well, human, and when kindly and honestly presented with facts, they eventually decide to at least look at ways to change the behavior causing the issue.

You'll always have customers and employees who have no desire to change, let alone listen. But stay with it. Critical conversations in highly charged situations are rarely once-and-done discussions.

Delivering Bad News to Clients

If you've been around business for more than a few years or have picked up a newspaper in the last 24 hours, you know that at some point in time businesses have less than fabulous news to give customers. This book isn't a public relations book, but public relations and critical conversations have much in common when it comes to talking to customers.

Public relations in companies, when done right and ethically, create an open and honest environment, and then present what's happening next, just like a critical conversation. While *Public Relations For Dummies,* 2nd Edition, by Eric Yaverbaum, Ilise Benun, and Richard Kirshenbaum (Wiley) gives you the lowdown on most of your PR questions, the following recommendations are great tools to add to any public relations strategy.

Creating an open and honest environment

It's far better to say, "We're finding out what's happening and will tell you as soon as we do know," than to try to make up something that you may later need to alter.

As a customer, which statement would make you want to continue working with another company or individual?

- ✔ **Initial statement:** "I didn't do it! We aren't wrong!" Two days later: "He was wrong." Four days later: "Well, maybe we were wrong." A week later: "Okay, I was wrong."

- ✔ **Initial statement:** "Something went wrong. We don't know what it is, but we're working to find out what happened. We will do everything we can to fix the problem after we figure out what happened. I'll keep you informed every day to let you know what's happening." One day later: "This is what happened, and this is what we're going to do to fix it."

I'd be much more inclined to continue the relationship with the company in the second scenario. Trust and a genuine desire to make things better are not only at the center of a critical conversation, but also at the center of customer relationships.

Identifying solutions together

After examining the facts and sharing them, one of the immediate next steps is to identify alternatives or solutions to the problem. This is true with a critical conversation with an employee or a discussion with a customer after a PR disaster. And luckily, the same terminology can help you create an environment of trust and find a solution that helps to not only resolve the problem but also build the relationship.

Here's what a critical conversation may sound like when working through a PR issue with a client.

> **Examine the facts:** "Our manufacturing line for trains and dolls broke down the last week in November, and our shipment to all the good little girls and boys is delayed."
>
> **Acknowledge feelings:** "I can understand how you may be upset because of the timing of the breakdown. Are you willing to work with me to help find a solution as quickly as possible?"
>
> **Decide on next steps:** "Our shipments will be ready the second to last week in December, and we can expedite the shipping with the help of little delivery trucks around the world, or I can help you partner with another supplier. Would any of these solutions work for you, or do you have another idea on how to fix the problem that we can agree to?"
>
> **The customer's response:** "I think we can work with one of those solutions. Thanks for your honesty and quick work."

Not having the trucks, trains, and dolls for the children on the other side of the mountain in late December could potentially shut down this company. By being honest with the facts and working together to resolve the problem in everyone's interest, the solution can be resolved.

Keeping Your Customers

Everyone makes mistakes, but it's how you recover from those mistakes that can make or break a business. Keeping clients in the face of failure, whether it's a PR issue or simply a customer service problem, depends on what happens after the initial conversation occurs. Sound familiar? It should. The critical conversation model is only as good as what happens after the discussion ends; that's why getting moving and evaluating the results are a big part of the conversation process.

Checking it twice

The way to use critical conversations to keep customers is to get moving on what you promise, and check back with them to make sure the problem is solved. Almost anyone can pick up this book and repeat a few phrases to customers when the company is faced with a tough PR or relationship issue. But it takes patience, consistency, and action to see real results from any conversation. After the conversation happens with a customer, what happens next is what matters most.

Can you imagine how a customer could react if a company said all the right things and did nothing? "Mr. Customer, I understand you're upset about getting a purple tutu when you ordered a green one. We'll get a new one in the mail right away." But what if that never happened? The company would probably soon be out of business. If you say you'll let your customers know what's happening with a potential PR issue in the next day, make every effort to really do it, and if you don't, let the customers know exactly why you aren't delivering on what you promised.

Renegotiating the future

Critical conversations with customers aren't just for solving customer complaints. Many business-to-business companies find themselves renegotiating contracts as they expire, adding additional work to a current contract, or even having to alter what the current agreement is as products and services change. Whatever the reason, you probably know that a critical conversation can help.

Although it may be hard to come to a client with disappointing news, or when a problem has hampered the relationship, it's possible to grow a relationship in the face of these conflicts if you listen to your client's perspective and genuinely want to resolve the issue.

Here's an example of being willing to find a solution, even in the face of a potential relationship breaker:

> "I know you've been a loyal customer of our steam model train engines for 20 years. Next year we're changing our product line to more modern model trains. I'd love to talk with you about how we can still serve you and your clients. Would you like to recommend some initial ideas, or would you like me to talk about options we have thought through?"

What goes well in this conversation? First, the initiator of the conversation demonstrates a willingness to solve the problem but doesn't push a solution on the receiver of the information. The initiator examines what's happening and then asks for the client's perspective. So often sales teams come in and present the "right solution" and then ask for the client's opinions. The critical conversation model turns the discussion around, letting the client speak his mind first. After asking for your client's perspective, it's appropriate to state your own and decide what each of you can and can't support.

Of course, in order for any conversation to work, the initiator has to be willing to listen and understand the client's point of view. Don't assume the client is wrong, but also don't assume that you know what's best for your customer. Ask for the customer's point of view and listen to what he has to say. This type of discussion opens up the opportunity for all ideas to be put on the table, and then both the initiator and the receiver can decide on the most favorable options for all parties.

Chapter 18

Hot Topics in Team Conversations

In This Chapter
▶ Building productive teams
▶ Improving the way teams work

*Y*ou can use the critical conversation model in almost any situation. If you look at critical conversations as a method of collaborating and making agreements, then you can use the tools and techniques almost anytime, anywhere, and for any reason.

In this chapter, I cover some hot topics where critical conversations can really shine. First off, I discuss how to help teams exceed goals and expectations by making decisions with the critical conversation model. Next, I show you how to facilitate group agreements that lead to action. And because critical conversations can happen to anyone, I give you tips on what to do if someone is having a critical conversation with you.

Creating a Productive Team

Many organizations are leaning toward a dynamic way of working together: building teams. The thought of different minds collaborating on a common goal is enticing and seems like a perfect way to conduct business. But in reality, very few groups of people really operate as a well-run team. Usually, employees do their own tasks, give updates on projects, and often pull information and work together in the end to achieve a large goal. For example, a team of technology consultants may have individual responsibilities within a large project. Each consultant focuses on a task or a piece of the project, and when it's time for the new technology to go live, all the parts are pulled together.

In Chapter 14, I walk through how to work through staff disputes, which occur within even the best of teams. Critical conversations can also help create an effective team by helping teams develop decisions and action plans everyone supports.

To move from a group working on a bunch of stuff to individuals accomplishing something greater than the sum of their parts, the group needs to openly discuss ideas and decisions together.

Facilitating team conversations

If you're ready to get a team together to collaborate and build real consensus that leads to world peace (or something like that), it's worth discovering one more element of critical conversations: how to facilitate conversations. The goal of facilitating group conversations is to help groups become teams that work together to solve problems. That, as you can guess, isn't an easy task, but by using these techniques, you get one step closer to creating a capable and effective team.

A wonderful by-product of facilitating team conversation is the exponential growth a team experiences. Team relationships are often challenged because the pace of the team or project is moving so fast that the members have little time to sit back and agree on a balanced approach to decision-making. By slowing down to go through developing agreements, a team is more likely to collaborate than to have conflict. Most people know that conflict often results in lost time, extra work, back-and-forth agreements, weak commitment, and everything else that makes team members bang their heads against a very jaded wall.

The art and science of facilitating

You've probably heard that facilitators can help guide a meeting or decisions, or perhaps you've been asked to do so in the past. Being a facilitator is both an art and a science. The science comes from putting the critical conversation method to use. By following the basics, a facilitator can ramp up the power of the conversation. Make sure to

✔ Examine options, ideas, and opinions.

✔ Acknowledge feelings.

✔ Assist the team (or group) in making a decision.

✔ Help the people in the room come up with next steps to get moving and evaluate results.

But the best facilitators know the art to the process as well. To be an effective facilitator, try putting some of the following artful concepts into action at your next meeting:

✔ Discern the tone and feeling of the meeting and know when the participants need a bit more focus or when the group needs a break. Facilitators do this by reading the environment for body language, tone of voice, and language use.

✔ Note whether people are crossing their arms, clenching their fists, and using a bunch of "they versus us" language. If they are, it probably means the group needs to work together a bit more to overcome emotions or differing views in the room.

✔ Look for the group members nodding their heads, leaning in, and using language that focuses on "us" and "we." If you hear this language, the group is most likely working as a team and is ready to make decisions as a team.

Four vital facilitation factors

Although artistry is best learned by practice, I can offer four areas to focus on as a facilitator of team decisions:

✔ **Look out for group dynamics.** (I tell you a little more about this topic later in this chapter.) Group dynamics include knowing the roles people play on teams, both formally and informally, and how individuals on the team interact with one another.

✔ **Listen for the underlying meaning, both the spoken and unspoken, of conversations.** Facilitators listen and take note when individuals aren't being heard or are talking too much; they also can sense when participants say one thing but may mean another. No, facilitators don't have a crystal ball or an omnipotent force behind the curtain in a place called Oz; they just listen closely and observe reactions from others in the room.

✔ **Provide feedback that has an impact.** It's one thing to observe a bully taking over the conversation, but it's quite another thing to be able to say, "Thanks, Bob, for that information. How about the rest of you? What are some of your views?" Giving feedback appropriately also means knowing when to intervene. Politely redirecting conversations may work, but facilitators also need to be prepared to talk to individuals who disrupt the group off-line about the consequences of their behavior.

✔ **Know how to ask questions that drive a discussion.** Luckily, if you're an expert in critical conversations, you have a leg up on the types of questions that create discussion rather than shut it down. Consider these questions: "What could we do together?" "How do we work together?" "What problems are we trying to solve?" These questions are "we" questions that generate discussion and commitment to solutions.

Facilitation in action

Many people on teams and in groups come to meetings, think they come up with a great decision and action plan, and then come back to the next meeting to discover that absolutely nothing happened. Or worse, progress on the project or idea has backtracked. Developing agreements that lead to action takes a leader, team member, or even an outside party that's actively involved. Facilitating critical conversations within teams is a lot more involved than just writing what people say on flip charts.

Dialogue builds agreements and action. Here are some of the questions a facilitator would use to help the group decide together:

✔ **Examine issues:** Ask, "Does everyone agree to work together to make a team decision?" People must be willing to work together before they can make any decisions. "What are the problems the team is facing?" A team facilitator shouldn't just assume that the organization needs to grow at a rate of 30 percent. Instead, the leader should first ask the team to identify the big changes or problems in the market that are putting pressure on profits and revenue. The series of questions would include: "What does the team think are the problems facing our financial performance, and why do we have these problems in the first place?" If the group seems to be conflicted about what the problem is, it may be useful to back up and ask, "What problem are we trying to solve?" In this example, the team may bring up anything from an old pricing strategy that caused margins to deteriorate or government regulations that opened the market to more competition. Whatever the answer, examining the issues as a team will launch a collaborative approach to finding a solution everyone can agree with.

✔ **Acknowledge opinions and feelings:** Some people may have an emotional stake in the old way of doing business. Before a decision is made to find a solution, you may need to acknowledge areas of contention or where disagreement may still lie. It may be impossible to thrill everyone with the outcome, but it is possible to ask whether everyone can support it. In highly charged situations, it may be helpful to recognize that until the emotional feelings are dealt with, a good decision probably won't be made. You may sense that the team has hit an emotional barricade. In this case, state what you're feeling and ask whether others feel the same. For example, you may say, "I feel like voices become a little tense when we talk about past solutions that didn't deliver expected results. Does anyone else feel this way?" Most likely, if you feel this, someone else feels it too.

✔ **Decide how to move forward:** Now is the time for the fun part — or at least the part many teams (and groups) jump into quickly: finding solutions. After everyone agrees on the problems, ask the team members how they recommend solving the problem. After ideas are voiced, the team can agree on the value of the options and then choose which decision everyone can support in the future. A team facilitator may first ask, "What solutions can we agree will benefit the company?" After these solutions are identified, ask, "Which of these solutions can everyone support as we move forward?" The first question is a safe question for the team to answer because it isn't asking for commitment. Then, after the team narrows down the solutions to those that will solve the problem, they will be more comfortable with identifying the one or two that they're willing to support.

Facilitating after the conversation

As with all critical conversations, the discussion during the conversation is truly critical, but the measure of the success of the conversation is what happens after the talking stops.

Create action plans to support decisions, and evaluate the success of those plans by identifying goals for each solution the team agreed on. Be sure to focus on SMART goal statements (see Chapter 4 for tips on creating goals that are specific, measurable, agreed-on and action-oriented, realistic, and time-bound). Also take the time to determine who's responsible for each goal and any critical success factors. *Critical success factors* are often milestones or goals that have tremendous downstream impact on the overall time line of a project. Critical success factors may be the approval of a budget before any further work can continue or the support of an executive before communication on a project or decision can be completed.

Decisions are best made as a group, but action planning and taking action can be done in small groups and then presented to the team for final agreement.

Making team decisions

Different organizations and different situations use different approaches to making decisions that will affect the group. When you use critical conversation techniques during the decision-making process, you often have better follow-through because more than one person is involved in making the decision. Following is a list of four common approaches to decision-making:

✔ **Decide and announce:** One person decides and announces the decision. When a leader controls the resources and output of the group (and therefore the group itself) she frequently tells people how to decide or makes the decision for them. In a critical conversation, a decision that will lead to change is a decision that's made together. If a leader makes decisions for the group, you can pretty much guarantee that the team is just a group of people who aren't really embracing change because they've had little or no input.

Suppose a company is rethinking its revenue streams because it wants to grow, and it needs to make a decision on what to do next. Using the decide-and-announce approach, the leader decides that all divisions in the company are required to make 30 percent more each year or their bonuses will be cut. This decision-making is most likely going to be met with rolled eyes, shaking heads, and individuals vying for their paychecks, even if that means people in the same company are competing against one another.

Sometimes decide-and-announce is necessary in business. If a CEO and CFO, and perhaps one other leader in the company, get together to decide something, it isn't a team decision — it's an executive decision.

✔ **Individual input sought and leader decides:** Another approach is when a leader seeks input from individuals, but then makes the decision on what to do on her own. This type of decision-making is a telltale sign that people are working individually on results, with little collaboration. In this type of decision-making, the leader consults people one-on-one and then uses that information to make a decision. Although the decision-maker listens to the members in the group, the group doesn't listen to one another. Therefore the group isn't a team, but just a cluster of people working on a project or goal.

For example, the CEO of the company asks a few of the senior people in the firm what they would do to increase revenue, and then the CEO sends out a memo with his decision. What's the result? Because she uses some input but not other input, the decision may be met with a lack of buy-in because not everyone contributed.

✔ **Team input sought and leader decides:** A leader may gather input from the team and then decide. Larger teams often operate quite well when their members are given the opportunity to examine options, acknowledge opinions and ideas, and then the leader or a subgroup of individuals on the team makes the decision. The key to the success in using this team decision-making approach is that the decision *reflects* the discussion. If a team works together as its members explore what's happening and possible solutions, and then the leaders who make the decision completely disregard the input, well, then this model is merely a façade and more of a decide-and-announce method. Additionally, after decisions are made, the leaders need to be present them back to the team. For example, a team may discuss the pros and cons of buying a new software system, and then a few people make the final decision. Before the decision is announced publicly, the decision is presented to the team.

This team decision-making model works well when a team frequently works together, has made decisions together in the past, and has a high level of trust within the team. Also, the teams need to be built of people that are trusted by employees who aren't part of the decision-making team. If the team members are just subsets of leaders, it isn't an improvement from decide-and-announce. During conversations that involve significant change, frontline councils and employee ambassadors are often ideal representatives to be involved in the discussion. For more on leading change and forming frontline council groups, check out *Leading Business Change For Dummies,* written by me and Terry H. Hildebrandt (Wiley).

✔ **Decide together:** Yes, collaboration takes time, but when a team is just forming or when the stakes are incredibly high or very personal, deciding together and agreeing to live with the decision is the best option. The goal of deciding together is to create a solution that the team can live with and support. When a team decides together, they also benefit from sharing information and ideas in real time.

Deciding together may take the most time, but when the team walks out the door after the decision has been made, you can pretty much guarantee that people will work together to accomplish the 30 percent increase in revenue target in the example from the first bullet point. You may have some compromise and some give-and-take, but if all the people on the team can live with and support the decision, they'll most likely do everything in their power to implement the decision.

Power of the pronoun

A little word can hold a lot of impact. If team members are using *us* and *we,* they're probably conscious that collaboration is essential. Productive team participants ask others for information, opinions, and ideas. A good conversation starter is "How do we want to address the problem?" But sometimes individuals simply state what they think without soliciting input (for example, using *I, me, you* or *they* more than *us* and *we*), or they start conversations with a more accusatory "You need to do this" or "That wasn't my responsibility." In these cases, the group is probably operating more in solos than in concert.

Making decisions by using the critical conversation principles not only elicits feedback from employees, but also helps you gain clarity over specific next steps by building consensus on what the team is solving. After all, a team that decides together produces together. But the wonderful world of teams doesn't stop there — teams that work together to decide (rather than just work as individuals) are ready to identify the right steps to move forward.

 Group think is when a group takes on its own persona and individual opinions on the team are either ignored or disregarded. An experienced facilitator can help steer teams away from a one-mind philosophy. In the absence of an expert facilitator, before making decisions on the problem or solution, ask, "Have we talked about and looked at all possible solutions?" Teams reaching consensus is wonderful, as long as the consensus is reasonable. If a group doesn't take all ideas and opinions into consideration, sometimes groups can make worse decisions than individuals.

Improving Team Behavior

How a team behaves gives the facilitator a tremendous view into how the members will handle a critical conversation and how capable they are of moving forward. But you don't need to be a facilitator to recognize group and team behaviors — any team or meeting participant can start looking at the strengths and weaknesses of a team by examining how a team behaves. For starters, look at

✔ **Roles, power, and influence:** As the conversation progresses, look for the different roles people play during the discussion. Does one person dominate discussions by talking too much or shutting down ideas before they have a chance to get up on a flip chart? Look out for individuals who take over meetings without letting all voices be heard. Additionally, are alliances being made during meetings? Minigroups can help direct teams toward making a decision, but they can also keep the participants not in the "in crowd" from voicing ideas and opinions.

✔ **Verbal and nonverbal cues:** A person who cuts off others in midsentence or speaks loudly may indicate an overly assertive individual. But also look for nonverbal cues to gauge how a team operates. Does everyone take the same seats, forming a visible pattern of who will talk when and who will lead the discussion? Do people start checking their phones and watches when a particular person starts talking? Watch for indicators of equality in the team. Not everyone has the same title, but in order for a team to use critical conversations to make decisions, every member of the team must have an equal opportunity to participate.

✔ **Group silence:** The rule in movie theaters is just as powerful for appraising team dynamics: Silence can be golden. When you notice silence in a team, look for whether people are eagerly thinking or simply anxious. The ability to pause and consider options while in the heat of a meeting is a signal that the group is able to work as a team to make decisions rather than just jump to the easiest answer and get out of there quickly. On the other hand, too much silence can also create problems. Check out Chapter 16 for more on how to engage individuals when silence is inhibiting productivity. For more on nonverbal skills like silence during a conversation, head to Chapter 7.

✔ **Conflict, consensus, and compromise:** Critical conversations can help overcome conflict, and often can create an even better relationship between parties than before the discussion began. As you observe group dynamics, look at how the team members work through conflict. Do they welcome it and use the exploring and acknowledging methods to build consensus in a decision? Or does the group compromise without any one person really feeling the team is better off than before the conversation began? Although compromise does happen on teams, highly functioning teams work to create a consensus on next steps during conflict rather than just giving in or finding the path of least resistance.

Observing how a team operates during the discussion provides insight into the areas the team can improve. The behaviors that occur during a conversation are often just as important as the decisions the team is making. For more on how to work through difficult behaviors that limit productivity, head back to Chapter 16.

Don't jump into a team meeting and start making judgments about whether the team is operating well. It's much better to look at team patterns. Everyone and every team can have a bad day, but a true team continues to rally respectfully during tough discussions and decisions.

Part V
The Part of Tens

"You're not going to go into one of your nit-picking, hotheaded, blowgun-hating rants, are you?"

In this part...

For anyone who knows Dummies books, this part provides chapters of ten tips to take you from rookie to master in eight or fewer pages. In this part you discover the personal benefits of leading a successful critical conversations (hint: get ready to see your career and relationships soar to new heights), how to keep your cool when others aren't (we all need that!), and how to manage (and stop) a conversation that's going south.

Chapter 19

Ten Benefits of Leading a Critical Conversation

In This Chapter

▶ Accelerating your career

▶ Influencing others through dialogue

▶ Creating a happier, healthier work environment

*M*astering the art of critical conversations is a big win for any organization. Employees discover how to deal with conflict, increase productivity, and, in turn, improve the overall performance of the organization. In addition, employees may realize that by mastering critical conversations, they find some powerful and lasting personal and professional benefits.

Increasing Leadership Potential

One of the biggest reasons people get promoted and become power players at work is because they show confidence in their leadership abilities. Results matter, but results alone aren't a guarantee that your career will continue to grow. Senior executives often judge leadership confidence by looking at these three traits:

✔ Asking for exactly what you want without being pushy, aggressive, or annoying

✔ Handling difficult personality types and situations at work with poise and ease

✔ Maintaining all these skills during change, crisis, and chaos

Guess what single tool can help develop all of these? You guessed it — critical conversation skills. By using critical conversation methods, you can handle difficult personalities and situations and ask for what you want and need without being overly aggressive. By acknowledging others' feelings and ideas, you'll be seen as someone who handles tough people with composure rather than someone who fights back. And although critical conversations are often easier with a little preparation time, after you have the basics down, the conversation method will become second nature, even during times of crisis.

Maintaining Confidence throughout Tough Situations

When faced with tough situations, it's very easy to let emotions fly and productivity sink. Critical conversations deal with tough situations directly by focusing constructive feedback on a specific issue, behavior, or problem, and by developing mutual agreement throughout the process. Most importantly, critical conversations take out the guess work by providing guidelines on what to say, and when and how to say it. Difficult circumstances are tough enough, so having a clear roadmap creates some certainty in uncertain times. All these benefits create confidence.

Knowing exactly which steps to go through frees you up to concentrate on how you're delivering messages and how the other party is responding to them — in other words, the art of critical conversations. By following the critical conversation method, you can have a discussion without being nervous about what is going to happen next.

Influencing without Overpowering

Many workforces are shifting from a top-down model to an information-based model where engineers, creative artists, consultants, finance professionals, and many service workers now hold the future of the company in their hands. "Boss A" is no longer the supreme dictator but rather a facilitator who makes sure that the real producers have the right tools to do their jobs. What does this shift mean? Influencing skills are more important than ever.

Critical conversations can help you influence outcomes by using supportive language rather than aggressive and dictatorial strategies. By making decisions *with,* rather than *for,* your team, you can proactively identify specific and tangible recommendations for moving forward.

I can't overstate the influencing power of data. Gathering and using data in a rational manner can help pinpoint where effort and resources should be focused. Guessing what the problem is or assuming what the problem is based on emotions tends to undercut even the most sincere efforts to make meaningful change through critical conversations.

Developing Healthy Work Relationships

Often, the more open and honest a working relationship is, the more credibility exists. Credibility takes time to develop. One of the best ways to build this kind of relationship is to give meaningful and timely feedback with the intent of helping employees, peers, and even managers increase their effectiveness. Even not-so-wonderful feedback in this context can build a more trusting environment.

Healthy working relationships are a two-way street. If you come to the table with a genuine interest in making positive change, in most healthy relationships the other party will provide the same respect and honesty. Yes, some individuals will be out for their own good — making you feel foolish for being honest and trusting when they're focused only on their own pocketbook and self-interest. Don't despair. Being an expert at critical conversations doesn't mean that you need to be the one who just lets everyone walk all over you. Quite the opposite is true. Using the method of examining what is happening and asking for agreement to do something about it is perhaps the most powerful and proactive way to build a working relationship.

Focusing on Teamwork

Critical conversations help all team members to be more open and direct with each other and to deliver on commitments by creating mutual agreements and ownership. Using the "Examine the Issues, Decide Together, Get Moving, and Evaluate" model, team members can be proactive by asking and giving input and deciding together how they want to act and implement solutions.

Teamwork isn't just about using conversations to get along. Teams using critical conversations often find myriad ways to solve issues, such as the best way to utilize scarce resources, because they examine and execute on priorities rather than wasting time on unproductive activities. By implementing a way to communicate clearly and follow up with the actions decided on by the team, everyone has less rework down the line.

By making critical conversation the way work gets done, teamwork can be focused on results and the content of decision-making, rather than on unproductive processes. Joint accountability and action planning go hand in hand and both are important aspects of the conversation. Action plans created during the conversation not only help make individual improvements in areas that are essential to the success of the team (in other words, where the team should focus its efforts) but also enable sharing areas of effective behavior that the team wants to model and continue.

Making Work Easier

When done correctly, critical conversations gather information that will support mutually-agreed-on action plans, build relationships and teams that are willing to work together, and allow individuals to identify and solve issues that are important to them. Although this environment may seem like just a dream, it is possible.

Critical conversations make life easier. Period.

Think about how much time individuals have spent making the same decision again and again and again. How many times have you felt that you're having the same conversation again and again and again? Although it may seem like a good amount of effort goes into a critical conversation, the price of poor communication quickly adds up when you consider the cost of decreased productivity and the low morale of co-workers who feel they're banging their heads on a brick wall.

Critical conversations make life and work easier by focusing on a targeted decision or outcome, rather than trusting random luck or gut instinct. Yes, you may spend more time up front examining what's happening than if you just jumped into solutions. But after the problem is agreed on, you have a high probability that the solution will fix the problem — saving time and energy.

Developing Rapport Quickly

Two things develop rapport quickly: confidence and authenticity. Critical conversations do both, and they do them fast.

When faced with tough situations, whether they're emotional, rational, or anything else, having a clear process makes people feel confident in your ability to lead. Before any conversation starts, set the tone by letting the parties in the discussion know that you want to follow a clear (and proven) process to find solutions, and then describe the critical conversation process. Even though you may not have the answers to everything, you can provide a path to follow to the answers. Tell the participants that you first want to examine what's going on and get everyone's perspective on the situation before jumping into solutions. This matter-of-fact approach sets the tone in a positive and non-accusatory way, which puts everyone at ease and positions you as a poised and rational leader. That's a great start to any relationship.

Authenticity builds rapport. Each critical conversation starts with the initiator expressing a desire to solve the problem at hand, with no hidden agenda. If you're authentic, all the parties will see it in your actions. In return they'll start trusting not only you but also others. In this process, they'll feel comfortable being open and honest as well.

Becoming a Better Coach

With budget constraints, growing workloads, and an increasingly diverse workforce pulling leaders in all directions, the time spent with employees is often limited to project status updates, dealing with workplace disputes, or the annual performance planning cycle. Critical conversations take managers out of the putting-out-fires role (which is quite tiring) and convert them into guides and navigators who help the employees come up with practical ways to build self-sufficient career skills and gain the knowledge required to do their own jobs better. You can spend days trying to convince an employee why he needs to see the value of something or why he needs to change, or you can ask the individual the following two questions:

- "Do you agree that it's important for our team to change/improve/deliver exceptional service?"
- "What do you want to work on to make this change a reality?"

These exploring questions that are part of a critical conversation help create agreements and take the pressure off you by sharing responsibility for making decisions.

Although many senior executives hire their own leadership coaches, coaching can also be part of a working relationship between employees, peers, managers, and employees. By helping employees identify areas they want to improve, creating an environment of support, and providing ongoing feedback about progress made, supervisors can help employees develop self-improvement skills they'll use for their entire careers and develop a more productive team that's ready to navigate the challenges ahead.

Encouraging Different Ideas

Using the critical conversation model to acknowledge that differences exist and to gain agreement on what you're trying to achieve are some of the easiest ways to solicit different ideas regarding how to get work done. Even though you may be passionate about one way of doing things, working through the critical conversation process can help all the parties involved recognize that the group has multiple ways to reach desired outcomes.

Critical conversations support innovation and different ideas in a few ways. First, individuals build collaboration and teamwork when they respect one another by coming to the discussion with a genuine desire to help, and when they're willing and able to listen to other opinions before making a decision. Second, part of the critical conversation model is to decide on solutions and next steps. By voicing your own ideas and allowing others to voice theirs, a number of possible solutions are more likely to be presented, rather than just one that was developed through tunnel vision.

Managing Conflict Like a Pro

Even in the most challenging conversations, you can find something that everyone can agree on and evaluate, especially if you come to the table genuinely wanting to improve the situation (being genuine is the golden rule of critical conversations; see Chapter 1).

Although critical conversations focus on a specific dialogue, almost all critical conversations are focused on resolving some type of conflict. As a master of the art and science of conversation, you'll become an expert in examining what's going on and working with different parties to decide what to do next.

When you see a problem developing or find yourself in the middle of a conflict, use this roadmap and your critical conversation skills to move toward resolution:

1. **Examine the situation by asking about the current situation, issue, or concern.**

2. **Continue to gain perspective by researching the facts from all perspectives.**

3. **Work with others to decide what to do next. Include every step in the process from gaining agreement to brainstorming solutions.**

4. **Come up with a mutually agreeable action plan to resolve the conflict.**

5. **Check in on progress frequently.**

The critical conversation steps are more than just a foundation to build on, because the steps really are the blueprints that tell you how to resolve almost any disagreement or conflict.

Keep in mind that conflict is never pleasant, and some conflicts are harder than others to resolve. After a tough discussion, it is a good idea to follow up face-to-face or by phone to reinforce that you want to resolve the issue for everyone. Acknowledge that although the team may have disagreement over how to solve the problem, you appreciate that everyone agrees with what the problem is. This statement gets back to the golden rule of critical communication: Come to the table with a genuine desire to help make the situation better.

Chapter 20

Ten Ways to Keep Your Cool When No One Else Is

In This Chapter

▶ Finding productive ways to walk away from a bad conversation

▶ Discovering how to keep the conversation moving forward

*Y*ou know critical conversations can help make decisions stick, work relationships grow, and teams operate better. But unless every person you have a conversation with picks up her own copy of *Critical Conversations For Dummies* (which I highly recommend), sometimes people will lose their cool and potentially set the discussion down the wrong path. In Chapter 21, I review ten ways to stop a conversation from going south in the first place, and in Chapter 16 I provide surefire ways to work with difficult people. This chapter turns the focus away from other participants and gives ideas on how to handle your emotions during a critical conversation, especially when someone is pushing your buttons.

Taking a Breath and a Break

Taking a breath and a break gives you time to collect your thoughts and physically slow down the conversation until you feel confident that your responses will be professional and productive. When you feel your blood pressure rising, it's perfectly acceptable (and encouraged) to nod your head, take a breath, and ask whether it's okay to take a quick break. Often as little as five minutes can bring the emotions back down and allow you time to focus on the process and content of the discussion and not take comments personally or say something that you'll later regret. The issues that cause a critical conversation to take place are usually stressful and can put almost everyone on edge. Most likely the individual receiving the information may want and need a break too.

If taking a five-minute break isn't feasible, the simple act of focusing on your breathing and pausing for five seconds can at least silence the conversation for a few seconds. During those five seconds, relax the tensest part of your body, and then continue with the conversation.

Make an effort not to sound like a sick dragon huffing and puffing when you're taking calming breaths. The effort may seem unnatural and could lead to more stress in the conversation. Normal breaths will do just fine.

Getting a Move On

I can't overstate the benefits of getting out and exercising before a critical conversation. I'm not talking about running a marathon; a short walk can provide a renewed perspective, perhaps even optimism about the conversation, and can also provide a chance for you to crystalize everything that you want to say, away from the distractions of the office. This chapter, however, is about what to do during the conversation. If someone else is losing her cool during the conversation (and causing you to do the same), unless you work for a running shoe company, it may be hard to stop the conversation and run a 10K. But that doesn't mean you can't get moving to help keep your cool.

You may say, "I feel I'm getting a bit worked up as we talk about this topic, and I've found that taking a quick walk helps to clear my mind and focus on the process. Are you okay if we take a little break and come back to the discussion afterward?" Even taking a walk to the break room to get a drink can help calm your nerves. You may even consider asking the other participants in the conversation to walk with you.

Go for a walk before the conversation starts and keep the option open as a way to clear your mind and feel better during the conversation as well.

Expressing Your Emotions

Expressing emotions at work is something that very few people do well. And expressing emotions during a critical conversation and maintaining professionalism and composure is even harder. Add to that having a critical conversation with someone who *is* losing their cool, perhaps even yelling at you, and you can see how the conversation can quickly unravel.

If someone is raising her voice or saying things that perhaps only pirates should say, it's fine to counter the negative attack by letting her know how you feel in a more professional manner. Although you may feel that someone is a complete ogre, you know that saying so isn't a good idea. But you can express how you feel about the ogre's behavior. Start with "I feel" or "I am" statements, rather than "you are" statements.

Saying "I feel I can't communicate my message effectively when you say my ideas are all rubbish," or "I feel uncomfortable with you raising your voice" is a rational way to express how you feel without accusing the other person of anything. And then leave it at that for a moment. Usually, helping the other party just realize the consequences of their behavior can be enough to stop the poor behavior then and there. Nobody likes to be told exactly what to do next, so leaving the option open for them to choose to apologize or stop the behavior is a good first step.

If the behavior doesn't stop or change, you can be a bit more direct with what actions should happen next. Explain how you feel and a possible solution to the problem: "When you raise your voice, I feel like you limit my ability to communicate and limit the dialogue between the two of us. I've found that when I receive feedback with which I don't agree, listening and then expressing my view professionally helps the conversation go forward." After expressing your feelings and a possible solution, it's useful to ask for another agreement: "Are you willing to work together to create an action plan?"

If the other party agrees, the conversation can continue and you've helped lower the emotions by expressing your position in a calm and controlled voice. However, if the other party doesn't agree to work together or tells you that she couldn't care less about how you feel, it may be time to go to a fallback plan: asking for help.

Asking for Help

Another way you can get support when you feel that the conversation is going downhill and you're about ready to lose your cool is to ask for outside help. The help may come from somebody in human resources, a professional mediator, your manager, or even a peer (for more on facilitation and mediation head to Chapter 15 for information about third-party options).

For example, you may say, "If we're going to reach agreement, we may need to bring in an outside party to help." This isn't a threat; it's just an option if the current conversation doesn't generate the results it needs to. It isn't a threat to say, "I know this conversation has a number of emotions attached to it. If you feel more comfortable, we can bring in a facilitator to help us create solutions that we both can live with and support."

 When you're having a critical conversation with a group, you have another great source for help — the support of the group itself. If someone else is losing his cool and you're about ready to do the same, first state the facts and then ask whether the rest of the group agrees. For example, "Bob, it seems like you're very passionate about the subject and have many ideas. I'm wondering if the rest of the group has other ideas they'd like to share." For an even more direct way, you may say, "Bob, it seems like you're raising your voice and disagreeing with a number of these ideas during the discussion. We need to hear everyone's ideas to find a solution. Would anyone like to share an idea to help us move forward?" Both of these examples stop the behavior that's causing emotions to fly, at least temporarily, gives you time to regain your composure, and takes you off the hook of having to control the conversation by yourself.

After you ask the team for support — versus trying to do it all on your own — you may find at least a few other people are starting to lose their cool as well and welcome the intervention.

Of course, some of these tactics may not work all the time. Critical conversations are, after all, both an art and a science. Nobody can predict another person's behavior perfectly. If you try to state how you feel, and ask the others in the room whether they feel the same way, and the other participant is *still* making her emotions the center of the discussion, you may need to call a break (as I discussed above). Approach the person who is causing the behavior and state that a third-party may be needed to help find a resolution.

Stating the Obvious

Stating the obvious very clearly is sometimes the only way to help curb your own emotions and get through to an individual who isn't responding to any other method of conflict resolution during a conversation.

One of the elements I discuss in Chapter 16 is to state the obvious and ask what the other individual is hoping to accomplish with his behavior. You may simply say, "Bob you're yelling at me and I'm wondering what you're trying to achieve with this behavior." Is this statement harsh? It could be. But if you're genuine in your desire to change the situation and use a sincere and professional tone of voice, the message will get across without sarcasm or anger.

If it's the first time an individual has lost her cool and you're in a group setting during the conversation, wait to state the obvious and ask what the individual hopes to accomplish with her behavior in an offline discussion. If the behavior is getting out of hand, ask for short break and approach the individual one on one with your concerns and questions about what she's hoping to achieve.

Finding the Positive

You didn't think you could get through an entire book written by a leadership coach and not have some pep talk, did you? You don't need to be a cheerleader, but you create tremendous power by thinking positively. When you look at the individual who's making you lose your cool, she's obviously behaving the way she is for a reason. If you're positive and try to find out what that reason is, you may find that you're able to keep your emotions in check. It's easy to get cynical during a conversation, especially when someone is habitually losing her cool, but try to do something different: look for the good in that person.

Maintaining a positive attitude can start with finding a common goal on what you're trying to accomplish. The other individual may have a completely different view of *how* to accomplish that goal, but often you can find at least one goal in common.

Look at it another way: You can almost guarantee that the conversation won't be positive if you respond to negative behavior with negativity. I can almost guarantee that the conversation will be negative if two people are yelling, arguing, or throwing around words that really shouldn't be said.

Need a little help channeling your inner cheerleader? Try phrases like "Let's see what's possible" or "It may be better if . . ." Instead of saying, "I just can't do that," try "Let's see what's possible for us to do." Rather than tell someone they must do something — "You must stop yelling, arguing, disagreeing with me" — offer a positive suggestion — "It may be best for us to talk rather than yell" or "It may be better if we look at all the possible solutions rather than assign blame to what happened in the past."

Keeping the Problem in Perspective

If you are getting caught up in the moment, it can be helpful to take a step back and keep the problem in perspective. First, make sure you are putting the real problem ahead of personal style, politics, and individual interests. You may find yourself spending more energy figuring out how you want to solve the problem than actually working on the solution.

Second, visualize the bigger picture. One great way to keep problems in perspective is to practice visualizing the bigger picture and goal. For example, imagine how you will feel when the issue is resolved. How is work different? How is your life different? If you visualize how life and work will be better once the conversation is successful and behaviors change, it is easier to remember and focus on why the conversation started in the first place rather than all the small details that may not be going perfectly. For more on visualization, check out *Creative Visualization For Dummies* by Robin Nixon (Wiley).

Knowing When to Walk Away

When your own emotions are almost ready to boil over, sometimes it's best to walk away from the situation.

You may feel that you're almost ready to lose your cool because what you're trying to accomplish is starting to seem pretty darn close to futile. If you're having a critical conversation, and the other individual truly has a completely different point of view and it seems like there are no agreements to be made, it may be better to just stop instead of blowing your top. But before you do, try to make one more agreement to close the conversation: the agreement to walk away and not make things worse. This means saying, "It seems like we're having a hard time agreeing to work together. Are you willing to make an agreement to put aside arguing with one another about the process and focus on our own work?" Leaving the conversation with the agreement to at least agree to disagree and work civilly with one another is sometimes the only agreement two people with vastly different views can agree too.

If the issue really is going around and around in circles, and walking away is the best option before your emotions explode, saying "I can't have this conversation anymore" can potentially close the door to any future conversation, which is probably not what you're hoping to do.

As you end the conversation, offer a solution even if the solution doesn't involve you. Or try saying, "I can appreciate that we have different views of the situation. Based on our conversation, I'm not sure I can agree on the problem without getting emotional about the issue. Would you be willing to agree that we can ask someone to come in and help?" Let the other party know that you've proposed a number of ways to come to agreement over how to work together/get better results, she is free to work with anyone that might be of help to her, and that you suggest your supervisor, human resources, or another trusted leader in the organization become involved in the conversation.

This way of cooling your emotions does have a few stipulations. One, you can accept the other person's behavior at some level. Two, taking the high road means you need to accept that an individual isn't going to change and you'll be able live with that. This method is an option when peers are having conversations with one another (as opposed to a manager and employee having a performance discussion) and when teams seem to be at an impasse.

If emotions are just too high, bowing out is better than blowing up.

Keeping Forward Movement

When people are under time constraints, stress and emotional outbreaks are a common and natural outcome. One way to bring those emotions back down is to reset your expectations and slow down the conversation. Although you may be stressed about the speed, realize that some behaviors take time to change, especially if the bad behaviors have been reinforced for years. As long as the conversation is moving, even if it isn't as fast as you may hope, taking away the clock and deadline can bring everyone's emotions down a notch and keep the movement going forward.

It doesn't need to take a year to resolve a staff dispute, but it may take longer than an hour. The outcome of the first meeting may be a decision that all the parties are willing to work together and start examining what's happening by making a list of what the problems are. Then the group can come back and acknowledge why the issue exists, discuss different perspectives on the issue, and determine whether the parties agree to resolve the issue. You may be thinking that using two meetings to agree to resolve an issue will surely make you lose it. But think of the alternative: everyone is fed up, all parties walk away in a huff, and nothing changes. After you agree to resolve the situation, all the parties can start deciding and agreeing on what to do next.

Maybe the conversation isn't moving along as fast as you hoped, but it is moving along. Critical conversations take time, but if you keep moving forward with the discussion by following the critical conversation steps, you'll eventually get to that finish line, and resolve the issue, behavior, or problem, once and for all. That will make even the most stressed out individuals smile.

Staying Flexible

Flexibility can go a long way toward helping to prevent getting caught up in the moment. If the conversation is going south, recognize that progress on decisions and changes in behavior will not happen until the immediate emotional situation is directly dealt with. Name the feeling you think is happening and then ask if the other individual is willing to address the emotional situation first and then get back to the main message in the conversation. For example, you may say, "I asked for this meeting to talk about the progress of the project, but I sense that there may be some concerns or emotions I was not aware of. Would it be okay for us to talk about those concerns first and then get back to how to make the project run more smoothly?" Letting the other individual lead the conversation is another way of examining what is happening.

You may also find that less is more when it comes to leading the conversation. If the conversation is trending in a negative direction, the other party may just be trying to find a way to take control of a tough conversation. If you and the other participant agree on the goal of the conversation, it may be a good idea to let go of any preplanned agenda. A successful critical conversation happens when all parties agree on how to move forward and an environment of trust is built. Neither of these implies that you need to dictate every step of the conversation. You may say, "I think we both agree our teams can work better together. Do you want to propose a way we can address this together, or would you prefer if I set the agenda?" If the end goal is met, it really does not matter who takes credit for leading the process to get to the end goal.

Chapter 21

Ten Ways to Manage a Conversation That's Going South

In This Chapter

▶ Engaging participants who can't get their phones out of their hands

▶ Pinpointing ways to keep agreements from unraveling

▶ Playing referee during the blame game

*T*he best laid plans can come unraveled when less-than-pleasant team members or employees start showing signs of reckless behavior. Whether you're having a one-on-one conversation or facilitating team agreements with the critical conversation tools, pack your toolkit with these surefire ways to manage a conversation that's going south.

Dealing with Texting, Typing, and Checking Messages

The beauty of being connected can be devastating for a conversation. Whether you're on a phone call and hear typing in the background, or someone starts looking at his phone habitually during a conversation (yes, this does happen!), try to stop the behavior then and there. If someone is doing something else, he isn't focusing on the conversation. Sure, someone may be checking the clock or seeing whether the phone call that was on vibrate was from his kid's school, but clocks and calls don't need to be checked every minute.

I don't mean to be too harsh, but if someone is texting, typing, or checking his phone during a critical conversation, have a frank discussion. Ask what's going on. A lighthearted but direct, "John, you keep looking at your phone. Do you need to be somewhere else?" will work just fine. Offer to be realistic about the expectations and timing of the meeting. For example, you may ask, "I see you are getting a number of calls. Is this time good for our conversation, or should we find a time that works better for your schedule when we can both put down our phones and talk?"

The response to this behavior is really not that much different if the critical conversation happens in a one-on-one setting. If someone's phone keeps vibrating while you're having the discussion, simply say, "I know that we're all busy, but the phone vibrating on the desk is making it hard for me to focus on our conversation. Is a better time for us to have the conversation later today when you can leave your phone at your desk?" As with so many disruptive behaviors, saying what's happening, what you're feeling, and a possible alternative is often the best bet to keep a critical conversation on track.

Meeting the Timekeeper

The evil and a bit outdated twin of the phone-checking guy or texting gal is the watch-checker. This is the individual who not only checks his watch but also lets you know exactly what the watch says. Following a two-point strategy can help put the time keeper and you at ease:

- ✔ **Appreciate and recognize the timekeeper's value.** Although some corporate cultures are notorious for always starting five minutes late, do your best to start conversations on time and to end on time. This may mean building in a few extra minutes for discussions and late arrivals.

- ✔ **Thank the timekeeper for keeping the meeting on time, and offer to schedule a conclusion to a meeting when needed.** As a facilitator or initiator of the discussion, use the last ten minutes (more if you have a bigger group) to review the agreements that were made during the meeting, and go over the next step after the conversation. Yes, this may mean breaking up a critical conversation, but that's a better option than rushing through agreements, opinions, and decisions that come apart soon after the meeting anyway.

However, if the timekeeper is preventing the meeting from moving forward, it may be best to deal directly with this as a challenging behavior. Take the time to head over to Chapter 16 to find out more ways to create positive solutions when you are faced with difficult behaviors.

Wording: Me-versus-You Language

Although you may come to the conversation with a genuine desire to make things better, not everyone is going to be in the same camp, at least not at the beginning. Recognize that this may happen and be prepared for it. Using the pronouns "we," "us," and "our" when you're talking about decisions and agreements can help create an environment of support and inclusion.

Me-versus-you language is often rooted in different opinions of how to solve a problem or what the problem is in the first place. For example, the individual may say, "You just don't understand how hard it is for me to do my job," or "You aren't working with these people on a day-to-day basis." In these situations, it's often useful to agree that there are different opinions or ideas and to acknowledge that the other party may be right. You can acknowledge behaviors and words neutrally by saying, "You may be right. You may be facing a situation I've never been in before." These statements address the problem without judgment.

Next, restate the purpose of the conversation and find out whether the other person is willing to work with you. You may try using pronouns like "we" and "us" to show your commitment to working together to solve the problem. For example, say, "I want to help make the situation better. Are you willing to work together to solve the issue? I know that if we work together, we have a better chance of solving the situation we've faced in the past."

Checking Body Language

Body language says a lot. Of course, you may not always have the luxury of seeing how someone is reacting if you can't have the conversation face to face, but even if you're 1,000 miles away, body language can make a conversation go south. If someone is tapping his feet, rolling his eyes, or crossing his arms, you may ask the individual to assess his own level of participation in the conversation. You could say, "I sense a bit of hesitation. Am I right?" If you're in a group conversation, you may stop and ask whether the others agree and what the group wants to do about the situation.

If you're in a one-on-one discussion, you can be even more direct and state what you see and ask what would help the other person become more involved in the conversation. Of course, some body language cues are simply nerves — so give yourself and the other individuals a break and accept that some people may have nervous or fidgety reactions to receiving tough news during a critical conversation. For more ways to read and work with nonverbal cues, check Chapter 7.

Observing When the Talker becomes Silent

Dealing with silent team members or individuals is often best done by creating opportunities for participation. You may try asking for their opinions or letting individuals think of solutions in a smaller setting or by themselves. These tactics work well when someone doesn't participate in a conversation. But dealing with a nonstop talker who immediately becomes silent takes a different approach.

The first option is to do absolutely nothing. Maybe the talker is done with all his comments. Maybe with your perfect conversation skills, the talker is finally processing information and discovering how to listen. There are plenty of possibilities, so be careful not to jump to conclusions too quickly.

However, if the person just stops participating in a group or in a one-on-one conversation and you need participation to build agreement about what to do next, it can be useful to state what you see. Saying, "I noticed that you aren't participating anymore," is a bit confrontational. To use more cooperative language that generates results, try saying, "I noticed that I've been doing much of the talking. I know you came to the meeting with so many ideas; can we start applying them to the problem at hand?" If you're in a larger group setting, it may be best to pull the person aside on a break to ask a similar question.

You may also want to give ownership of the issue back to the currently silent talker. You can help drive this accountability by targeting questions more directly. For example, saying, "This action plan is our responsibility — not just yours or mine — so I'd like your input into what you're willing to agree to," is a kind yet direct way of saying, "Speak now or forever hold your peace."

Getting Defensive

People naturally defend themselves and their opinion when they receive feedback. When someone goes on the defensive, don't back down — doing so undercuts the conversation. Instead, recognize the individual's opinion and ask him to focus on the purpose of the meeting before defending his position. For example, you may say, "I can see how you may have strong opinions about the feedback. I'm hoping we can work together to get clarity on the real reasons for the issue, and then we can look at the pros and cons of possible solutions." By delaying the defensive reaction, you may find that the other individual starts to understand the rational facts, instead of just voicing his emotional reaction.

State what's happening and explain that conflict over problems, solutions, and ideas is natural. Then ask whether the other person is willing to focus on gaining a clear understanding of the problem before making judgment.

If the defensive behavior is focused on everything that could go wrong or what went wrong in the past — talk about what could happen and what is possible. For example, you could say, "I see that there are many reasons why things didn't work in the past. This conversation is about fixing these issues in the future. Are you willing to focus on the future and what can be done to make change happen?" This statement doesn't discount the past, but it's really hard to make excuses for things that are going to happen in the future. It may also be helpful to have a back-up plan for all the items on the action plan. If you have a clear plan for what to do when something unexpected happens, you can limit the number of excuses you may hear in the future.

Handling the Situation When the Offense Strikes Back

Of course the opposite of going on the defensive is letting someone else go on offense and attack others. Perhaps the individual is pushing buttons or being overly aggressive. If you're in a group conversation, try to redirect the conversation by asking others to participate in the discussion. First, acknowledge their participation and then turn to others in the room and ask, "How about the rest of you? What are some of your views?" An offensive participant can become dominating quickly, so try to diffuse the situation by actively including others.

If you're having a one-on-one discussion and the individual starts going on the offensive, perhaps by telling you what you need to do ("You need to be a better manager," "You need to give me more time," or "You need to brush your teeth more"), acknowledge his statements, and then turn the discussion back to the purpose. For example, you may say, "I recognize that I can do things differently to support you. If you feel confident that we have a clear understanding of the problem, let's look at what you, I, and we can do together to make things better." Acknowledge that improvement isn't a one-way street, but in the end the other individual needs to be willing to take responsibility for changing his behavior (with your support, of course).

Ending the Blame Game

Even worse than a defensive or offensive participant is someone who loves to throw blame around, often not taking any responsibility or ownership for anything. A good place to start putting an end to this behavior is to follow some of the tips for working with difficult behaviors in Chapter 16.

Someone who blames others is often doing one of two things (sometimes both): hiding his own insecurities or just trying to get away with doing nothing. If someone is insecure about his job, abilities, or skills, do your best to build rapport and let him know that you're there to help — not to lay blame. But if someone is just trying to get away with doing nothing, you may also employ two other stealth tactics. First, you can simply say that you're confused about why there's so much blame when the goal of the conversation is to gain a clear understanding of what's happening and to find potential solutions — not to harp on who did or didn't do what. Ask the individual to take a break from pointing fingers and to focus on the process.

And, of course, you can always play the humor card. If you play it without being sarcastic or blaming others, humor can help redirect the blame, For example, try saying, "It seems like there's plenty of blame to go around — I'm wondering whether there are just as many ideas for solving the problem."

In some cases, especially in a group conversation when the blame game starts, you may need to take a break and talk off-line about the consequences of blaming others.

Keeping Agreements in Tact

When agreements unravel during a conversation, you may feel like all that work to get to an agreement went to waste. But quite the contrary is true. Agreements in a critical conversation are put in place throughout the process so that regrouping is easy when conversations start going south.

In Chapter 1, I lay out the key agreements that critical conversations need to have. These agreements aren't just for fun — they help keep conversations on track and help build support for decisions and actions. If the first agreement is to sit in a room and have a discussion, when someone starts arguing, the participants are reminded that they made an agreement to work together. Then they can decide whether that agreement is still in place. Often this slight push is enough to refocus the conversation.

If the conversation is truly struggling or derailing because of a lack of agreement rather than personal conflicts, ask whether the conversation is still focused on the agreed-on problem or solution or whether something else is going on. You may interject with something like, "We agreed to work together to solve the problem. Then we agreed that all the issues were on the table, but now we're having trouble coming up with solutions. Do we need to revisit the problem, or is something else going on here?" This method works just as well in a small group or one-on-one setting as it does in a larger conversation.

A final opportunity to redirect a conversation when agreements unravel is to refocus on the process. You may simply restate the agreed-on process, and ask whether the participant wants a little more information about how the process works. Stepping back to explain the process and gaining agreement to move forward takes little time and can deliver big results in the effort to move the conversation forward.

Tempering Emotions

When the other party or parties in the conversation are so upset or emotional that they can't focus on tasks, the conversation may come to a screeching halt, or worse, turn into a complete wreck. First, don't get caught up in the emotions — even if you completely agree or disagree with the agreement — or force decisions. Sometimes progress on finding solutions or even discovering the problem can't happen until the emotion is resolved or at least dealt with. There is tremendous value in dealing with the emotions because it can lead to progress.

Second, call a spade a spade. Name the feeling, emotion, or behavior you're experiencing or sensing in the room. By simply saying, "I sense there is tension in the room," you open the possibility of others wanting to resolve that tension or even recognizing its presence.

After you voice the feeling, you or the facilitator can help the team agree on ways to address the emotional situation first and then get back to the purpose of the meeting. This step often looks like a critical conversation within a critical conversation. Recommend to the group that it examine and acknowledge the feelings and opinions of others, and then make a decision about whether the meeting or discussion can continue.

Finally, if you're in a large group conversation, ask that everyone support others who may be emotional. Some people are better at dealing with the emotions of highly charged situations, and some people need to cry it out. If you're in a one-on-one conversation, simply state (and mean) that you understand or at least recognize what the other person may be feeling.

Index

• *Numerics* •

360-degree communication
    review, 124

• *A* •

accommodating words, turning
    confrontational into, 95–96
accountability, employee, 188
accusations, 91
acknowledgment
    in customer conversations,
        252, 253, 260
    dominator of conversation, 35
    of feelings in team conversations,
        220, 221, 266–267
    of feelings in workplace
        complaints, 220, 221
    of feelings of others, 207
    of losing your cool, 144
action
    building trust with, 140
    as motivation, 134
action plans
    agreeing on goals and
        expectations, 160–161
    characteristics of, 65–66
    for difficult behaviors, 239–242
    elements of, 161–164
    example plan, 162
    performance, 27, 191–192
    responding to ignored, 167–168
    SMART goals, 161
    team conversations, 267
    what will happen, 161–163
    when will it happen, 163–164
    who will make it happen, 163
active listening
    active silence, 109–110
    assessing nonverbal cues with, 112
    to build rapport, 140
    clarifying questions, 110–111
    listening *versus*, 108

    reflecting before responding, 110
    steps in, 109
active silence, 109–110
advice, giving unsolicited, 208
agenda, 132–133
agreeing to disagree, 156
agreements
    acknowledgment of the problem, 17
    on action plan, 160–161
    approach to finding a solution, 18
    asking for, 52
    assertive communication
        style for, 119–121
    building early on, 63–64
    in customer conversations, 258
    examples of, 63–64
    keeping intact, 296–297
    in mediated conversation, 227
    by passive communicators, 117, 118
    passive-aggressive behavior
        and, 119, 122
    on performance expectations, 73
    recapping and rephrasing
        previous, 156–157
    reinforcing during conversation, 64
    SMART, 64–65
    in staff disputes, 208–209
    in team conversations, 267
    willingness to work together, 17
alternatives, discussing
        possible, 62–63
anger
    nonverbal expressions of, 107,
        245–246
    in staff disputes, 207, 208
anxiety, 25–26
argumentative language, 91, 95–96
arms, crossed, 102–103
art of conversation, 15–16, 17–18
assertive communicators
    conversation example, 120–121
    described, 119
    managing style under
        stress, 124–125

assertive communicators *(continued)*
  qualities of, 119
  using to move to action, 121
assumptions
  assuming the worst, 237
  clarifying, 125–126
attitude
  bad, 138
  building trust and rapport
    with, 139–141
  maintaining positive, 137–138
audience, distracted, 33, 34, 37–38
authenticity
  being authentic, 39
  rapport built with, 279
avoiding critical conversations, 29–31
awareness, asking about, 97–98

• *B* •

back-stabbing gossiper, 244–245
bad attitudes, 138
bad behaviors. *See* difficult behaviors
bad news, shying away from, 29–30
Bailey, Keith (*Customer Service For Dummies*), 254
behavior
  actionable, 19
  asking about awareness of, 97–98
  describing impact or
    consequences of, 59
  evaluating change in, 67–68
  identifying desired, 62
  improving team, 270–272
  linking consequences to, 19
  mirroring, 102, 140
  obnoxious, 210–211
  offensive, 210
  passive-aggressive, 119, 122
  patterns of behavior within the
    group, 72
  phone-checking, 291–292
  resolving difficult, 231–247
  rewarding right, 241–242
  separating from the person, 149, 233
  watch-checking, 291–292
benefits of critical conversations,
  13–14

Benun, Ilise (*Public Relations For Dummies*), 259
bias, 72, 76
blame, 76, 224, 296
body language
  checking, 293
  crossed arms, 102–103
  cultural differences, 102
  of direct communicators, 115
  effective and ineffective
    compared, 101
  in example conversations, 100
  hand gestures, 104
  mirroring, 140
  relaxed and open, 103
break, taking, 283–284
breath
  calming, 283–284
  focus on breathing, 284
building relationships, 24–25
buzz words, 91

• *C* •

challenging behaviors. *See* difficult
  behaviors
challenging situations
  handling the unexpected, 148–149
  keeping tough discussions
    encouraging, 149–154
  losing your cool, 144–146
  mistakes, righting, 143–144
  refocusing off-track conversations,
    157–158
  resistance, dealing with, 154–157
change, possibility of, 138
checking messages, during
  conversation, 291–292
check-ins, 68, 165–166
clarifying questions, 110–111
closing the conversation
  action plan creation, 160–164
  best methods for, 66
  crucial nature of, 66, 159–160
  follow-up note, 164–165
  formal documentation, 166–167
  goal of, 66
  scheduling follow-up meetings,
    165–166

coach
  becoming better, 279–280
  discouraging, 151
  motivating, 151
coaching
  benefits of leadership, 279–280
  described, 176
  difficult behaviors, 239–240
  employee performance, 195
  finding coachable moments, 179
  manager-to-employee discussion
      compared, 177–178
  methods, 176–179
  role models and mentors, 241
collaboration, 91
commitments
  action plan development, 65–66
  building agreements early on, 63–64
  coachable moments, 179
  gaining, 20, 65–67
  keeping, 39
common ground, 97
communication. *See* nonverbal
      communication; verbal
      communication
communication review,
      360-degree, 124
communication style
  adapting to build rapport, 140
  assertive, 119–121, 124–125
  assessment of, 114, 121–123
  clarifying assumptions, 125–126
  described, 113–114
  direct, 114–116, 121, 125
  feedback on, 123–124
  managing under stress, 124–125
  passive, 116–119, 121, 125
  problems facing communicators,
      124
  sharpening your, 123–126
compassion, firing employees
      with, 195–197
complainers, 232, 233
complaints, customer. *See* customer
      conversations
complaints, workplace
  addressing, 215–220
  confidentiality of, 223, 224, 228, 229

defining, 216–217
duration of issue, 216
emotions in, 222–223
ethical concerns, 218, 219
legal concerns, 216, 217–219
mediator use in, 225–227
morale issues, 219
moving forward after, 227–229
not addressed by critical
      conversations, 217–219
off-the-wall inquiries, 220
overview of, 215–216
separating personal issues from
      valid grievances, 224
severity and risk of, 216
that benefit from a critical
      conversation, 219–220
using critical conversations,
      220–221
compromise, in team
      conversations, 271
concerns, combining or grouping, 79
confidence, 276
confidentiality
  employee performance
      and, 197–198
  location for conversations, 13
  by third parties in critical
      conversations, 46
  in workplace complaints, 223, 224,
      228, 229
conflicts
  avoidance by passive
      communicators, 117, 118
  managing, 280–281
  necessary, 201–202
  staff disputes, 199–214
  steps to resolve, 204–206
  in team conversations, 271
  turning into positive
      experience, 207–208
  unnecessary, 200–201
  unresolved, 25
confrontational language
  avoiding, 92–95
  turning confrontational words into
      accommodating words, 95–96
confrontational triggers, 93–94

consensus, in team conversations, 271
consequences
    clarifying, 61
    describing, 59
    linking behavior to, 19
    prioritizing multiple issues, 78
contemplative questions, 132
conversation-ready cultures, 182–183
conversation-resistant cultures, 183
cooperative language, 91–98, 294
corporate speak, 91, 137
Covey, Stephen (leadership guru), 31
Creative Visualization For Dummies
    (Nixon), 288
critical conversations
    agreements in, 17–18
    art and science of, 15–18
    benefits, 13–14
    building relationships with, 24–25
    closing, 66, 159–168
    described, 10–11
    difficulty of, 28–32
    EDGE model, 18–21
    examples of, 27
    foundation analogy, 9
    fundamentals of, 44
    goals for, 39–40
    golden rule of, 14–15
    guidelines, 57
    kicking off, 51–55
    length of, 51
    managing performance with, 26–27
    parties involved in, 12, 21–22,
        27, 44–46
    pitfalls of, avoiding, 32–42
    preparation for, 46–51
    resolving issues with, 25–26
    roles in, 44–46
    shying away from, 29–31
    that go south, 290–298
    traps in, 14–15
    walking away from, 288–289
    when to have, 11, 50, 69, 74–77
    where to have, 13, 51
    why they matter, 23–27
critical success factors, 267
Cross-Cultural Selling For Dummies
    (Lee, Roberts, and Kraynak), 102

crossed arms, 102–103
crying in the workplace, 213–214
culture, organizational, 182–183
customer(s)
    giving in to, 250
    hostile, 257–258
    internal and external issues
        compared, 254–255
    keeping, 260–262
    satisfaction, 251, 256
    service, 251–252, 256, 257
    that cross the line, 256–259
    upset, 255–256
    wanting talk with manager, 256–257
customer conversations
    check back with customers, 261
    closing the conversation, 66
    delivering bad news, 259–260
    examples, 250, 251–252, 257
    with hostile customers, 257–258
    key elements, 252–254
    knowing what upset customers
        want, 255–256
    openness and honesty in, 259–260
    renegotiating the future, 261–262
Customer Service For Dummies
    (Leland and Bailey), 254

• *D* •

data, influencing power of, 277
day-to-day conversations, 180–182
debate, 92
decision-making approaches
    decide and announce, 268
    decide together, 269–270
    individual input sought and leader
        decides, 268–269
    organizational culture and, 182, 183
    team input sought and leader
        decides, 269
defensive reaction, 47, 294–295
destruction, nonverbal expressions
    of, 107
dialogue, components of, 86
differences
    acknowledgment of, 280
    stating existence of, 98

difficult behaviors
    action plans for, 239–242
    anger and hostility, 245–246
    coaching and support, use
        of, 239–241
    complainers, 232, 233
    critical conversations for, 237–238
    defining, 232–233
    education and mentoring,
        use of, 241
    examples of, 232, 243–246
    gossip, 234, 244–245
    intent of, 233–235
    labeling, 235–236
    pattern of, 247
    resolving, 231–247
    rewarding right behaviors, 241–242
    screaming, 238
difficulty, acknowledgment of, 97
direct communicators
    assertive communicators
        compared to, 121
    assumptions about, 116
    behaviors of, 114–116
    described, 114
    managing style under stress, 125
direction, common, 33, 35, 39–42
disagreements, 156
DiSC (assessment), 72, 114
discrimination, 217, 222–223
disrespect, nonverbal expressions
    of, 107
distortion of message meaning, 86
distracted audience, 33, 34, 37–38
diversity, valuing, 214
documentation
    action plan, 162
    during follow-up meeting, 166
    follow-up notes, 164–165
    formal, 166–167
Dodd-Frank Act, 218
dress and appearance
    effective and ineffective
        compared, 101
    in example conversations, 100
    professional, 103–104

• *E* •

EDGE model
    customer conversations, 253, 260
    deciding on options to move
        forward, 19–20, 62–65
    evaluation of impact, 20–21, 67–68
    examining facts/data, 19, 58–61
    firing employees, 196
    following action steps and
        agreements, 167–168
    gaining commitments, 20, 65–67
    in hiring employees, 172
    overview of, 18–21, 57
    in performance conversations,
        187–192
    in workplace complaints, 221
education, for changing
    behaviors, 241
ego, 138
elephant issues, 76–77
e-mail, 31–32
emotional intelligence, 146, 214
Emotional Intelligence For Dummies
    (Stein), 146, 214
emotional statement, 16
emotions
    acknowledgment in team
        conversations, 266–267
    anger, 107, 207, 208, 245–246
    anxiety, 25–26
    confrontational language, 92
    control yours, 237
    crying, 213–214
    difficult behaviors and, 237
    expressing during critical
        conversations, 206
    expressing to keep your
        cool, 284–285
    fact *versus,* 28–29
    festering, 50
    hot buttons, 136–137, 231, 232, 233
    keeping your cool, 283–290
    losing your cool, 144–146
    managing high, 54–55
    mediation and, 225

emotions *(continued)*
  preparation for conversation, 133–138
  reflected in nonverbal cues, 99, 107
  self-awareness of, 146
  tempering, 297–298
  uncontrolled, 130
  in workplace complaints, 222–223
empathy, 151, 207, 223, 237
employee letter, formal, 166–167
employees
  ability to improve, 193
  accountability of, 188
  asking for perspective of, 26
  confidentiality, 197–198
  consequences for, 188
  evaluating progress, 193–194
  everyday conversations, 180–182
  exceptional performance, 175–176
  expectations in writing, 188
  firing, 66, 67, 195–197
  hiring, 172–173
  job description, 188
  morale issues, 219
  performance conversation, 185–195
  performance management, 174, 175–176
  staff disputes, 199–214
  willingness to improve, 193
  workplace complaints, 215–229
encouraging environment, maintaining, 149–154
English Grammar For Dummies (Woods), 88
enthusiasm, level of, 105–106
EQ (emotional intelligence), 146
ethical concerns
  that also break the law, 218
  workplace complaints, 219
evaluations
  of customer conversations, 254
  in EDGE model, 20–21
  employee development, 175–176
  follow-up meetings, 68
  of staff dispute conversations, 206
everyday conversations, 180–182

examination of facts
  in EDGE model, 19, 58–61
  in performance conversation, 187–189
  in workplace complaints, 220–221
Example icon, 6
excuses, 137, 295
exercising, 284
expectations
  agreeing on in action plans, 160–161
  of employees in writing, 188
  performance, 73–74
  realistic, 138
  unmanaged, 130
expressions. *See also* nonverbal communication
  crossed arms, 102–103
  cultural differences, 102
  effective and ineffective compared, 101
  facial, 101, 103
  paying attention to, 100, 102
eye contact
  effective and ineffective compared, 101
  in example conversations, 100
  maintaining appropriate, 103

• F •

facial expressions
  effective and ineffective compared, 101
  using genuine, 103
facilitating team conversations
  in action, 266–267
  art and science of, 264–265
  facilitating after conversation, 267
  vital factors in, 265–266
facilitators
  finding neutral party, 147
  focus on process, 146
  leader role compared, 202–203
  role in critical conversations, 46, 147
  in staff disputes, 202–203, 207
  of team conversations, 264–267

fact-action messages, 196
facts
  asking for additional information,
    59–60
  defined, 88
  emotions colliding with, 28–29
  examination in EDGE
    model, 19, 58–61
  examination in performance
    conversation, 187–189
  examination in workplace
    complaints, 220–221
  focus on, 59
  leading with, 96
  objective-focused conversations, 70
  presenting as facts, 88
  starting with, 206
fair warning, giving, 49–51
feedback
  approaches to giving, 47–48
  building trust with, 39
  coaching, 177, 178
  on communication style, 123–124
  creating results with, 180–182
  defensive reaction to, 294
  to develop relationships, 231
  initiator's role in, 44
  meaningful, 39
  open climate for, 27
  positive, 181–182
  preparing to give, 47–48
  providing impactful, 265
  providing to employees, 188
  recognition, 241–242
  reflecting current actions, 75
  rules for, 181–182
  in team conversations, 265
  tips for presenting negative, 189
  as two-way street, 182
  on workplace complaint process,
    229
  writing down, 48
feelings. *See also* emotions
  acknowledgment in team
    conversations, 266–267
  acknowledgment in workplace
    complaints, 220, 221
    of customers, 252, 253, 260
  "I feel" statement, 204
fight-or-flight reaction, 209
firing employees, 66, 67, 195–197
flattery, by imitation, 102
flexibility
  of assertive communicators,
    119, 120
  with boundaries, 154–155
  dealing with resistance, 154–155
  in difficult conversations, 290
  off track conversation, 131
focus
  on actions, not generalizations, 75
  on behaviors rather than labels,
    235–236
  clarifying, 158
  dealing with resistance, 154–155
  on process, 146, 150
  refocusing the conversation,
    157–158
  teamwork, 277–278
follow-through
  follow-up meeting, 165–166
  follow-up note, 164–165
  scheduling follow-up conversations,
    165–166
forward movement, maintaining,
  289–290

• *G* •

genuine, being, 14–15, 138
goals
  in action plan, 65, 160, 161, 162
  being clear on, 39–40
  coachable moments, 179
  common, 97
  of conversation closure, 66
  finding common, 24–25
  for performance conversations,
    186, 191
  performance management, 174, 175
  realistic, 64–65
  resolving staff disputes, 203
  SMART, 64–65, 174, 175, 191, 267
  team conversations, 267

golden rule of critical conversations, 14–15
gossip, 88, 234, 244–245
ground rules, setting, 154–155
group conversations
  creating a productive team, 163–170
  decision-making approaches, 268–270
  facilitating, 264–267
  improving team behavior, 270–272
group dynamics, 265, 271
group think, 270
grudges, 211–212

• *H* •

hand gestures, 104
handling the unexpected, 148–149
harassment, 210, 218
healthy lifestyle, 131
help
  after losing your cool, 145
  asking for, 145, 285–286
  from facilitators, 146–147
  to keep your cool, 285–286
  from other party, 147–148
hidden agenda, 14–15
high stakes, managing, 54–55
Hildebrandt, Terry H. (*Leading Business Change For Dummies*), 44–45, 183, 269
hiring, 172–173
honesty
  building trust and rapport with, 139–140
  in customer conversations, 259–260
  difficult behaviors and, 237, 238
hostility
  dealing with hostile customer, 257–258
  impatience and, 31
  nonverbal expressions of, 107
  resolving behavior, 245–246
hot buttons, 136–137, 231, 232, 233

human resources department
  role in critical conversations, 46
  working with, 195, 198
  workplace complaints and, 216, 217, 218, 221, 228
humor, use of, 54–55, 296

• *I* •

"I feel" statement, 204
"I" statements
  to avoid defensive reactions, 47
  confrontational language and, 95
  to describe your perspective, 206
  examples of use, 30
  to keep your cool, 285
  use in staff disputes, 207
  use of word, 90–91
  working with difficult behaviors, 235
icons, used in book, 5–6
ideas, encouraging different, 280
imitation, 102
impact
  assessing performance conversation, 192–194
  evaluating, 67–68
  of poor behavior, 59
impatience, 31
improvement, evaluating employees, 193–194
indicators for critical conversations
  objective issues, 70
  performance issues, 72–74
  subjective issues, 70
  workplace dynamics, 71–72
influence
  levers of, 153–154
  use without overpowering, 276–277
information, asking for additional, 59–60
inherited issues, 75–76
initiator of the critical conversation, 44–45
inner drive, source of, 135
innovation, 179

intelligence, emotional, 146, 214
intent
    asking about, 59–60
    of difficult behaviors, 233–235
interactions between individuals in
        the workplace, 71–72
interruptions, 137
intervening in staff disputes, 202–203
interviews, 173
intimidation, nonverbal expressions
        of, 107
issues, examining in team
        conversations, 266

• J •

jargon, 91
job description, 188

• K •

keeping your cool
    asking for help, 285–286
    exercising, 284
    expressing emotions, 284–285
    flexibility, 290
    forward movement, maintaining,
        289–290
    perspective, 288
    positive attitude, 287
    stating the obvious, 286–287
    taking a breath/break, 283–284
    walking away, 288–289
Kirshenbaum, Richard (*Public
        Relations For Dummies*), 259
knowledge, sharing of, 182, 183
Kraynak, Joe (*Cross-Cultural Selling
        For Dummies*), 102

• L •

labels, 235–236
language
    body language, 100, 101, 102–103,
        115, 293
    confrontational, 91–96
    cooperative, 91–98, 294

leader
    decision-making approaches
        of, 268–270
    facilitator role compared, 202–203
    mediated conversations
        concerning, 226
leadership style assessments, 72
*Leading Business Change For
        Dummies* (Schlachter and
        Hildebrandt), 44–45, 183, 269
leading conversations, benefits of
    coaching improvement, 279–280
    confidence, 276
    conflict management, 280–281
    ease of working life, 278
    encouragement of different
        ideas, 280
    healthy working relationships, 277
    increasing leadership potential,
        275–276
    influence, 276–277
    rapport development, 279
    teamwork focus, 277–278
leading questions, 132
Lee, Micheal Soon (*Cross-Cultural
        Selling For Dummies*), 102
legal issues
    discrimination, 217, 222–223
    harassment, 210, 218
    mediation and, 226
    safety issues, 218
    separating personal issues from
        valid grievances, 224
    workers' compensation, 217–218
    workplace complaints and,
        216, 217–219
Leland, Karen (*Customer Service
        For Dummies*), 254
length of critical conversation, 51
listening
    active, 108–112, 140
    to all parties, 14
    blocked by confrontational
        language, 92
    by leader, 146
    to others, 24
    by passive communicators, 116
    talking more than, 115

Lloyd, Ken (*Performance Appraisals & Phrases For Dummies*), 174
location for critical conversation, 13, 51
lose-lose outcome, 80
losing your cool, 144–146

• M •

manager, customer conversations with, 256–257
Maslow's hierarchy of needs, 135
"me" language, 293
meaning, underlying, 267
mediation, 225
mediators
  benefits of using, 226–227
  role in critical conversations, 46
  selecting, 225
  steps in professionally-mediated conversation, 227
  when to work with, 225–226
mentoring, 176, 241
me-*versus*-you language, 293
mirroring, 102, 140
money, as motivation, 134
morale issues, 219
motivations
  action, 134
  coachable moments, 179
  with everyday conversations, 180
  identifying other person's, 40–42
  identifying your, 80, 134–135
  money, 134
  of others, 40–42, 136
  recognition, 134
  respect, 134
  results from, 150–151
  teamwork, 134
  voicing, 135
motivation-seeking questions, 41
multiple issues
  creating win for everyone, 79–80
  dealing with, 77–78
  patience, 81
  prioritizing, 78–79
Myers-Briggs (assessment), 72, 114

• N •

name-dropping, 15
needs
  meeting, 135–136
  supporting others', 151–152
nerves
  acknowledging and controlling, 104
  expressions of, 101
nervous habits, 101
neutral party, finding, 147
Nixon, Robin (*Creative Visualization For Dummies*), 288
nodding, 102, 103
nonverbal communication
  active listening, 108–112
  assessment of, 112
  body language, 100, 101, 102–103, 115, 293
  crossed arms, 102–103
  described, 99
  dress and appearance, 100, 101, 103–104
  emotions reflected in, 99, 107
  example, 100
  expressions, 100–104
  eye contact, 100, 101, 103
  facial expressions, 101, 103
  mirroring, 102, 140
  mistakes, 107
  nerves and stress, 101, 104
  nodding, 102, 103
  paying attention to, 100, 102
  silence, 106
  space, 106–107
  in team conversation, 271
  voice, 101, 104–106
note, follow-up, 164–165

• O •

objective
  keeping focus on, 55
  setting for meeting, 48–49
objective issues, addressing with critical conversations, 70
objective statements, 49

obnoxious co-worker, dealing with, 210–211
offensive comments, 210
offensive participants, 295
one-sided conversation, 33, 34, 35–37
open-ended questions, 38, 111, 132
opening the discussion, 51–53
openness
  body language and, 103
  building trust and rapport with, 139–140
  in confrontational situation, 97
  in customer conversations, 259–260
  voice tone and, 105
opinions
  acknowledging others, 19
  acknowledgment in team conversations, 266–267
  definition of, 88
  expressing when starting conversations, 206
  validating, 155
options
  leading with, 96
  to move forward, 19–20
organizational culture, 182–183
"our" language, 293
overcommunicating, 246
overdue critical conversations, 74–77

● *P* ●

pace of conversation, 115, 131
paraphrasing, 111
participation
  creating opportunities for, 294
  by passive communicators, 118
parties involved in conversations, 12, 21–22, 27, 44–46
passive communicators
  assertive communicators compared to, 121
  behaviors of, 118
  conversation examples, 116–117
  described, 116
  managing style under stress, 125
  participation of, 118

passive-aggressive behavior, 119, 122
patience
  multiple concerns and, 81
  realistic expectations, 138
  slowing down in relationships, 31
  in staff disputes, 207
  voice tone, 106
perceptions
  acknowledging other, 58–61
  clarifying, 111
Performance Appraisals & Phrases For Dummies (Lloyd), 174
performance conversation
  action plan, 191–192
  assessing impact of, 192–194
  check-ins, 192
  clarifying what's not working, 187–190
  crying, 213–214
  examination of facts, 187–189
  example of poor, 186–187
  goals for, 186, 191
  looking for options, 190–191
  preparing for, 185–186
  questions to prompt positive actions, 190
  tips for presenting negative feedback, 189
  unfavorable reviews, 186–194
performance expectations
  overview of, 73–74
  when to intervene, 73
performance improvement
  action plan for, 27, 191–192
  closing the conversation, 66
  continuing, 194–195
  employee ability to improve, 193
  employee willingness, 193
  evaluating, 193–194
  options for, 190–191
  role of critical conversation in, 26–27
performance issues, as critical conversations indicator, 72–74
performance management, with EDGE model, 174, 175–176
personal safety concerns, 218

personal styles, differing, 214
perspective
  acknowledging others, 19
  asking for employee, 74
  describing yours with "I"
      statements, 206
  keeping problem in, 288
  in workplace complaints, 221
phone conversations, 51
phone-checking, during
      conversation, 291–292
phrases, key for results, 96–98
pitfalls
  avoiding with preparation, 130
  distracted audience, 33, 34, 37–38
  lack of trust, 33, 35, 38–39
  not heading in same direction,
      33, 35, 39–42
  one-sided conversation, 33, 34,
      35–37
  table of, 34–35
point of views, appreciating
      others', 205
positive attitude
  building trust and rapport with,
      139–141
  to keep tough discussion
      encouraging, 150
  to keep your cool, 287
  maintaining, 137–138, 287
  nonverbal cues, 109
positive spin, 60
postponing conversations, 12
power
  distribution in meeting, 146
  in team conversations, 270–271
  wise use of, 152–154
practice, 150
pre-framing success, 52
preparation for critical conversations
  agenda, 132–133
  avoiding pitfalls through, 130
  building rapport and trust, 138–141
  emotional, 133–138
  feedback, 47–48
  giving fair warning, 49–51

for mediated conversation, 227
  objective, setting the, 48–49
  physical, 131–133
  practice the conversation, 150
  question design, 132
prioritizing multiple issues, 78–79
problems, acknowledgment of, 17
problems in critical conversations
  distracted audience, 33, 34, 37–38
  lack of trust, 33, 35, 38–39
  not heading in same direction, 33,
      35, 39–42
  one-sided conversation, 33, 34,
      35–37
  table of, 34–35
process, focus on, 95–96, 146, 150
progress, evaluating, 67–68
pronouns, 90–91, 270, 293
public relations, 259, 260
Public Relations For Dummies
      (Yaverbaum, Benun, and
      Kirshenbaum), 259

• Q •

questions
  assertive communicators use of, 119
  clarifying, 110–111
  contemplative, 132
  designing, 132
  interviewing, 173
  leading, 132
  neutral, 207
  open-ended, 111, 132
  to prompt positive employee
      actions, 190
  to spur discussion, 119
  for team conversations, 266–267
  yes-no, 38, 132

• R •

rapport
  building, 138–141
  defined, 139
  development of, 279

recapping and rephrasing previous agreements, 156–157
recipient, role in critical conversations, 45
recognition
  behavior reinforcement with, 241–242
  as motivation, 134
redirecting the conversation
  for distracted audience, 37–38
  keeping agreements in tact, 297
  in one-sided conversation, 35–37
reflecting before responding, 110
refocusing the conversation, 157–158
relationship influence, 153
relationships
  building, 24–25
  healthy working, 277
  slowing down in, 31
relevance of concerns, 75, 79
Remember icon, 6
rescheduling a meeting, 145
resistance, dealing with, 154–157
resolving issues, 25–26
respect
  as motivation, 134
  word choice and, 88
results, with motivated people, 150–151
rewards
  in conversation-ready environments, 183
  motivation and, 242
Roberts, Ralph R. (*Cross-Cultural Selling For Dummies*), 102
role models, 241
roles
  in critical conversations, 44–46
  initiator, 44–45
  recipient, 45
  in team conversations, 270–271
  third parties, 45–46
  unclear, 130
Rule of Three, 59
rumors, 224
rushed conversations, 106

• S •

safety
  concerns, 218
  staff disputes and, 203
sarcasm, 37–38, 137, 238
satisfaction, source of, 135
scheduling
  critical conversation, 50–51, 131
  follow-up meetings, 165–166
  rescheduling a meeting, 145
Schlachter, Christina Tangora (*Leading Business Change For Dummies*), 44–45, 183, 269
science of critical conversation, 16–18
scope of the conversation, badly defined, 130
screamers, 243
secondhand issues, 76
"should," use of word, 90
shying away from conversations, 29–31
silence
  active, 109–110
  benefits of, 207
  group, 271
  by passive communicators, 118
  by previous talker, 294
  in team conversations, 271
  as tool dealing with resistance, 156
  use of, 106
situation, identification of, 58
situational context, 112
small talk, using, 53–54
SMART agreement, 64–65
SMART goals
  in action plan, 161
  performance management, 174
  team conversations, 267
smiling
  to build rapport, 140
  facial expression, 101, 103
  sincerity creation, 109
snowball effect, 77

solutions
  agreement on approach to, 18
  alternatives, 62–63
  assertive communicators and,
    119, 121
  in customer conversations, 256, 260,
    261–262
  finding to fit everyone, 14
  key phrase for results, 98
  for problems in critical
    conversations, 34–42
  to staff disputes, 205, 208–209
space
  in staff dispute, 207
  use of, 106–107
specificity, in performance
    conversation, 73
speed of conversation, 104, 106
speed of talking, 115
spin, positive, 60
staff disputes. *See also* workplace
    complaints
  crying, 213–214
  grudges, 211–212
  necessary conflicts, 201–202
  obnoxious co-worker, 210–211
  offensive comments, 210
  solving future problems, 208–209
  steps to resolve conflict, 204–206
  turning into positive experience,
    207–208
  unnecessary conflicts, 200–201
  values and style differences, 214
  when to intervene, 202–203
  when to step aside, 200–202
starting a critical conversation
  managing high stakes and high
    emotions, 54–55
  opening the discussion, 51–53
  small talk, use of, 53–54
stating the obvious, 286–287
Stein, Steven J. (*Emotional Intelligence
    For Dummies*),
    146, 214
stopping the conversation, 155–156
Strengths Deployment Inventory
    (assessment), 72

stress
  expressions of, 101
  fight-or-flight reaction, 209
  managing your communication style
    under, 124–125
  reduction with healthy lifestyle, 131
  schedule-associated, 131
  style, adapting, 41
subjective issues
  addressing with critical
    conversations, 70
  workplace dynamic
    conversations, 71
success
  critical success factors, 267
  pre-framing, 52
superstar employees, 175–176
support
  difficult behaviors and, 239–241
  of needs of others, 151–152
  showing, 25
supporting the discussion, 54
surprises, avoiding, 50

• *T* •

team conversations
  creating a productive team, 163–170
  decision-making approaches,
    268–270
  facilitating, 264–267
  improving team behavior, 270–272
teamwork
  focusing on, 277–278
  as motivation, 134
technology, use of, 31–32
texting, during conversation, 291–292
"them," limiting use of word, 90
"they," limiting use of word, 90
third parties, role in critical
    conversations, 45–46
Thomas-Kilmann Conflict Mode
    Assessment (assessment),
    72, 114
360-degree communication
    review, 124
time line, action plan, 163–164

timekeeper, 292
time-out, 145
Tip icon, 6
tone of voice
  calm and patient, 106
  enthusiasm level, 105–106
  friendly and open, 105
  importance of, 104–105
trust
  building, 35, 39, 138–141
  defined, 139
  lack of, 33, 35, 38–39
  tips for, 35, 39
tunnel vision, 280
typing, during conversation, 291–292

• *U* •

unexpected, handling of, 148–149
"us" language, 265, 270, 293

• *V* •

validating opinions, 155
value, adding with performance
    conversation, 73–74
values
  differing, 214
  organizational culture and, 182, 183
venting, 197
verbal communication. *See also*
    words
  cooperative language, 91–98
  corporate speak, 91
  examples of poor, 86–87
  how it is sent and received, 86
  key phrases for results, 96–98
  pronouns, 90–91
  in team conversation, 271
viewpoints, appreciating others', 205
violence, workplace, 203
voice quality
  effective and ineffective
      compared, 101
  speed of delivery, 104
  watching for extremes in, 104

voice tone
  calm and patient, 106
  enthusiasm level, 105–106
  friendly and open, 105
  importance of, 104–105

• *W* •

walk, taking short, 284
walking away, 288–289
Warning! icon, 6
watch-checking behavior, 292
"we" language, 90–91, 265, 270, 293
willingness, to improve, 193
win-lose outcome, 80
wins, creating immediately
    achievable, 162
win-win outcome, 79–80
Woods, Geraldine (*English
    Grammar For Dummies*), 88
words
  corporate speak, 91
  importance of, 87, 88, 90
  poor choices, 89
  pronouns, 90–91, 270, 293
  turning confrontational words into
      accommodating words, 95–96
workers' compensation benefits,
    217–218
workplace complaints
  addressing, 215–220
  confidentiality of, 223, 224,
      228, 229
  defining, 216–217
  duration of issue, 216
  emotions in, 222–223
  ethical concerns, 218, 219
  legal concerns, 216, 217–219
  mediator use in, 225–227
  morale issues, 219
  moving forward after, 227–229
  not addressed by critical
      conversations, 217–219
  off-the-wall inquiries, 220
  overview of, 215–216
  separating personal issues from
      valid grievances, 224

workplace complaints *(continued)*
  severity and risk of, 216
  that benefit from a critical
    conversation, 219–220
  using critical conversations,
    220–221
workplace dynamic critical
  conversations, 71–72

• Y •

Yaverbaum, Eric (*Public Relations For
  Dummies*), 259
yelling, 243
yes-no questions, 38, 132
"you" language, 90, 293

Apple & Mac

iPad 2 For Dummies,
3rd Edition
978-1-118-17679-5

iPhone 4S
For Dummies,
5th Edition
978-1-118-03671-6

iPod touch For
Dummies, 3rd Edition
978-1-118-12960-9

Mac OS X Lion
For Dummies
978-1-118-02205-4

Blogging & Social Media

CityVille For Dummies
978-1-118-08337-6

Facebook For Dummies,
4th Edition
978-1-118-09562-1

Mom Blogging
For Dummies
978-1-118-03843-7

Twitter For Dummies,
2nd Edition
978-0-470-76879-2

WordPress For
Dummies, 4th Edition
978-1-118-07342-1

Business

Cash Flow For Dummies
978-1-118-01850-7

Investing For Dummies,
6th Edition
978-0-470-90545-6

Job Searching with Social Media
For Dummies
978-0-470-93072-4

QuickBooks 2012
For Dummies
978-1-118-09120-3

Resumes
For Dummies,
6th Edition
978-0-470-87361-8

Starting an Etsy
Business For Dummies
978-0-470-93067-0

Cooking & Entertaining

Cooking Basics
For Dummies,
4th Edition
978-0-470-91388-8

Wine For Dummies,
4th Edition
978-0-470-04579-4

Diet & Nutrition

Kettlebells
For Dummies
978-0-470-59929-7

Nutrition For Dummies,
5th Edition
978-0-470-93231-5

Restaurant Calorie
Counter For Dummies,
2nd Edition
978-0-470-64405-8

Digital Photography

Digital SLR Cameras
& Photography For
Dummies, 4th Edition
978-1-118-14489-3

Digital SLR Settings
& Shortcuts
For Dummies
978-0-470-91763-3

Photoshop Elements 10
For Dummies
978-1-118-10742-3

Gardening

Gardening Basics
For Dummies
978-0-470-03749-2

Vegetable Gardening
For Dummies,
2nd Edition
978-0-470-49870-5

Green/Sustainable

Raising Chickens
For Dummies
978-0-470-46544-8

Green Cleaning
For Dummies
978-0-470-39106-8

Health

Diabetes For Dummies,
3rd Edition
978-0-470-27086-8

Food Allergies
For Dummies
978-0-470-09584-3

Living Gluten-Free
For Dummies,
2nd Edition
978-0-470-58589-4

Hobbies

Beekeeping
For Dummies,
2nd Edition
978-0-470-43065-1

Chess For Dummies,
3rd Edition
978-1-118-01695-4

Drawing For Dummies,
2nd Edition
978-0-470-61842-4

eBay For Dummies,
7th Edition
978-1-118-09806-6

Knitting For Dummies,
2nd Edition
978-0-470-28747-7

Language & Foreign Language

English Grammar
For Dummies,
2nd Edition
978-0-470-54664-2

French For Dummies,
2nd Edition
978-1-118-00464-7

German For Dummies,
2nd Edition
978-0-470-90101-4

Spanish Essentials
For Dummies
978-0-470-63751-7

Spanish For Dummies,
2nd Edition
978-0-470-87855-2

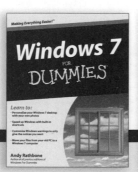

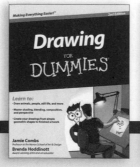

Math & Science

Algebra I For Dummies,
2nd Edition
978-0-470-55964-2

Biology For Dummies,
2nd Edition
978-0-470-59875-7

Chemistry For
Dummies, 2nd Edition
978-1-1180-0730-3

Geometry For Dummies,
2nd Edition
978-0-470-08946-0

Pre-Algebra Essentials
For Dummies
978-0-470-61838-7

Microsoft Office

Excel 2010 For
Dummies
978-0-470-48953-6

Office 2010 All-in-One
For Dummies
978-0-470-49748-7

Office 2011 for Mac
For Dummies
978-0-470-87869-9

Word 2010
For Dummies
978-0-470-48772-3

Music

Guitar For Dummies,
2nd Edition
978-0-7645-9904-0

Clarinet For Dummies
978-0-470-58477-4

iPod & iTunes
For Dummies,
9th Edition
978-1-118-13060-5

Pets

Cats For Dummies,
2nd Edition
978-0-7645-5275-5

Dogs All-in One
For Dummies
978-0470-52978-2

Saltwater Aquariums
For Dummies
978-0-470-06805-2

Religion & Inspiration

The Bible For Dummies
978-0-7645-5296-0

Catholicism For
Dummies, 2nd Edition
978-1-118-07778-8

Spirituality For
Dummies, 2nd Edition
978-0-470-19142-2

Self-Help &
Relationships

Happiness For Dummies
978-0-470-28171-0

Overcoming Anxiety
For Dummies,
2nd Edition
978-0-470-57441-6

Seniors

Crosswords For Seniors
For Dummies
978-0-470-49157-7

iPad 2 For Seniors
For Dummies, 3rd
Edition
978-1-118-17678-8

Laptops & Tablets
For Seniors For
Dummies, 2nd Edition
978-1-118-09596-6

Smartphones & Tablets

BlackBerry For
Dummies, 5th Edition
978-1-118-10035-6

Droid X2 For Dummies
978-1-118-14864-8

HTC ThunderBolt
For Dummies
978-1-118-07601-9

MOTOROLA XOOM
For Dummies
978-1-118-08835-7

Sports

Basketball For
Dummies, 3rd Edition
978-1-118-07374-2

Football For Dummies,
2nd Edition
978-1-118-01261-1

Golf For Dummies,
4th Edition
978-0-470-88279-5

Test Prep

ACT For Dummies,
5th Edition
978-1-118-01259-8

ASVAB For Dummies,
3rd Edition
978-0-470-63760-9

The GRE Test For
Dummies, 7th Edition
978-0-470-00919-2

Police Officer Exam
For Dummies
978-0-470-88724-0

Series 7 Exam
For Dummies
978-0-470-09932-2

Web Development

HTML, CSS, & XHTML
For Dummies, 7th
Edition
978-0-470-91659-9

Drupal For Dummies,
2nd Edition
978-1-118-08348-2

Windows 7

Windows 7
For Dummies
978-0-470-49743-2

Windows 7
For Dummies,
Book + DVD Bundle
978-0-470-52398-8

Windows 7 All-in-One
For Dummies
978-0-470-48763-1

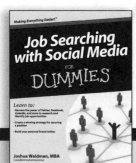

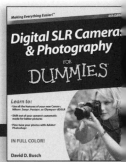

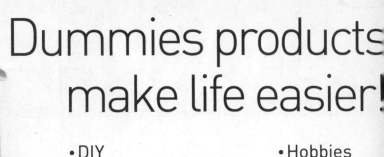